BTEC FIRST AWARD

BUSINESS

ALWAYS LE[ARNING]

PEARSON

Published by Pearson Education Limited, Edinburgh Gate, Harlow, Essex, CM20 2JE.

www.pearsonschoolsandfecolleges.co.uk

Text © Pearson Education Limited 2012
Typeset by Phoenix Photosetting, Chatham, Kent, UK
Original illustrations © Pearson Education Limited 2012
Illustrated by Adrian Barclay/KJA-artists.com and Phoenix Photosetting
Cover design by Pearson Education Limited and Andrew Magee Design
Front cover photos: Plainpicture Ltd: Scanpix
Indexing by Indexing Specialists (UK) Ltd

The rights of Carol Carysforth, Paul Bentley, Lisa Chandler-Corris, Mike Neild and Karen Glencross to be identified as authors of this work have been asserted by them in accordance with the Copyright, Designs and Patents Act 1988.

First published 2012.

17 16 15 14 13
10 9 8 7 6 5 4 3

British Library Cataloguing in Publication Data
A catalogue record for this book is available from the British Library

ISBN 978 1 447935 56 8

Printed in the UK at Ashford Colour Press, Gosport, Hants

Websites
There are links to relevant websites in this book. In order to ensure that the links are up to date, that the links works, and that the sites aren't inadvertently links to sites that could be considered offensive, we have made the links available on our website at www.pearsonhotlinks.co.uk. Search for the title BTEC First Business Award Student Book or ISBN 978 1 447935 56 8.

Copies of official specifications for all Pearson qualifications may be found on the website: www.edexcel.com

A note from the publisher
In order to ensure that this resource offers high-quality support for the associated BTEC qualification, it has been through a review process by the awarding organisation to confirm that it fully covers the teaching and learning content of the specification or part of a specification at which it is aimed, and demonstrates an appropriate balance between the development of subject skills, knowledge and understanding, in addition to preparation for assessment.
While the publishers have made every attempt to ensure that advice on the qualification and its assessment is accurate, the official specification and associated assessment guidance materials are the only authoritative source of information and should always be referred to for definitive guidance.
No material from an endorsed book will be used verbatim in any assessment set by BTEC.
Endorsement of a book does not mean that the book is required to achieve this BTEC qualification, nor does it mean that it is the only suitable material available to support the qualification, and any resource lists produced by the awarding organisation shall include this and other appropriate resources.

Contents

Acknowledgements

The publisher would like to thank the following for their kind permission to reproduce their photographs:

(Key: b-bottom; c-centre; l-left; r-right; t-top)

Alamy Images: AlexSegre 13, Art Directors & TRIP 116, Corbis Bridge 190, Directphoto.org 78, Elizabeth Leyden 109, Eric Nathan 71, GeoPhotos 79, GeoPhotos 79, Gregory Wrona 205, Janine Wiedel Photolibrary 111, Jeff Gilbert 24, Jeremy Sutton- Hibbert 90, Juice images 125, Justin Kase zsixz 148, Londonstills.com 152, Martyn Goddard 112, Nathan King 20, Paul KIngsley 26, Peter Phipp / Travelshots.com 200, Robert Johns 128, Robert Stainforth 81, 87, Robert Stainforth 81, 87; **Ben Moss:** 131; **Caroline Gooder:** 193; **Chris Reid:** 61; **Copyright (c) The LEGO Group:** 76; **Corbis:** Drew Myers 156, Helen King 142, Mika 100, Randy Faris 40, Ren Zhenglai / Xinhua Press 110, Roy McMahon 217, Simon Kimber / Demotix 89; **Daniel Chang:** 14; **Big Funky Pictures Ltd:** Jason Gilliat 17; **Getty Images:** AFP 203, Chris Ryan / OJO Images 35, Colorblind / Stone 97, Erik Dreyer / Stone 104, Helen Ashford / Workbook Stock 167, Inti St. Clair / Digital Vision 121, Inti St. Clair / Digital Vision 121; **innocent ltd:** 92; **Lowri Roberts:** 165; **Pearson Education Ltd:** Clark Wiseman / Studio 8 144, Gareth Boden 120, Rob Judges 6, QUAD-U2, Jules Selmes 96; **Revolver World:** 95; **Science Photo Library Ltd:** Victor De Schwanberg 160; **Shutterstock.com:** AISPIX by Image Source 58, Andresr 22, Andrew Bassett 137, Andrey Popov 208, Banner-U8, Andrey Popov 208, Banner-U8, Boris Djuranovic 38, Dmitrijs Dmitrijevs Banner-U3, Dmitriy Shironosov 187, Emran Mohd Tamil 213, erobanks 194, Fleming Photography 180, Goodluz 31, hxdbzxy 145, Banner-U6, hxdbzxy 145, Banner-U6, Kamira 11, Kurhan 83, leungchopan 166, Losevsky Pavel 127, Martin Haas 107, Max Earey 75, Maxx-Studio 77, Monkey Business Images 2, 51, Monkey Business Images 2, 51, moshimochi 57, Netrun78 3, Norman Pogson 176, Otna Ydur Banner-U2, pcruciatti 84, Portokalis 29, PT Images 70, R. Nagy Banner-U1, Rido 74, Serge64 175, Sergey Furtaev 34, Serhiy Shullye 47, StockLite 184, 195, StockLite 184, 195, wavebreakmedia ltd 119, Yuri Arcurs 138, 170, Banner-U4, Banner-U5, Banner-U7, Yuri Arcurs 138, 170, Banner-U4, Banner-U5, Banner-U7, Yuri Arcurs 138, 170, Banner-U4, Banner-U5, Banner-U7, Yuri Arcurs 138, 170, Banner-U4, Banner-U5, Banner-U7, Yuri Arcurs 138, 170, Banner-U4, Banner-U5, Banner-U7; **Sonya Clarkson:** 219; **SuperStock:** Cultura Limited 135; **The Gro Company:** 23

Cover images: *Front:* **Plainpicture Ltd:** Scanpix

All other images © Pearson Education

In some instances we have been unable to trace the owners of copyright material, and we would appreciate any information that would enable us to do so.

Authors' acknowledgements

The authors would like to thank all the people and organisations who have helped us by providing information on their business activities. This has enabled us to produce a book which accurately reflects current business practice and is appropriate for today's BTEC First learners.

For agreeing to be featured in WorkSpace features and help with other case studies we are hugely indebted to: Sam Clayton, a talented self-employed photographer; Daniel Chang, the creator of the Dream Sheep app; Ben Fox, whose vision led to On your Bike (Recycle) Ltd; James Plant and James Moss, who own and run Plant and Moss Ltd, Birmingham; Chris Reid, the brains and energy behind Connect Technology Group; Steve Wells and Eric Metcalf at Brook Food Processing Equipment for their help with bakery costings; Paul Birch, the MD of Revolver World; Ben Moss, manager at R A Bennett & Partners estate agents; Lowri Roberts, the owner of Siop Cwlwm in Oswestry; Caroline Gooder, Engineering Administrator at Cummins Turbo Technologies; Sonya Clarkson, Head of Employment Services at East Lancashire Hospitals NHS Trust.

As always, thanks are also due to the team at Pearson who worked so hard to produce this book, especially Lewis Birchon, our publisher, for his constant help and support and Laura Bland our editor, for her patience and calm efficiency.

We hope this book will help teachers and tutors to deliver the new BTEC First Award with ease and confidence and provide a useful and inspirational resource for their students.

About this book

This book is designed to help you through your BTEC First Business Award and is divided into the 8 units of the qualification.

About your BTEC First Business

Choosing to study for a BTEC First Business qualification is a great decision to make for lots of reasons. This qualification will prepare you for virtually any career by equipping you with financial skills, organisational ability, marketing knowledge and the ability to present your ideas clearly. The principles of business underpin every shop, office and organisation in the UK economy, meaning that you will have skills and knowledge that will be valued by employers in every sector. In addition, a BTEC First Business qualification can help you to progress to the next level of study.

About the authors

Paul Bentley worked in retail management before training as a teacher. He currently works at St Edmunds Catholic School in Wolverhampton where he is a lead practitioner and the coordinator of vocational education. Paul is a doctoral research student at a Russell Group university and is also an experienced author, having written and co-written tutor support materials, delivery guidance, and journal articles.

Carol Carysforth has enjoyed a varied business career. In addition to being involved with two family businesses, she has worked in HR, travel and tourism, manufacturing and sales and marketing. She has worked both for private industry and in the public sector. During her teaching career she specialised in teaching business studies and administration to FE and HE students and became Deputy Dean of Faculty of Business and Management at Blackburn College. She has worked as a consultant on several curriculum development projects at national level.

Lisa Chandler-Corris taught BTEC in school and college for many years before working as a Training Consultant. In this role, she produces teaching and training materials, reviews educational resources and gives advice on teaching and training.

Karen Glencross was an IT trainer in a multinational engineering company in the North East of England before working in the Further Education sector. She moved to Redcar and Cleveland College and during that time held the post of Head of Faculty for Business Information and Technology. She is now self-employed working as a Qualifications Manager for a training provider.

Mike Neild started his post-graduate career as a research scientist at GCHQ in Cheltenham. A move north resulted in a complete change of career to production manager for a large international company. After studying for higher level management qualifications, Mike's interest in teaching was aroused and he started his teaching career at Blackburn College, specialising in business and management. Mike became Senior Tutor at the College and headed two different departments before deciding to focus on writing full-time.

How to use this book

This book contains many features that will help you use your skills and knowledge in work-related situations, and assist you in getting the most from your course.

These introductions give you a snapshot of what to expect from each unit – and what you should be aiming for by the time you finish it.

How this unit is assessed

Learning aims describe what you will be doing in the unit.

A learner shares how working through the unit has helped them.

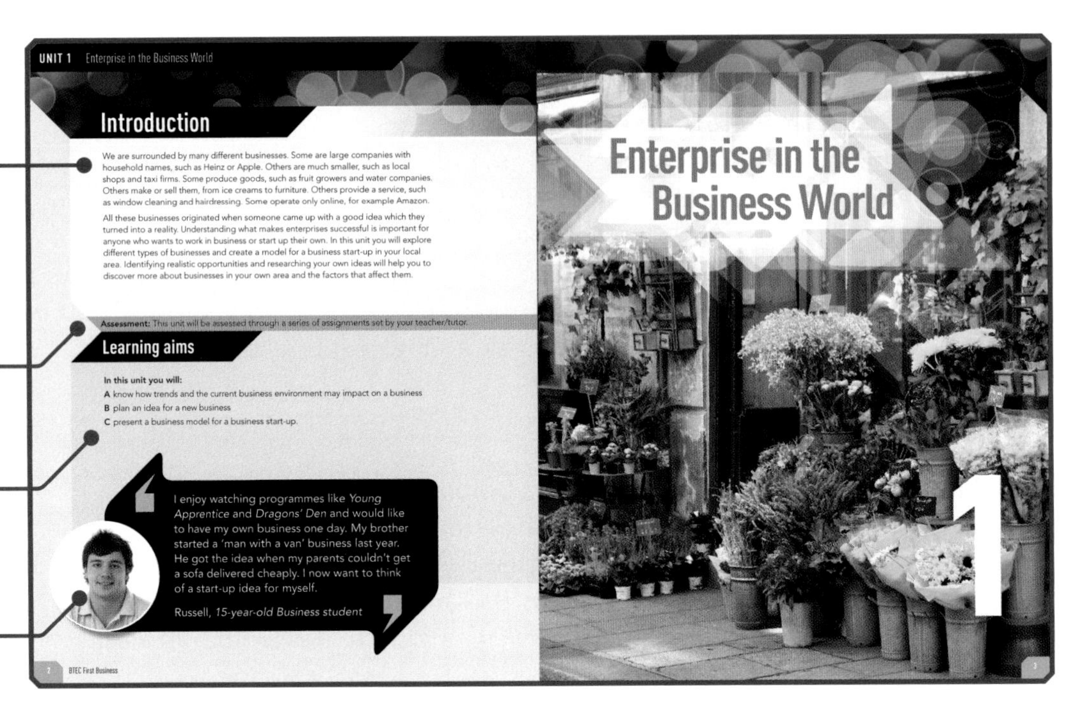

UNIT 1 Enterprise in the Business World

Introduction

We are surrounded by many different businesses. Some are large companies with household names, such as Heinz or Apple. Others are much smaller, such as local shops and taxi firms. Some produce goods, such as fruit growers and water companies. Others make or sell them, from ice creams to furniture. Others provide a service, such as window cleaning and hairdressing. Some operate only online, for example Amazon.

All these businesses originated when someone came up with a good idea which they turned into a reality. Understanding what makes enterprises successful is important for anyone who wants to work in business or start up their own. In this unit you will explore different types of businesses and create a model for a business start-up in your local area. Identifying realistic opportunities and researching your own ideas will help you to discover more about businesses in your own area and the factors that affect them.

Assessment: This unit will be assessed through a series of assignments set by your teacher/tutor.

Learning aims

In this unit you will:

A know how trends and the current business environment may impact on a business

B plan an idea for a new business

C present a business model for a business start-up.

I enjoy watching programmes like *Young Apprentice* and *Dragons' Den* and would like to have my own business one day. My brother started a 'man with a van' business last year. He got the idea when my parents couldn't get a sofa delivered cheaply. I now want to think of a start-up idea for myself.

Russell, *15-year-old Business student*

Enterprise in the Business World

1

Features of this book

There are lots of features in this book to help you learn about the topics in each unit, and to have fun while learning! These pages show some of the features that you will come across when using the book.

Topic references show which parts of the BTEC you are covering on these pages.

Getting started with a short activity or discussion about the topic.

Key terms boxes give definitions of important words and phrases that you will come across.

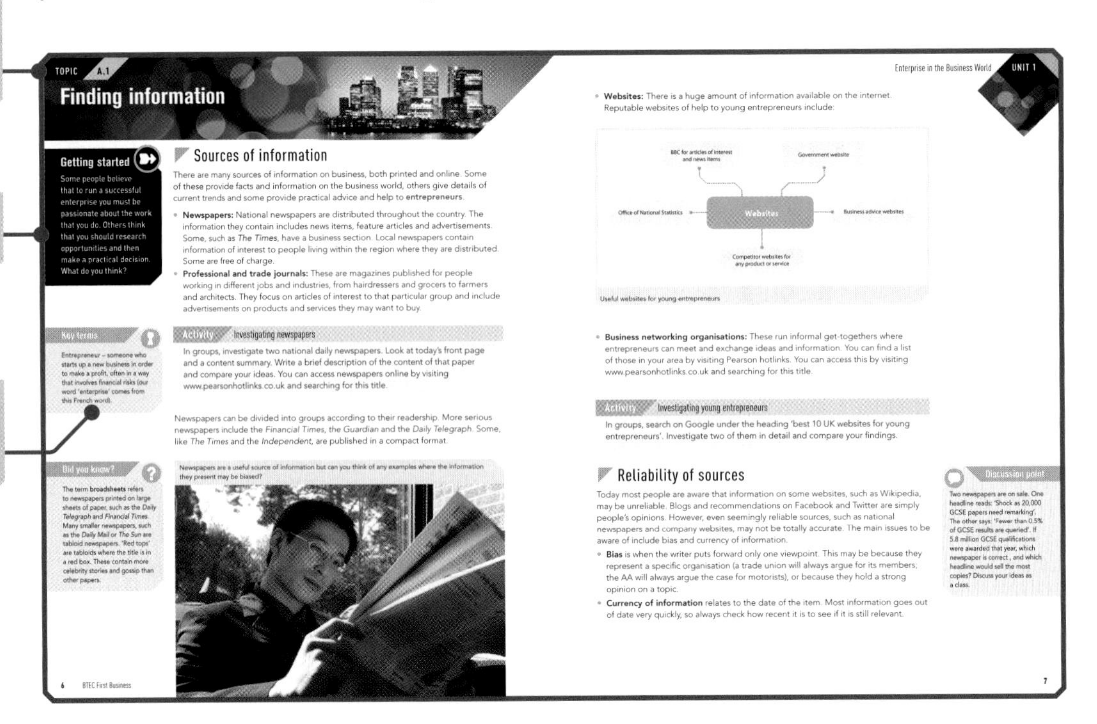

TOPIC A.1

Finding information

Getting started

Some people believe that to run a successful enterprise you must be passionate about the work that you do. Others think that you should research opportunities and then make a practical decision. What do you think?

Sources of information

There are many sources of information on business, both printed and online. Some of these provide facts and information on the business world, others give details of current trends and some provide practical advice and help to **entrepreneurs**.

- **Newspapers:** National newspapers are distributed throughout the country. The information they contain includes news items, feature articles and advertisements. Some, such as *The Times*, have a business section. Local newspapers contain information of interest to people living within the region where they are distributed. Some are free of charge.
- **Professional and trade journals:** These are magazines published for people working in different jobs and industries, from hairdressers and grocers to farmers and architects. They focus on articles of interest to that particular group and include advertisements on products and services they may want to buy.

Key terms

Entrepreneur – someone who starts up a new business in order to make a profit, often in a way that involves financial risks (our word 'enterprise' comes from this French word).

Activity Investigating newspapers

In groups, investigate two national daily newspapers. Look at today's front page and a content summary. Write a brief description of the content of that paper and compare your ideas. You can access newspapers online by visiting www.pearsonhotlinks.co.uk and searching for this title.

Newspapers can be divided into groups according to their readership. More serious newspapers include the *Financial Times, the Guardian* and the *Daily Telegraph*. Some, like *The Times* and the *Independent*, are published in a compact format.

Did you know?

The term **broadsheets** refers to newspapers printed on large sheets of paper, such as the *Daily Telegraph* and *Financial Times*. Many smaller newspapers, such as the *Daily Mail* or *The Sun* are tabloid newspapers. 'Red tops' are tabloids where the title is in a red box. These contain more celebrity stories and gossip than other papers.

Newspapers are a useful source of information but can you think of any examples where the information they present may be biased?

6 BTEC First Business

Enterprise in the Business World UNIT 1

- **Websites:** There is a huge amount of information available on the internet. Reputable websites of help to young entrepreneurs include:

BBC for articles of interest and news items
Government website
Office of National Statistics
Websites
Business advice websites
Competitor websites for any product or service

Useful websites for young entrepreneurs

- **Business networking organisations:** These run informal get-togethers where entrepreneurs can meet and exchange ideas and information. You can find a list of those in your area by visiting Pearson hotlinks. You can access this by visiting www.pearsonhotlinks.co.uk and searching for this title.

Activity Investigating young entrepreneurs

In groups, search on Google under the heading 'best 10 UK websites for young entrepreneurs'. Investigate two of them in detail and compare your findings.

Reliability of sources

Today most people are aware that information on some websites, such as Wikipedia, may be unreliable. Blogs and recommendations on Facebook and Twitter are simply people's opinions. However, even seemingly reliable sources, such as national newspapers and company websites, may not be totally accurate. The main issues to be aware of include bias and currency of information.

- **Bias** is when the writer puts forward only one viewpoint. This may be because they represent a specific organisation (a trade union will always argue for its members; the AA will always argue the case for motorists), or because they hold a strong opinion on a topic.
- **Currency of information** relates to the date of the item. Most information goes out of date very quickly, so always check how recent it is to see if it is still relevant.

Discussion point

Two newspapers are on sale. One headline reads: 'Shock as 20,000 GCSE papers need remarking'. The other says: 'Fewer than 0.5% of GCSE results are queried'. If 5.8 million GCSE qualifications were awarded that year, which newspaper is correct, and which headline would sell the most copies? Discuss your ideas as a class.

7

Activity Researching ethical trading

Research ethical trading and then find out which businesses you know are members of the Ethical Trading Initiative.

Activities will help you learn about the topic. These will be done in pairs or groups, or sometimes on your own.

Question 1

Ashraf has started his own car valeting business. Divide the following items into start up costs and running costs. [4]

(a) Pressure washer

(b) Car shampoo and polish

(c) Promotional leaflet

(d) Telephone bill

A chance to practise answering the types of test questions that you may come across in your test. (For Unit 2 only.)

Assessment activity 1.1 *Maths* 2A.P1 | 2A.P2 | 2A.M1 | 2A.M2 | 2A.D1

You have been asked to produce your own booklet for young entrepreneurs in your area. This will describe the local business environment and identify trends and changes that may affect a start-up business. Your booklet should be divided into three sections:

1. The first section should focus on the current business environment that exists in your own area. You should also be aware of changes that can take place and explain how these can affect a start-up business.
2. The next section should focus on trends you have researched. If you wish, you can focus on trends and that could affect your own idea for a start-up business. You need to compare how two trends have impacted on a start-up business.
3. The final section should focus on the current risks, opportunities and trends in the current business environment for a start-up business. Your assessment should be based on the data you have researched and you should focus on appropriate guidance for an entrepreneur.

Tip

You **assess** information by carefully considering all the factors or events that apply and identifying which are the most important or relevant. Use your research to provide evidence for your conclusions.

You **compare** by identifying the main factors in two or more situations. Point out the similarities and differences and, if appropriate, say which is best and why. Or explain the effects these factors have had.

Activities that relate to the unit's assessment critera. These activities will help you prepare for your assignments and contain tips to help you achieve your potential. (For all units **except** Unit 2.)

Just checking

1. What is inflation and why is high inflation bad for businesses?
2. Why do the government and business entrepreneurs both want employment levels to be high?
3. List four types of taxes paid in the UK.

Use these to check your knowledge and understanding of the topic you have just covered.

Someone who works in the business industry explains how this unit of the BTEC First applies to the day-to-day work they do as part of their job.

This section also gives you the chance to think more about the role that this person does, and whether you would want to follow in their footsteps once you've completed your BTEC.

BTEC Assessment Zone

You will be assessed in two different ways for your BTEC First in Business. For most units, your teacher/tutor will set assignments for you to complete. These may take the form of projects where you research, plan, prepare, and evaluate a piece of work or activity. The table in this BTEC Assessment Zone explains what you must do in order to achieve each of the assessment criteria. Each unit of this book contains a number of assessment activities to help you with these assessment criteria.

The table in the BTEC Assessment Zone explains what you must do in order to achieve each of the assessment criteria, and signposts assessment activities in this book to help you to prepare for your assignments.

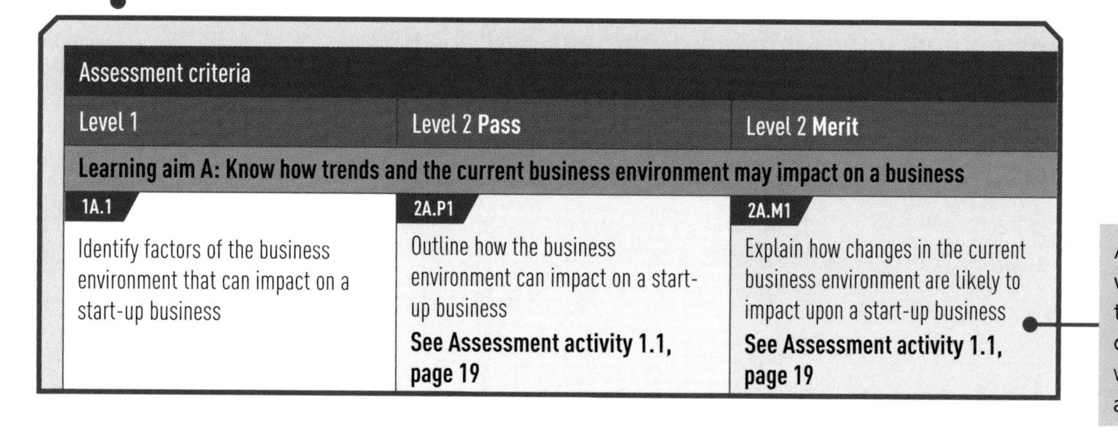

Assessment criteria		
Level 1	Level 2 **Pass**	Level 2 **Merit**
Learning aim A: Know how trends and the current business environment may impact on a business		
1A.1 Identify factors of the business environment that can impact on a start-up business	**2A.P1** Outline how the business environment can impact on a start-up business **See Assessment activity 1.1, page 19**	**2A.M1** Explain how changes in the current business environment are likely to impact upon a start-up business **See Assessment activity 1.1, page 19**

Activities in this book will show you the kinds of task you might be asked to do to meet these criteria when your tutor sets an assignment.

Question 1

Which two of these items are fixed costs for a florist? [2]

Click on **two** *of these boxes:*

- Staff wages ☒
- Flowers ☐
- Monthly rent ☒
- Ribbons and wrapping paper ☐

For Unit 2 of your BTEC, you will be assessed by an onscreen test. The BTEC Assessment Zone in Unit 2 helps you to prepare for your tests by showing you some of the different types of questions you may need to answer.

Planning and getting organised

The first step in managing your time is to plan ahead and be well organised. Some people are naturally good at this. They think ahead, write down commitments in a diary or planner and store their notes and handouts neatly and carefully so they can find them quickly.

How good are your working habits?

Improving your planning and organisational skills

1 Use a diary to schedule working times into your weekdays and weekends.

2 Also use the diary to write down exactly what work you have to do. You could use this as a 'to do' list and tick off each task as you go.

3 Divide up long or complex tasks into manageable chunks and put each 'chunk' in your diary with a deadline of its own.

4 Always allow more time than you think you need for a task.

Take it further

If you become distracted by social networking sites or texts when you're working, set yourself a time limit of 10 minutes or so to indulge yourself. You could even use this as a reward for completing a certain amount of work.

Sources of information

You will need to use research to complete your BTEC First assignments, so it's important to know what sources of information are available to you. These are likely to include the following:

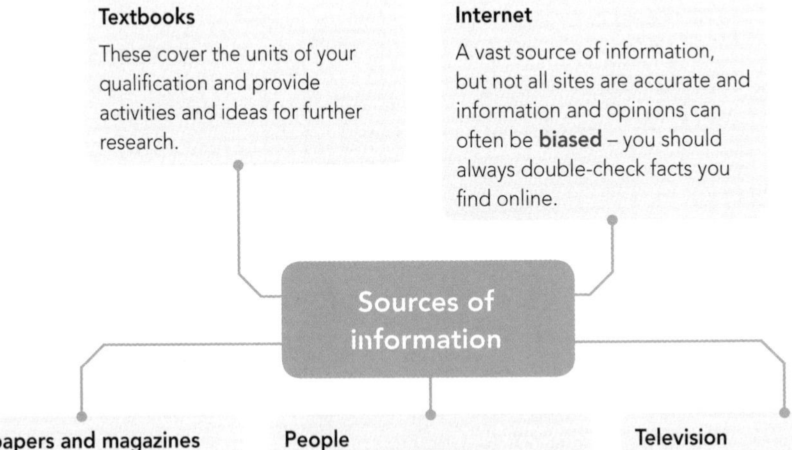

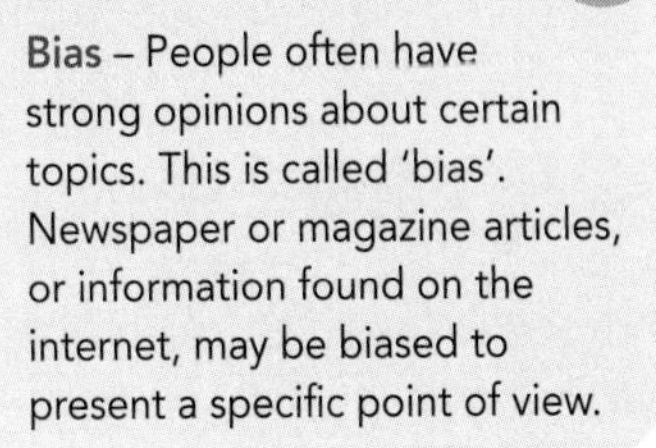

Key terms

Bias – People often have strong opinions about certain topics. This is called 'bias'. Newspaper or magazine articles, or information found on the internet, may be biased to present a specific point of view.

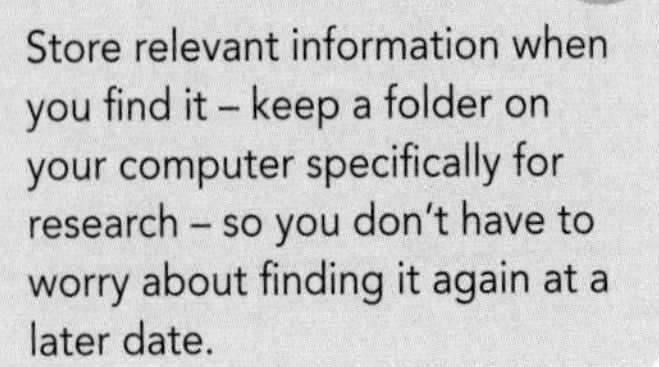

Remember!

Store relevant information when you find it – keep a folder on your computer specifically for research – so you don't have to worry about finding it again at a later date.

Organising and selecting information

Organising your information

Once you have used a range of sources of information for research, you will need to organise the information so it's easy to use.

- Make sure your written notes are neat and have a clear heading – it's often useful to date them, too.
- Always keep a note of where the information came from (the title of a book, the title and date of a newspaper or magazine and the web address of a website) and, if relevant, which pages.
- Work out the results of any questionnaires you've used.

Selecting your information

Once you have completed your research, re-read the assignment brief or instructions you were given to remind yourself of the exact wording of the question(s) and divide your information into three groups:

1. Information that is totally relevant.
2. Information that is not as good, but which could come in useful.
3. Information that doesn't match the questions or assignment brief very much, but that you kept because you couldn't find anything better!

Check that there are no obvious gaps in your information against the questions or assignment brief. If there are, make a note of them so that you know exactly what you still have to find.

Key terms

Plagiarism – If you are including other people's views, comments or opinions, or copying a diagram or table from another publication, you must state the source by including the name of the author or publication, or the web address. Failure to do this (when you are really pretending other people's work is your own) is known as plagiarism. Check your school's policy on plagiarism and copying.

Presenting your work

Before handing in any assignments, make sure:

- you have addressed each part of the question and that your work is as complete as possible
- all spelling and grammar is correct
- you have referenced all sources of information you used for your research
- all work is your own – otherwise you could be committing **plagiarism**
- you have saved a copy of your work.

Introduction

We are surrounded by many different businesses. Some are large companies with household names, such as Heinz or Apple. Others are much smaller, such as local shops and taxi firms. Some produce goods, such as fruit growers and water companies. Others make or sell them, from ice creams to furniture. Others provide a service, such as window cleaning and hairdressing. Some operate only online, for example Amazon.

All these businesses originated when someone came up with a good idea which they turned into a reality. Understanding what makes enterprises successful is important for anyone who wants to work in business or start up their own. In this unit you will explore different types of businesses and create a model for a business start-up in your local area. Identifying realistic opportunities and researching your own ideas will help you to discover more about businesses in your own area and the factors that affect them.

Assessment: This unit will be assessed through a series of assignments set by your teacher/tutor.

Learning aims

In this unit you will:

A know how trends and the current business environment may impact on a business

B plan an idea for a new business

C present a business model for a business start-up.

I enjoy watching programmes like *Young Apprentice* and *Dragons' Den* and would like to have my own business one day. My brother started a 'man with a van' business last year. He got the idea when my parents couldn't get a sofa delivered cheaply. I now want to think of a start-up idea for myself.

Russell, *15-year-old Business student*

1 Enterprise in the Business World

This table shows you what you must do in order to achieve a **Pass**, **Merit** or **Distinction** grade, and where you can find activities in this book to help you.

Assessment criteria			
Level 1	**Level 2 Pass**	**Level 2 Merit**	**Level 2 Distinction**
Learning aim A: Know how trends and the current business environment may impact on a business			
1A.1 Identify factors of the business environment that can impact on a start-up business	**2A.P1** Outline how the business environment can impact on a start-up business **See Assessment activity 1.1, page 19**	**2A.M1** Explain how changes in the current business environment are likely to impact upon a start-up business **See Assessment activity 1.1, page 19**	**2A.D1** Maths Assess the current risks, opportunities and trends in the business environment for a start-up business **See Assessment activity 1.1, page 19**
1A.2 Identify current trends that may impact on a start-up business	**2A.P2** Maths Explain how current trends will impact on a start-up business **See Assessment activity 1.1, page 19**	**2A.M2** Maths Compare how two trends have impacted on a start-up business **See Assessment activity 1.1, page 19**	
Learning aim B: Plan an idea for a new business			
1B.3 Identify the features of successful businesses	**2B.P3** Describe, using relevant examples, the features of successful businesses **See Assessment activity 1.2, page 27**	**2B.M3** Compare the features, strengths and weaknesses of two successful businesses **See Assessment activity 1.2, page 27**	**2B.D2** Maths Justify how the initial plan for a business idea has potential for success in relation to existing local businesses **See Assessment activity 1.2, page 27**
1B.4 English Maths Prepare an initial plan for a business idea for the local area	**2B.P4** English Maths Prepare a realistic initial plan for a business idea suitable for the local area **See Assessment activity 1.2, page 27**	**2B.M4** Maths Explain how the initial plan for a business idea has the potential to respond to market needs **See Assessment activity 1.2, page 27**	
Learning aim C: Present a business model for a business start-up			
1C.5 Outline the choice of format selected for a business start-up	**2C.P5** Explain the reasons for the choice of format selected for a business start-up **See Assessment activity 1.3, page 33**	**2C.M5** English Present a realistic business model for a business, explaining how the format and business model will enable it to carry out its activities successfully **See Assessment activity 1.3, page 33**	**2C.D3** English Present a realistic business model for a business, explaining how the format and supporting evidence justifies the initial business idea **See Assessment activity 1.3, page 33**
1C.6 English Present, with guidance, a business model for a business start-up	**2C.P6** English Present a realistic business model for a business start-up **See Assessment activity 1.3, page 33**		

English Opportunity to practise English skills **Maths** Opportunity to practise mathematical skills

How you will be assessed

The unit will be assessed by a series of internally assessed tasks. You will research your own ideas for a start-up business and prepare an initial plan which shows that you have considered current trends and the needs of your local business environment. You will then plan your business model, deciding which would be the best format for your own business and giving reasons for your choice. You will need to prepare explanatory notes to support your model before you present it.

Your evidence for this unit will be collected and prepared throughout your course and stored in a portfolio, together with any observation records or witness statements.

Your assessment could be in the form of:

- a business model with explanatory notes
- a presentation in which you put forward your ideas and/or business model and answer questions about it

More about your portfolio

Your portfolio must contain the information you have researched, your notes and other evidence that led you to make certain decisions about your proposed business.

This should be divided into the following sections:

- Ideas for your start-up business
- Research for the start-up business
- Initial plan for a business idea
- Format of business start-up and reasons for choice
- Business model
- Presentation
- Observation records/witness statements. These may be from your teacher/tutor, other learners in your group or other contacts you have made as part of your investigations or research.

You will find activities to help you to assemble your research materials as well as assessment activities that cover all the criteria as you progress through the unit.

Remember

As you work through this unit, date all your reference and research notes and keep them safely in a folder or your portfolio, so that you don't lose anything.

TOPIC A.1

Finding information

Getting started

Some people believe that to run a successful enterprise you must be passionate about the work that you do. Others think that you should research opportunities and then make a practical decision. What do you think?

Sources of information

There are many sources of information on business, both printed and online. Some of these provide facts and information on the business world, others give details of current trends and some provide practical advice and help to **entrepreneurs**.

- **Newspapers:** National newspapers are distributed throughout the country. The information they contain includes news items, feature articles and advertisements. Some, such as *The Times*, have a business section. Local newspapers contain information of interest to people living within the region where they are distributed. Some are free of charge.
- **Professional and trade journals:** These are magazines published for people working in different jobs and industries, from hairdressers and grocers to farmers and architects. They focus on articles of interest to that particular group and include advertisements on products and services they may want to buy.

Key terms

Entrepreneur – someone who starts up a new business in order to make a profit, often in a way that involves financial risks (our word 'enterprise' comes from this French word).

Activity Investigating newspapers

In groups, investigate two national daily newspapers. Look at today's front page and a content summary. Write a brief description of the content of that paper and compare your ideas. You can access newspapers online by visiting www.pearsonhotlinks.co.uk and searching for this title.

Newspapers can be divided into groups according to their readership. More serious newspapers include the *Financial Times*, *the Guardian* and the *Daily Telegraph*. Some, like *The Times* and the *Independent*, are published in a compact format.

Did you know?

The term **broadsheets** refers to newspapers printed on large sheets of paper, such as the *Daily Telegraph* and *Financial Times*. Many smaller newspapers, such as the *Daily Mail* or *The Sun* are tabloid newspapers. 'Red tops' are tabloids where the title is in a red box. These contain more celebrity stories and gossip than other papers.

Newspapers are a useful source of information but can you think of any examples where the information they present may be biased?

- **Websites:** There is a huge amount of information available on the internet. Reputable websites of help to young entrepreneurs include:

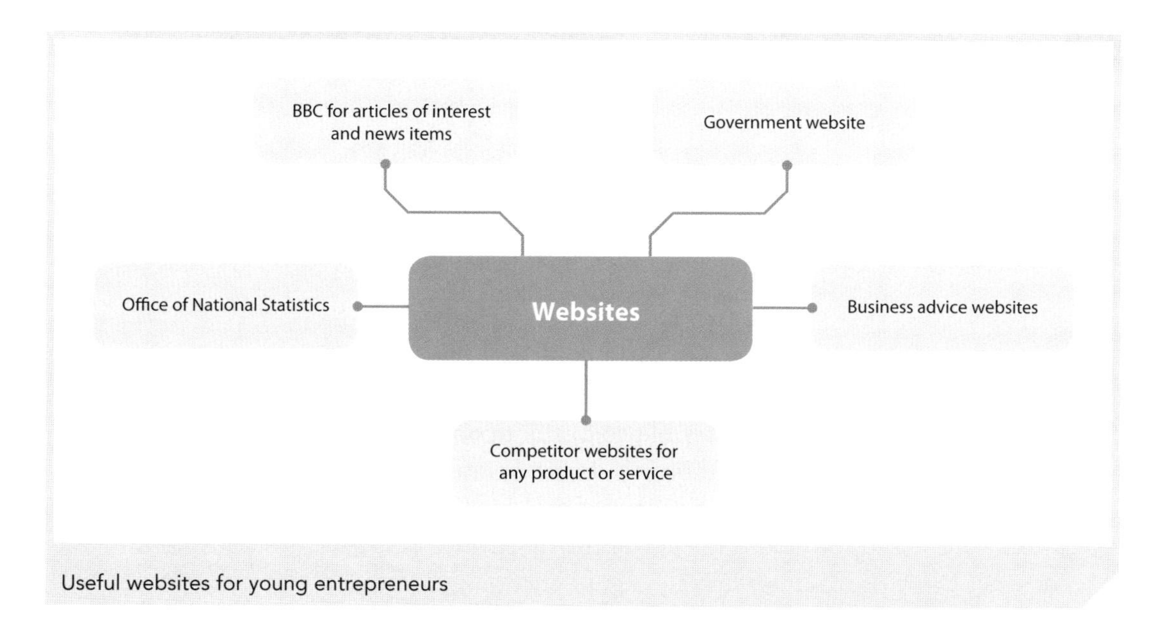

Useful websites for young entrepreneurs

- **Business networking organisations:** These run informal get-togethers where entrepreneurs can meet and exchange ideas and information. You can find a list of those in your area by visiting Pearson hotlinks. You can access this by visiting www.pearsonhotlinks.co.uk and searching for this title.

Activity Investigating young entrepreneurs

In groups, search on Google under the heading 'best 10 UK websites for young entrepreneurs'. Investigate two of them in detail and compare your findings.

Reliability of sources

Today most people are aware that information on some websites, such as Wikipedia, may be unreliable. Blogs and recommendations on Facebook and Twitter are simply people's opinions. However, even seemingly reliable sources, such as national newspapers and company websites, may not be totally accurate. The main issues to be aware of include bias and currency of information.

- **Bias** is when the writer puts forward only one viewpoint. This may be because they represent a specific organisation (a trade union will always argue for its members; the AA will always argue the case for motorists), or because they hold a strong opinion on a topic.
- **Currency of information** relates to the date of the item. Most information goes out of date very quickly, so always check how recent it is to see if it is still relevant.

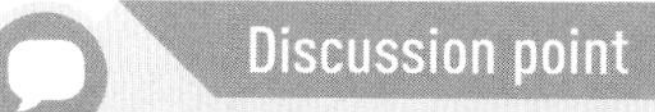

Two newspapers are on sale. One headline reads: 'Shock as 20,000 GCSE papers need remarking'. The other says: 'Fewer than 0.5% of GCSE results are queried'. If 5.8 million GCSE qualifications were awarded that year, which newspaper is correct, and which headline would sell the most copies? Discuss your ideas as a class.

Factors to consider in the current business environment

Getting started

What is the business environment like in your area? Which types of business are thriving and which are not? Compare your ideas as a class.

Introduction

All businesses are affected by the current business environment. This means the local and national factors that will affect it. They include the location of the business and its customers and the political and economic situation that prevails at the time.

National factors

Some people are not interested in politics or the **economy** unless something bad happens to them, such as losing their job. In 2011, unemployment rose, especially among young people. Few people received pay rises, but fuel and energy prices increased. This meant people had less money to spend. This affects all business because sales and profits then fall.

It is important that anyone thinking of starting a business understands the national factors that can affect them.

Key terms

Economy – the system by which a country's money and goods are produced and used.

Exchange rates – the value of an individual currency against other currencies.

Interest rates – the cost of borrowing money.

Political issues

There are three main political parties in the UK – Conservative, Labour, and Liberal Democrat (Lib Dem). In 2010, a coalition government was formed between the Conservatives and the Lib Dems because no single party gained an outright majority share of the vote. The coalition will govern the country until the next General Election.

Activity Finding out about voting

The date of the next General Election is given on the Government website. There are two reasons why a General Election might be held sooner. Go to Pearson hotlinks to find out about what these are and to learn more about voting.

Did you know?

The government gets its money through taxation and by borrowing money. The government uses this money to provide public services in Britain, such as education, the NHS and road networks.

Type and level of government support for business

All political parties want businesses in the UK to thrive and more overseas firms to operate here. The reasons are simple:

- If jobs are available and people are working, then they pay tax and fewer people need benefits. This means the government receives more money and pays out less and therefore has more money to spend.
- If people feel positive about the future and think the government is doing a good job, they are more likely to re-elect that political party next time.

To help businesses, governments aim to have a stable and growing economy. They may also offer assistance by providing loans or grants. The government has introduced a National Loan Guarantee scheme to make it easier for small firms to borrow money and entrepreneurs to raise funds to start up a business. It provides online help for businesses at Business Link and on the BIS (Department for Business Innovation and Skills).

Taxation

The main taxes collected by Her Majesty's Revenue and Customs (HMRC) are:

- **Income tax** – paid by employees on a PAYE (pay as you earn) basis
- **National Insurance** – paid by both employers and employees
- **Value added tax (VAT)** – added to many sales transactions. VAT-registered businesses can reclaim the VAT they pay on most purchases
- **Corporation tax** – paid by limited companies and based upon the profit made.

The economy

The 'economy' refers to a country's wealth and resources and how much money it earns by producing goods and services. This determines the standard of living of the people who live there. It is much better to live in a country with a stable and growing economy.

Figure 1.1 is a simple description of how the economy operates. Consumers buy goods from firms which use this money to hire workers and pay wages. These workers then buy more goods, and so on. The more this happens, the greater the number of people employed and the richer they can become.

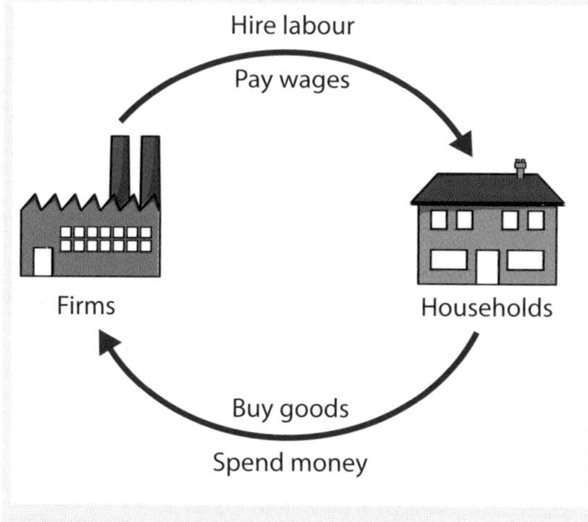

Figure 1.1 How the economy operates

Indicators that show how well the economy is working include:

- **Level of employment:** If this is high, people have more money to spend so the economy is likely to grow.
- **Inflation:** Low inflation means that prices and wages only increase a small amount each year. This is better for businesses as the costs involved in running the enterprise should remain about the same.
- **Exchange rates:** These determine whether British goods and services are cheap or expensive to overseas buyers. The more we sell overseas the more money Britain earns. However, when UK residents buy foreign goods, money leaves the country. Ideally we want to earn more on exports than we spend on imports.
- **Interest rates**: These are also referred to as the cost of loans. If these are low, businesses are more likely to borrow money to invest in better machinery, equipment or buildings. This enables UK businesses to stay up to date and competitive.

Activity Susie's cuddly toys

Susie's cuddly toys sell well in America. To meet a new order Susie needs to borrow £5,000 to buy more equipment. The order is worth US$30,000.

1 If interest rates are 7.5% and she borrows the money for a year, how much will she repay?

2a If one pound sterling is currently worth $1.5, how much is the order worth in sterling?

2b If, by the time the goods are sent, £1 = $1.6, will she make more money or less?

Give a reason for your answer.

CONTINUED ▸▸

Did you know?

The late Steve Jobs (Apple) started his business in a garage, Rob Law (who designed Trunkies®, the ride-on children's cases) started his business in his flat and JK Rowling wrote the first Harry Potter book in a café. According to Enterprise Nation, over 2,000 new businesses a week are started from homes in the UK.

Local factors

The type of enterprise will influence the premises that are needed and where they should be situated. Many small businesses are run from home. The advantages are that there is no rent to pay, no travelling costs and no commuting time, but you need to be self-disciplined as there are often distractions at home!

Location

The best location is the cheapest place which provides enough space and easy access to customers and suppliers. If you start an eBay business, you can work from home easily. If you open a retail outlet you need to be near shoppers – whether on a high street, in a market or in a mall. If you start a sandwich shop, you need passing trade, so a busy main road (with parking) is better than a side street or housing estate.

Requirements for resources

All businesses need resources. The main aspects to consider are summarised in Table 1.1.

Table 1.1 Resource factors to consider

Resources	Factors to consider
Premises	These may be a shop, office, workshop or small industrial unit. The appearance is important if customers visit you, and so is nearby parking. Small business and enterprise centres provide accommodation at reasonable rates with many services, such as electricity and wi-fi, included.
Staff	Any staff you employ must be able to reach you easily. If unemployment is high in the area, labour costs may also be lower.
Equipment and other supplies	A dog walker needs little equipment, whereas a DJ needs equipment plus transport. A car valeting firm needs a supply of water, cleaning materials and a forecourt. Allow enough space to store and use any necessary items.
Stocks of goods and raw materials	How large are these items, how many will you need to store? If they are valuable, you may need a safe. If they are perishable, such as flowers or ice cream, you will need a cold room or freezer.
Location of suppliers	If you are dependent on regular supplies of materials or fresh food, then you will save money on travel or delivery costs if you are near to a major outlet or producer. You will also need less storage space if you replenish stocks regularly.
Customers	Customers are essential to your business survival. If you visit customers, aim to keep travel time and costs down. If they come to you, then location and 'your image' is more important. Will they book an appointment or do you want to attract passers-by? Where are your main competitors, and why? Should you be near them?

What factors should you consider when choosing premises for your business?

Activity Finding accommodation

Many local councils support new business start-ups and also offer accommodation in specially built units and centres. Search online to find those available in your local area.

Impact of factors

When you decide which factors are relevant to your own business idea, you must consider how any decision you make would affect a target group of customers.

Ideally, your target group will consist of people who would use your services or buy your products and whom you can ask for feedback. You can then find out if you are on the right track by testing out your ideas. If the feedback is generally negative, you might have to consider swapping your business proposition for an alternative!

Just checking

1. What is inflation and why is high inflation bad for businesses?
2. Why do the government and business entrepreneurs both want employment levels to be high?
3. List four types of taxes paid in the UK.

Activity Factors affecting your business

Factors that will influence the location of a coffee shop are: the proximity of other shops and businesses; plenty of space for customers; good wi-fi access; easy access for suppliers to deliver; passing trade; nearby parking and availability of staff. Produce your own list of factors that will influence the location of a different type of enterprise. Now add any other factors that may affect your idea for a business. Keep your notes safely in your folder.

TOPIC A.3

Trends affecting business

Getting started

Some experts think that all 'point and shoot' cameras will soon be obsolete now that everyone can take photos with their mobile phones. Do you agree?

All businesses are affected by changes in the world around them. These can provide new opportunities but they can also threaten the survival of organisations that fail to adapt. In 1888 Kodak made its name by producing the first cameras and rolls of film that people could easily use. In 2011 it filed for bankruptcy. The company had failed to adapt quickly enough to new developments in digital photography.

The types of trends that affect business are shown in Figure 1.2:

Figure 1.2 Trends affecting business

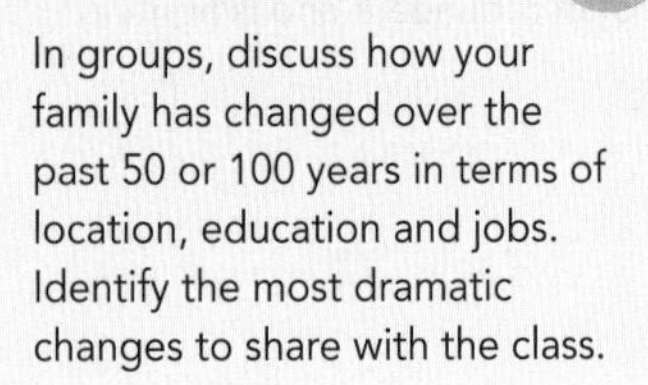

Discussion point

In groups, discuss how your family has changed over the past 50 or 100 years in terms of location, education and jobs. Identify the most dramatic changes to share with the class.

Social trends

These involve the way we live and behave. Sixty years ago fewer people owned a car or went abroad on holiday and borrowing money was considered shameful. Today driving to the airport to catch a plane and paying by credit card is considered normal. Society has changed a lot in a short time. So how does this affect business?

- **Population changes** – the population of Great Britain increased by over 20 million people between 1911 and 2011, according to ONS Census figures, and there are more elderly people because life expectancy has increased as a result of improved diet and healthcare. This presents opportunities for organisations like Saga who target 'silver spenders'. A more culturally diverse population has provided opportunities for ethnic speciality shops, from kosher butchers to Asian wedding planners.
- **Households and families** now often consist of a 'blended' family where parents, step-parents, children and step children live together. Couples may opt to cohabit rather than marry. In the UK, civil partnerships between same-sex couples are now legal and accepted by society.

- **Education** has improved with more young people achieving good GCSE and A-level grades and attending university. Some students now choose to study near their home to keep their living costs down.
- **Labour market** changes have seen more women working and more families reliant on good quality childcare. Employment laws have given workers more protection and have allowed employees to request flexible working. Many people work from home, and some have more than one part-time job. There is more temporary work available and people expect to have several different jobs during their working life.
- **Increasing travel for work** – many people endure long commutes to their workplace, often to avoid the high cost of housing in city centres. In some families, one person may work away during the week, or work abroad on a short-term contract, while their partner and children remain at home. Some people emigrate to improve their career prospects.

Why do you think so many people commute to work?

Activity Brainstorming business opportunities

Today most people are far more aware of health and fitness. In groups, brainstorm the business opportunities that have occurred as a result. Then choose one other social or lifestyle trend and make a similar list. Compare your ideas as a class.

Did you know?

The decline in demand for stand-alone satnavs has meant that Halfords has now refocused its operations on selling bicycles and car maintenance products. Meanwhile, TomTom (a satnav producer) has made 10% of its staff redundant and is fighting the competition by issuing an iPhone and an iPad app.

Technology trends

These not only affect what people buy and how they work and spend their leisure time, but also mean that some products rapidly become obsolete. Videotapes gave way to DVDs, now there are internet-ready Blu-ray players and high definition TVs. 3D and Smart televisions are now on sale and an integrated iTV from Apple is a possibility, too. As Internet connection speeds increase, DVDs and Blu-ray disks may take second place to movie streaming on demand.

Today most people have a computer. For personal use, laptops, smartphones and tablets now outrank PCs and provide almost continuous access to the internet. Banking and shopping, communicating, researching information, social networking and sharing photos are common online activities and a fundamental part of many people's lives. Cloud computing will mean that in the future, programs and data are stored remotely, rather than on computers themselves.

CONTINUED ▸▸

Case study

Two new technology trends have been the rise in online buying by mobile phone (300% higher at the end of 2012 than 2011) and the massive increase in application or 'app' downloads.

This has led to increased income for app stores and for developers, and has tempted many people to try their hand at creating an app. As over 50% of downloaded apps in the UK are games, this is probably the best place to start.

Certainly Daniel Chang thought so. Daniel already worked for a well-known animation studio but spent much of his spare time over eight months developing 'Dream Sheep', an addictive game involving floating sheep, lethal stars and fluffy clouds. The basic game is free from the iTunes Store.

Daniel honed his skills designing the game, writing the music and carrying out the programming. However, basic guidance is given at many sites online, so all you need is a very good idea, money to pay a developer and friends who will spread the word on Facebook and Twitter!

Dream Sheep

1. What has caused the surge in demand by consumers for downloaded apps?
2. Suggest two reasons why writing a game app is a good idea, especially if you have the skills?
3. Given the number of apps available, what do you think Daniel's biggest challenge is now?
4. Find out more about 'Dream Sheep' by visiting Pearson hotlinks. If you have an iPhone, iPod Touch or iPad, try it out yourself and tell your friends if you like it!

Did you know?

Many businesses have made a feature out of being 'green', such as Ecover products and The Natural Nursery. The Green Oil business was started in a garden shed by Simon Nash. Use the internet to find out more about these businesses.

Environmental trends

Most people are aware of the negative effects of some consumer and commercial actions on the environment. They know that the planet's resources will not last for ever, that sustainability is important and that pollution of any type is a bad thing.

- **Renewable energy** comes from natural sources, such as the sun or wind. Therefore solar power and wind power are renewable, whereas oil, gas and coal are not.
- **Recycling** means that items are reused instead of being thrown away. People now expect suppliers to incorporate recyclable materials in their products and packaging.

Ethical trends

Ethics relates to principles and standards of behaviour. Consumers now expect businesses to behave ethically and to give something back to the community. What does this actually mean? Ethical issues are often closely linked to environmental concerns and include:

- **Carbon footprint,** which is calculated by the amount of emissions produced by an activity. The aim is to become 'carbon neutral' by using less energy and compensating for unavoidable use, such as by tree planting or investing in schemes to provide renewable energy in developing countries.
- **Responsible sourcing** of all types of supplies. Although timber has had the most publicity, because of the global effects of destroying the rainforests, ethical companies also look at many other aspects relating to their suppliers. These include a ban on child labour, and insisting on fair pay rates, reasonable working hours and good working conditions.
- **Animal welfare** in the UK is now covered by the Animal Welfare Act which governs the way animals must be treated by breeders, those who keep working animals and pet owners.

Remember

In practical terms, being ethical means that you will always source and supply reputable products, never mislead a customer to make a sale and never make promises that you cannot fulfil.

Activity Researching ethical trading

Research ethical trading and then find out which businesses you know are members of the Ethical Trading Initiative.

Business and the community

Responsible businesses do not wait for the law to tell them what to do. They identify their own values and write an ethical code which states the actions they will and will not take.

Many businesses also have charitable trusts or foundations which enable them to contribute to the welfare of their suppliers, the local community or other needy causes.

Business in the Community is a charity which promotes responsible business practice and gives awards to outstanding organisations and projects.

In 2011, there were protests across the world against wealthy bankers who were held responsible for the worldwide financial crisis and the huge pay rises awarded to some top executives. Should it be socially and ethically unacceptable to be paid a massive salary, no matter what you do? What effect would this have? Research the issue further, then debate it as a class.

Activity Research trends and changes

Research the main trends and changes that could affect your ideas for a start-up business. Divide these into risks that would threaten your business and opportunities from which you would benefit. Keep your notes safely in your folder.

TOPIC A.4

Size of business and type

Introduction

Businesses come in all shapes and sizes. In 2012, there were about 4.8 million business enterprises in the UK. Over 60% of these were owned by one person, often working without any other staff.

Key terms

SMEs – stands for 'small and medium enterprises'.

Microbusiness – a business which has fewer than ten staff.

Types of business

Most businesses in the UK are small and are known as **SMEs** (small and medium enterprises). **Microbusinesses** are even smaller. Each category is defined by the number of people they employ, as shown in Table 1.2.

Table 1.2 Types of business enterprise

Type of enterprise	Number of employees	Number of enterprises in the UK at start of 2012	Total number of people employed (thousands)
Microbusiness	Up to 9	1,022,695	3,848
Small enterprise	10–49	177,950	3,471
Medium enterprise	50–249	29,751	2,909
Large business	250 or more	6,455	9,763

(Source: Department for Business, Innovation and Skills)

Did you know?

74% of enterprises have no employees and 3.83 million people work from home.

Activity: Calculating SMEs

Use Table 1.2 to calculate the total number of SMEs in the UK and the number of people they employ.

Start-ups and existing businesses

Start-ups are new businesses, whereas existing businesses are those that are already open and trading. Over 200,000 new enterprises were set up during 2011 but unfortunately not all of them were successful. The Office of National Statistics figures show that about 20,000 businesses close down every year. Many of these are small enterprises.

The government is trying to encourage more new start-ups because successful businesses help everyone and some will grow. They provide an income for the entrepreneur, provide employment for staff, give customers more choice and help to keep prices low because there is more competition for goods and services.

Discussion point

Why do some businesses fail while others survive? Is it because the owner is poor at running the enterprise or for some other reason? Discuss this in groups and see how many reasons you can suggest.

Activity: Researching a website

Russell's brother has a 'man with a van' business. Visit Pearson hotlinks to visit the AnyVan site. You can access this by going to www.pearsonhotlinks.co.uk and searching for this title. Customers can list jobs and ask for quotes. Can you suggest two benefits of the website for customers and for small business enterprises?

WorkSpace

Sam Clayton

Photographer

Many would-be entrepreneurs struggle to start their own enterprise because they don't have the skills or cannot raise the money required. In that case, they could do worse than to follow Sam Clayton's example. Sam successfully runs one of the millions of one-person businesses in the UK.

After leaving school, Sam trained to become a nursery nurse and spent several years working with children. Working in a nursery and watching a photographer take photos of the children, she remembered her previous interest in photography. Her father was a keen photographer. Sam decided to take a course in photography and borrowed her father's camera to create her own photos. She created her own darkroom at home and persuaded the nursery managers to let her become the official nursery photographer.

It wasn't until Sam photographed her manager's wedding that she realised she wanted to start a photographic business.

Sam continued to work full-time to finance her growing business. She carried out research, attended training courses and looked for photographers and images which inspired her. She made some mistakes, spending money on advertising that wasn't effective and buying unnecessary equipment, and she struggled to price her skills when people asked her to quote for a job. An online American forum for wedding and portrait photographers was a great help to Sam. Exchanging views with like-minded photographers on Facebook and Twitter helped, too.

In April 2006, five years after starting her business, Sam took the plunge and set out as a fully self-employed photographer. She has never looked back.

Think about it

1. How did Sam overcome the problem of raising finance to run her business?
2. In what way did Sam's previous experience come in useful? How do you think it helps her now?
3. How can Facebook and Twitter help Sam to promote her business?
4. To be successful, businesses need a USP (unique selling point) that makes them stand out. Look at Sam's website by visiting Pearson hotlinks. Identify her USP and suggest why she receives so many referrals by word of mouth from clients.

TOPIC B.1

How business ideas can be successful

Getting started

All entrepreneurs spend time and risk their savings to make their idea a reality. They also risk failure. What skills and abilities are needed to be an entrepreneur? Discuss your ideas as a class.

Introduction

Some businesses are very successful, others are not. Why is this? Can you guarantee success if you have a good idea? In this topic, you can find out.

Did you know?

- When Phil Mundy found he couldn't use his iPad during a skiing holiday, he invented iPrints – small strips that attach to the fingertip of a glove allowing you to use a smartphone or tablet in a cold environment.
- Global Entrepreneurship Week takes place each November. Find out what happens and how this can inspire young entrepreneurs.

Successful business ideas

There are usually good reasons why some business ideas are successful and others are a disaster.

These are the main reasons why some ideas are so successful:

- **Finding innovative solutions:** Solving a problem by thinking of something new is always a good idea. Recent innovations include the SkyBox (which can pause live programmes) and the electric car. James Dyson built his business on innovative solutions such as the bagless vacuum cleaner and bladeless fan.
- **Meeting customer needs:** This means selling products or services that people want to buy at the right price. Clever businesses offer additional services to beat their competitors, such as free delivery and a personal service. If you do all this *and* offer something different, you should have a recipe for success.
- **Identifying new needs:** Focusing on a new and growing area is always a good idea.
  - Mentoring and coaching are techniques used to help people to develop their full potential in many areas, from work or communication skills to sports and fitness.
  - Using digital media, such as social media websites, to target customers more effectively is now the aim of many businesses.
- **Continuing to meet established customer needs:** Some customer needs, such as transport, food, toiletries and clothes are standard, but there are still opportunities in these areas. Look at what is on offer, identify any gaps and then review and improve your idea. For example, many taxi firms now offer stretch limos or minibuses (for hen or stag parties) and airport services. Speciality foods cater for different tastes, and luxury toiletries and fashionable accessories are also in demand.
- **Being entrepreneurial** means taking risks, having good ideas and being persistent. Find examples of inspirational entrepreneurs such as Tanya Budd, who designed the HypoHoist; Rose Grimond, the business woman behind Orkney Rose, Mark Zuckerberg who founded Facebook, or someone else.
- **Importance of having a strong vision and seeing it through:** The late Steve Jobs, the co-founder of Apple, always had faith in his own belief, even when things went wrong. The key is to learn from a problem and not give up.

- **Measures of success:** These relate to methods of checking the success of a business, for example:
  - Financial – by looking at sales and revenue figures
  - Social – by checking out how many people like the business on Facebook or are following it on Twitter
  - Customer satisfaction – by obtaining feedback from customers who use the product or service.

Assessment activity 1.1 *Maths*

2A.P1 | 2A.P2 | 2A.M1 | 2A.M2 | 2A.D1

You have been asked to produce your own booklet for young entrepreneurs in your area. This will describe the local business environment and identify trends and changes that may affect a start-up business. Your booklet should be divided into three sections:

1. The first section should focus on the current business environment that exists in your own area. You should also be aware of changes that can take place and explain how these can affect a start-up business.
2. The next section should focus on trends you have researched. If you wish, you can focus on trends and that could affect your own idea for a start-up business. You need to compare how two trends have impacted on a start-up business.
3. The final section should focus on the current risks, opportunities and trends in the current business environment for a start-up business. Your assessment should be based on the data you have researched and you should focus on appropriate guidance for an entrepreneur.

Tip

You **assess** information by carefully considering all the factors or events that apply and identifying which are the most important or relevant. Use your research to provide evidence for your conclusions.

You **compare** by identifying the main factors in two or more situations. Point out the similarities and differences and, if appropriate, say which is best and why. Or explain the effects these factors have had.

Link

You can read more about sales and revenue figures in *Unit 2: Finance for business.*

Business ideas

Introduction

Some people think that brilliant ideas come unexpectedly – they call these a 'light bulb' moment. Others believe they come through research and experience. What do you think?

Did you know?

Cirque du Soleil is French for Circus of the Sun. The name was chosen to suggest youth and energy.

The founder of Cirque du Soleil, French Canadian Guy Laliberté, slept on a bench in Hyde Park on his first visit to London when he was a teenage busker with no money. Today he is estimated to be worth £1.6 billion. He argues that there is no such thing as a new business idea only a variation on someone else's. He thought circuses were outdated and developed a spectacular that features human performers, not animals.

Key term

Unique Selling Point (USP) – a special feature of a product (or service) that makes it easy to promote and sell.

Discussion point

Twitter was the result of a brainstorming session. Brainstorming is a short, focused discussion where you suggest ideas. The trick is to be open to all suggestions and see where they lead. Work in groups to identify 'the best business idea for a lifetime' and see what happens.

In the last topic you saw examples of how business ideas can be successful and you may have already thought of some good ideas yourself. If not, then this topic will help.

What is the **Unique Selling Point (USP)** of Cirque du Soleil?

Activity Identifying your skills

Guy Laliberté built on his talents as a street performer. A teenage Tommy Hilfiger started his business because he kept being asked where he bought his clothes. List your skills, abilities, interests and hobbies to see if they trigger any good business ideas.

Researching the market

You often hear people ask why a certain product is not made or why they cannot buy something. **Market research** aims to find out what potential customers think or want. This can identify gaps in the market and potential opportunities to provide what people want.

A successful example of market research is Moonpig®. The website was launched to satisfy the demand for greetings cards that could be individually customised.

There are two methods of research you can use:

- **Primary research** is the collection of original data. This is the way to get new ideas, to find out about people's individual buying habits and establish individual customer needs.
- **Secondary research** is desk-based and means researching online and in books and newspapers. Use this to check whether the **market** is growing or declining, how large it is, the range of goods or services provided, who sells them and the prices they charge.

Key terms

Market – the customers for a particular product or service

Market research – finding out customer views and opinions

Activity Carrying out research

1. Work in small groups to find out what ideas your friends and family have for new or updated products or services that would meet their needs. Design a short questionnaire to find out. Talk to people, send emails and texts, use Facebook. Try to find answers from 10 people to compare with your group.
2. Go online to find out what types of enterprises other people are setting up at Enterprise Nation. List any that appeal to you.
3. Mintel is a large market research agency. Check its blog to find current trends.
4. Investigate your own ideas further. Remember that some useful sources were given at the start of this unit.

Keep all your notes safely as you will need them for your next assessment activity.

Selecting a product or service

Do you make or sell a product or offer a service? What is the difference?

- **A product** is an item that is produced to satisfy the needs of the market. You can make a product yourself or buy items ready-made and then sell them to customers.

  Making products like clothes or jewellery means you need suitable equipment or facilities. Producing any type of food means you must check out the regulations that apply (see next topic). All products must be good quality and value for money if you want repeat sales.
- **A service is** a task you perform – such as valeting a car or walking a dog. Some services, such as mowing lawns and DJ-ing, mean you will need transport and some basic equipment.

  To get a good reputation your work must be of high quality and you must be totally reliable.

Remember

Offering a quality product or professional service is essential if you want repeat business and your customers to recommend you to others.

CONTINUED ▸▸

▸▸ CONTINUED

Targeting customers

Your target customer is the person who will benefit most from your product or service. Small enterprises usually do better by specialising in supplying items or services to a certain group, known as the **niche market.** This is smaller than the **mass market** which is a term used to describe goods that everyone buys, such as shampoo or chocolate. It makes it easier for you to set a competitive price but it is vital that you target your customers accurately. For example, if you plan to sell children's mittens, you will have an entirely different target customer than if you sell gardening gloves.

Did you know?

Niche markets provide greater opportunities for small enterprises because there is less competition from large suppliers.

Activity: Finding a niche

Check out some niche markets yourself on Amazon. Simply click on a major category, such as accessories, then pick an item, such as gloves and see how many different types you are offered!

The main ways in which customers can be targeted are shown in the table below.

Table 1.3 Categories of target customers

Category	Focus on	Examples
By age	Babies, toddlers, pre-school, teenagers, young adults, older or retired customers	Children's party entertainers, face painting, many types of books, magazines, music, films and TV programmes
By gender	Male or female	Many toys, toiletries and clothing shops
By location	The local community, national market or selling internationally	Local sandwich shop or market stall, eBay store, website with e-commerce facilities
By interests concerns	Culture, lifestyle, hobbies, health or needs	Henna tattoos, juice bars, computer games, exercise classes, mobility aids, pet services.

Create a profile for this customer. What products and services do you think she's interested in?

Meet the needs of your target customer

You will only meet the needs of your **target customer** if you understand what they want and why they want it. This means finding out how they think, where they buy, how often they shop and how much they spend.

Put this information into a **customer profile**. This is a snapshot of your customer that summarises:

- their age and lifestyle
- where they live
- what they like and dislike, worry about and value
- how much they would be prepared to pay
- their shopping and spending habits.

Activity Creating a customer profile

Create a customer profile that represents your own class. Compare your ideas. Then think about how it would change for a different age group or by location.

Remember

Lulu is a grandmother and Alan Sugar is a grandfather – both are fit, lively and intelligent! Avoid making assumptions about different groups of people and research your target customer properly.

Benefits versus features

Your target customer will buy your product or service because of the benefits they obtain. The features are less important. For example, the benefit of a microwave oven is that you can heat and defrost food quickly and have some meals ready in minutes. Features (such as pre-programmable settings) are useful but less relevant.

Case study

Providing a major benefit can guarantee success. The Gro-clock enables parents to pre-programme a sun icon to appear to indicate when it's time to get up. This helps the early-waking tot to learn to stay in bed longer – which benefits the parents, too! For most buyers this is their reason for purchase.

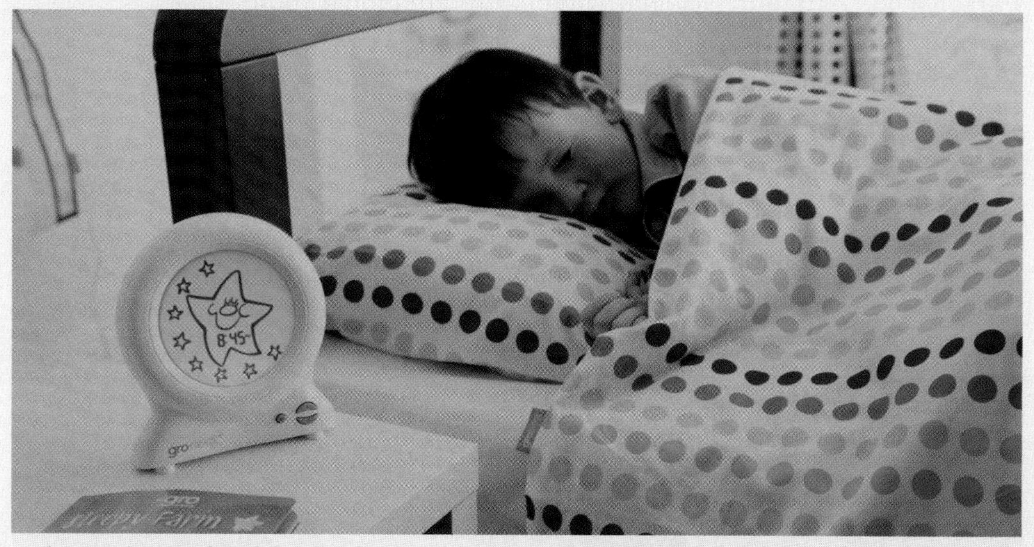

What are the benefits of the Gro-clock?

The Gro Company started with a Grobag Baby Sleep Bag – a smaller size sleeping bag designed by two parents when they needed to keep their own baby warm at night. Read their success story online by accessing their website via Pearson hotlinks and see what other products they make.

1 Who is the target customer for the Gro-clock? Give a reason for your answer.
2 Why was the Grobag Baby Sleep Bag so popular?
3 Suggest two reasons why The Gro Company itself has been so successful.

Key terms

Mass market – all the consumers in one market

Niche market – a small group of customers for a specialised item

Target customer – the customer that a business aims to supply

Customer profile – the main features of a particular group of customers.

Activity Thinking about benefits

List the benefits of your planned product or service. Remember, these must meet the needs of your target customer.

Assessing the suitability of a business idea

Introduction

Once you have come up with your business ideas, you need to assess them to find out which are the most suitable. This means putting your enthusiasm to one side for a while, and thinking carefully about the prospects of success.

Did you know?

Many church halls and community centres rent out their premises for short periods during the week. They can be used by anyone who wants to offer aerobics, yoga or Zumba dance classes, for example.

The resources required

Although you might dream of starting an airline business or competing with Facebook, you are unlikely to do so, given the resources required. It is easy to get carried away with an idea without considering the resources you would need.

- **Time and skills:** How much **time** is needed to develop the idea? Do you need help from other people? Do you have all the necessary **skills** and expertise? If not, who has? How much would it cost you to hire them?
- **Personal commitment:** How much energy and **personal commitment** are you prepared to invest? Would you be happy to neglect your social life for several months to work on it? What are your other commitments and how high would this project rank on your list of priorities?
- **Finance, premises, materials and equipment:** Some start-up businesses need all of these, others need very few. If you aim to work from home, then your life is easier. Even if you rent premises to save money, you will have to pay a deposit equivalent to several months' rent. If all you need is a desk and a computer (and you already have both), then you will need to buy less than if you plan to offer a gardening service.

What resources would you need to run a dance class?

Selecting the most appropriate idea

The most appropriate idea is not necessarily the one that requires the least resources, but is unlikely to be the one that needs the most. At this stage you should be able to eliminate any non-starters and should be left with some ideas that are still feasible.

Activity Identify your resources

List the resources required for each of your business ideas. Estimate the likely cost of each one in terms of time, skills, commitment, finance, premises, materials and equipment. Rank each idea according to how appropriate and feasible you think it is. Keep your notes safely in your folder.

Likelihood of success or failure

You now need to decide which one of your remaining ideas is most likely to be a success. You can do this by:

- identifying your prospective customers and deciding how easy it would be to contact them and tell them about your business
- looking at existing demand for your product or service to find out whether it is growing or declining in your area
- estimating how profitable your idea would be – for example, for each item you make or each service you offer, how much money could you make?

Identification of major barriers to entry

'Barriers to entry' is the term used when it is difficult to start a new business because there are many problems and requirements to consider. These could include:

- **large start-up costs** because of the type of premises or amount of equipment needed
- **cash flow issues** because you have to spend money on start-up costs but would not be paid by customers for some time (see Unit 2: Finance for Business)
- **licences** to operate, insurance and other regulations to consider, such as food handling requirements. If you aim to work from home, you need to check that the type of enterprise you plan would be allowed by your local authority.
- **competitors** who are already well established in the area.

Remember

It is essential to come up with a good business name that people will remember. It should summarise what the business is all about. You must not copy competitors' names, although it is helpful to bear them in mind when coming up with ideas yourself.

Activity Assess your business ideas

Assess your own business ideas by carrying out the following activities.

1. Review the business ideas you have come up with so far. Identify the ones that are most likely to be successful by considering which are innovative and will meet new needs or established customer needs.
2. Provide evidence for your views by researching your market and identify gaps or opportunities.
3. Create a profile for your target customer.
4. Assess how easily you will be able to access these customers and the problems or barriers that you might face setting up the business.

Keep your notes safely in your folder.

TOPIC B.4

Producing an initial plan for a business idea

Introduction

You should now have enough information to select the most suitable business idea and produce an initial business plan.

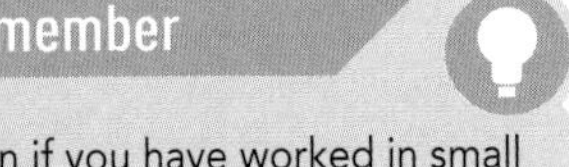

Remember

Even if you have worked in small groups on researching an idea for a start-up business, the initial plan and rationale must be your own work.

What is a rationale?

Your rationale explains why you think your idea is realistic and is worth pursuing further. It must include the following:

- **Your vision**: How do you see your enterprise at the start? What problem will it solve or what customer needs will it fulfil? How will your product or service do this? What will make it different from products and services offered by existing competitors? (For an example of a vision, see the 'On your Bike' case study later in this unit.)
- **The concept**: Provide a clear description of your business idea and how the business will operate, that is, how the business will make money.

Supporting evidence

This is all the information you have researched and collected throughout this unit. As well as providing this, you need to list the evidence you have obtained and explain why this supports your vision and business concept, for example:

- **Possible customers**: By now you should have prepared a customer profile. It is helpful if you also know the potential size of the market and trends that are affecting it.

Who is the target customer for your product or service?

- **Possible routes to market:** How do you plan to supply your goods or service or deliver them to your customers? What alternatives are there?
- **Your strategy (plan) for dealing with competitors:** Do you intend to offer a different product or service, operate in a different location or have a different pricing strategy? Do you have a USP like Sam Clayton (see the WorkSpace feature earlier in this unit)? How is your idea better than the competition?
- **Ideas for financing:** This should be linked to the resources that you have identified will be needed.
- **Ideas for implementation:** How do you see your plan becoming a reality? How would you put it into practice and over what timeframe? How would you cope until the business started making a profit? Do you have all the necessary skills and, if not, what are your plans for acquiring these or getting someone else to help you?

Assessment activity 1.2 *Maths English* 2B.P3 | 2B.P4 | 2B.M3 | 2B.M4 | 2B.D2

Prepare a presentation in which you will outline your own initial plan for a business idea in your local area and explain why it will succeed against others. You will also summarise the research that you have carried out, and the information you have obtained to support this idea. This must include:

1. Your own description of the features of successful businesses you have personally identified and a comparison of the features, strengths and weaknesses of two successful businesses.
2. Your own realistic plan for a business together with a rationale including your vision and concept. Your plan should include the resources you would require and any barriers you have identified as well as your ideas for financing and implementation. You should also refer to the research you have carried out to explain why your plan is suitable for your own area and how your business idea has the potential to respond to market needs. This means showing that you have researched gaps in the market, created a customer profile and identified the best routes to market.
3. Your own justification for how your idea has the potential for success in relation to existing local businesses.

Tip

Justify your views by giving evidence to support your conclusions, for example by explaining your USP and how you will deal with competitors. You should also demonstrate that you have considered the factors that have made other local businesses successful.

Choice of business format

Introduction

The **business format** relates to the way a business is legally owned and operated. All entrepreneurs must choose the format that they think is the most appropriate for their business at the time. The format options are described in the table below.

Did you know?

Some well-known businesses are franchises, such as Body Shop, KFC and Subway. The owner (franchisor) allows other people (franchisees) to use the name and set up an identical business in their own area in return for a fee and, often, a share of the profits.

Table 1.4 Different business formats

Business format	Description/comments	Benefits	Issues
Sole trader – the smallest and most popular type of business in the UK	The business is owned by one person with or without employees. The owner is personally responsible for every aspect of the business, from keeping the premises clean to doing the accounts.	• Easy to set up – just register with HMRC (the tax office). • After paying tax, all the profits are yours. • Record keeping is simple. • You can trade under your own name without needing permission.	• Illness or holidays may mean there is no income. • You need business skills. • You are personally responsible for paying all debts, otherwise you could be declared bankrupt. This is called **unlimited liability**.
Partnership – owned by two or more people who share responsibility for running the business	Drawing up a Partnership Agreement stating each person's role and share of profits helps to prevent disputes.	• Partners can share skills and ideas. • Problems can be discussed and different views taken into account. • The business will still operate if one partner is ill or on holiday.	• Partners may disagree or not contribute equally. • Profits must be shared. • Decision- making is slower. • Partners still have unlimited liability unless they form a Limited Liability Partnership (LLP).
Private limited company – many family firms have this format. The name always ends with 'Ltd'	The business is registered at Companies House as a limited company. Each person invests money in the business and receives shares in return. The company now pays corporation tax on its profits.	• The owners have **limited liability** for debts. If the business fails, they are only liable up to the amount they invested in the business. • Banks are more willing to lend money.	• Shares in a private company cannot be sold to the public. • Limited companies must comply with more laws and send their accounts to Companies House each year. • All directors and company officers have certain legal duties and obligations.
Public limited company – the largest type of privately owned enterprise in the UK. The business name always ends 'plc'	Many started as private limited companies and were then **floated** on the Stock Exchange. This is the term used when a public limited company is launched. Now anyone can buy shares in the company.	• The business receives far more capital which can be used to grow the company. • If the business is successful, the value of the shares will increase, which will increase the overall value of the company. • Some of the profit, after tax, can be paid to the shareholders as dividends.	• The company must comply with more rules and its accounts are reported in the press. • An Annual General Meeting must be held each year and all shareholders are invited. • If the shares fall in value, many shareholders may sell which lowers the value of the company.

Activity Starting a limited company

Find out more about starting and registering a limited company at the Companies House website.

Social enterprises

A **social enterprise** is a business formed with the aim of using any profit or surplus to fulfil social objectives. It may be run as a sole trader, a partnership or a limited company. The format will depend on the type of business, its operations and its objectives.

Case study

On your Bike (Recycle) Ltd is a charitable social enterprise and was started by Ben Fox in July 2010. Ben loves bikes, is passionate about sustainability and detests the fact that the UK dumps over 2000 used bikes into landfill every day. His charity works with schools, hospitals and businesses to obtain and recycle bikes that have been donated or dumped. All the bikes are checked and repaired before being sold to new owners.

Can you think of any other social enterprises that support sustainability?

Ben's vision goes beyond repairing and recycling bikes. He wants to teach students how to check and repair bikes, provide training for the unemployed, promote cycling for health and train people to cycle safely. He also wants to set up a cycle hire with his local authority.

You can find out more about Ben's business by visiting www.pearsonhotlinks.co.uk. If you are a cyclist living in Somerset, do pass on any old bikes to him!

1 Explain Ben's vision in your own words.
2 Explain the difference between a limited company that is not a social enterprise and one that is.

Key terms

Social enterprise – a business which uses its profits or surplus to fulfil social objectives, such as helping others.

Business format – the way a business is legally owned and operated.

Unlimited liability – the owners are personally responsible for all debts, even if this means selling personal possessions.

Limited liability – the owners are only responsible for debts up to the amount they have invested in the business.

Floating – launching a public limited company on the Stock Exchange.

Activity Assess business formats

Assess the advantages and disadvantages of each type of business format for your own business idea. Keep your notes safely in your folder.

Sources of help and support in developing a new business

Getting started

Megan argued there was so much to do before she started her enterprise that she couldn't afford the time to ask for advice or support. Her father replied that she couldn't afford not to. What did he mean? And who is right?

Introduction

There are many sources of help and support available to new entrepreneurs which offer advice and help to prevent unnecessary mistakes.

Sources of help

You may need help in various ways, for example:

- **finance:** Most high street banks employ advisers who will provide entrepreneurs with help and guidance. They also give advice on their websites, run free online courses and publish guides and case studies.
- **start-up capital:** This is the money needed to pay for your initial requirements before you receive any revenue. Options for raising this money include:
  - a loan from family, a bank or specialist organisation (such as The Prince's Trust)
  - selling shares to friends and family
  - an overdraft – arranging with the bank to let you spend more than is in your account, on a temporary basis.
- **further research on your chosen idea:** Your best sources are other similar enterprises. If they are located in a different area which means you would not be a direct competitor, they may be willing to provide information and advice. Otherwise, check their website and investigate case studies online and in newspapers and magazines.
- **independent advice:** This is available, free of charge, from the Business Link website. The portal StartUp Britain was also set up by the government to help entrepreneurs. You can visit this website and search the National Enterprise Network at Pearson hotlinks to find your nearest centre. The StartUp website also offers useful advice on many topics.

Did you know?

- The StartUp website has a special section for young entrepreneurs.
- James Caan, formerly of *Dragons' Den*, is promoting a government scheme to offer start-up loans to young people with ideas. Read about this on their website which can be accessed through Pearson hotlinks at www.pearsonhotlinks.co.uk.

Activity — Researching business support

In small groups, divide up and share out the research tasks below.

- Identify five major banks and investigate each one to find the help and services it provides.
- Find out about The Prince's Trust, how it works and what it can offer young entrepreneurs.
- For a business idea your group has come up with, investigate what your competitors have to offer.
- Check out three different sources of independent advice.
- Search on Google under the heading 'Sources of Business Advice' to see what else you can find!

Each group should give a short presentation to summarise its findings as well as provide a brief handout.

Support networks

Talking to people about business worries or problems is a useful way of obtaining advice. Several support networks exist to promote contact between business people:

Why is it helpful to talk over your ideas with someone else?

- **Chambers of Commerce** are a network of organisations that offers support and advice to their members who run local businesses. Find your local branch by visiting Pearson hotlinks. You can access this by going to www.pearsonhotlinks.co.uk and searching for this title.
- **Trade associations** provide specific help and guidance to their members who work in a particular trade, from aromatherapists to builders. Check the list by visiting Pearson hotlinks.
- **Professional bodies** represent professionals, such as doctors, lawyers and architects. Many also set and mark professional examinations.
- **Friends and family** can be an invaluable support, particularly if you know people who run a business or are experienced in finance or accounts.
- **Charities and voluntary organisations** include The Prince's Trust and UnLtd which supports social entrepreneurs. ADP (Association of Disabled Professionals) provides help and support to anyone who is disabled and wants to set up a business.

Did you know?

The government has set up a mentoring programme to enable entrepreneurs to receive advice and guidance from experienced professionals. Visit Pearson hotlinks to find a link to their website.

Activity Researching two organisations

The Federation of Small Businesses represents thousands of small businesses and provides advice on its website. Shell LiveWIRE, funded by Shell UK limited, provides free information to young people on running a business and enables them to network with other entrepreneurs and talk to online mentors. It also runs an annual competition.

Find out more about both organisations on their websites.

Remember

Keep all your research materials safely in your folder. You will need them when you prepare your business model.

TOPIC C.3

Business model

Did you know?

Many business models are a variation on other similar businesses. For example, a restaurant, a fast-food outlet, a sandwich bar and a party caterer are all in the food trade, but their business models are very different.

Introduction

A business model is a description of a business which explains exactly how it will operate. Your task now is to use all your research to create your own description, based on your own realistic idea for a business start-up.

Your business model must include all the components and functions of your business and state the revenues it will generate, the expenses it will incur and show how you will make a profit. A more detailed list is given in the table below.

Table 1.5 Components of a business model

Component	Explanation
Research results	The results of researching your chosen market. This must include: • a description of your potential customers (and whether these are businesses or individual consumers) • information about your main competitors.
Goods or services	What you intend to produce or offer for sale. If you are selling goods, you must state whether you intend to make these yourself, or buy them and resell them.
Means of delivering to the customer	How do you intend to sell your good(s) or service(s) – over the internet or by making direct sales? Or both? Would you consider taking on a franchise or not. Why?
Business aims	These are your long-term goals, i.e. what you want to achieve over the next three to five years.
Business objectives	These are short-term targets you want to achieve in the first few months or year. The most effective objectives are SMART, for example someone who makes jewellery may aim to create 15 individual items a week. • This is **Specific**, because it focuses on one target • This is **Measurable** because they can check how many are made • This must be **Achievable** with the resources they have if they work hard • This must be **Realistic** in the time available • This is **Time-related** because 'a week' has been specified.
Stakeholders and their influence	Stakeholders are those people directly affected by your business. They include: • the owners, including any business partners who will have views on what you should do • employees who have opinions and also legal rights • customers who will have opinions about what they want to buy, the quality they expect, the price they think is reasonable and associated services, such as delivery • financiers, i.e. anyone who lends you money such as a bank, charitable organisation or your shareholders. If they fear their money is at risk, they could ask for it back! • suppliers who will rely on you for orders but will also influence your profits, especially if their prices increase. They will want to be paid promptly or may refuse to supply you • the local community who may object if you want to set up a noisy business or one from home with constant visitors, but otherwise will support you and may become customers.

Table 1.5 Components of a business model

Component	Explanation
Finances and start-up costs	You need to list all the start-up costs that you have identified and how you intend to obtain the finances needed to open your business.
Evidence to justify why the idea will succeed	This must be more than wishful thinking! It should include projected sales figures and sales income, based on your chosen pricing policy. You need to estimate your running costs and forecast your potential profit and when this will be achieved. You can also include details of similar successful businesses and how your business model is an improvement on those.

Assessment activity 1.3 *English*

2C.P5 | 2C.P6 | 2C.M5 | 2C.D3

You are to meet a local group of business financiers who may be interested in supporting a realistic and original business idea that has the potential to be successful. Your task is to prepare a presentation to illustrate your idea and business model and to give a short sales pitch to explain it. To support your arguments, you should ensure that your portfolio is up to date and includes all the relevant evidence. Be prepared to discuss your presentation, explain how your idea has developed and the components of your model, and to answer any questions.

Your presentation should include the following information:

- an outline of the format you have chosen for your business start-up with an explanation of the reasons that made you choose this particular format rather than any other
- your business model together with all the essential components, such as your aims and objectives, method of operation, projected revenues and expenses
- a definition of what success is, using your business plan and comparisons to existing businesses to show how likely it is that your business will be successful.

Provide evidence to show why your model is realistic.

In your sales pitch, you should:

- explain how the format and model will enable the business to carry out its activities successfully. This must be based on its potential for success in relation to existing local businesses. You will need to identify and explain how it has the necessary features to respond to market needs by giving reasons for its suitability and explaining why you rejected other ideas
- explain how the format and supporting evidence justifies your initial idea. You could illustrate this by tracing the steps you have taken from your original business ideas to your final vision. This should include how you evaluated the different ideas you had using the sources of information you had obtained, and why you continued to develop this particular one.

Tip

Use your presentation as an opportunity to demonstrate the alternatives you considered, the timeline over which you have been working and your creativity in responding to market needs. Practise explaining your ideas and use the materials in your presentation to prompt you.

Introduction

Every business must be financially healthy to survive. In this unit, you will learn that to achieve this, the amount of money a business spends (its costs) must be less than the money it receives (its revenue). When this happens, the difference between these two figures is known as profit.

This does not happen by accident; it requires careful planning and there are several 'tools', or techniques, that help businesses to do this. These include predicting when a profit will be made by preparing a break-even analysis, and budgeting to ensure that revenue is as predicted and spending is within planned limits. It also means monitoring the money the business has in the bank and can be expected to receive and pay out in the future.

Preparing key financial documents also enables the business to measure its success and identify areas where improvements are needed. You will learn how to prepare these documents as well as the main techniques used by businesses to plan and monitor their financial situation.

Assessment: You will be assessed using an onscreen test lasting one hour.

Learning aims

In this unit you will:

A understand the costs involved in business and how businesses make a profit

B understand how businesses plan for success

C understand how businesses measure success and identify areas for improvement.

My sister is a really good hairdresser but struggled when she started up her own business. Luckily her friend was good at finance and showed her what to do. She says understanding cash flow has been crucial to her survival – so I'm looking forward to learning about business finances.

Tom, *16-year-old Business student*

2 Finance for Business

TOPIC A.1

Understand the costs involved in business

Getting started

What costs are involved in setting up and running a sandwich shop? In small groups, list these and then compare your list with other groups.

Introduction

Even the smallest business has various costs. For example, a local newsagent has to buy stock items of newspapers, magazines, confectionery and crisps, pay staff wages (including people delivering newspapers), pay rent and business rates for the property as well as bills for gas, electricity and telephone.

How much will it cost Sam to start up his business?

Key terms

Start-up costs – the amount of money spent setting up a business before it starts trading.

Operating costs (or running costs) – money spent on a regular basis to keep a business running.

Income – money which is paid into a business.

Understand and identify the costs of a business

The costs incurred in running a business can be split into two main categories:

- **start-up costs**
- **operating costs** (or running costs).

Start-up costs

When people start a new business from scratch, there are various items that are required before they can start trading. A driving instructor needs a car; a print shop needs a computer and a copier. Both will need to advertise their business to attract customers. The main point about start-up costs is that these are incurred *before* any **income** is received and the owner has to find this money. It may come from savings but often is obtained as a loan, perhaps from family or from a bank.

Running costs

These are the day-to-day costs incurred in the running of a business. A driving instructor must buy fuel for the vehicle, and a print shop has to buy paper and pay for electricity.

Did you know?

The total amount of money required to start a new business is known as start-up capital.

Activity — Separating your costs

Divide your list of costs for a sandwich shop into start-up costs and running costs.

Understand, define and identify different types of running costs

The running costs of a business can also be split into two types:

- **fixed costs** (or **indirect costs**)
- **variable costs** (or **direct costs**).

Fixed costs

These have to be paid no matter how many products the business makes or sells or how many customers it has. Driving instructors must tax and insure their cars, whether they have one client or fifty. The print shop must pay for heating and lighting. These are often called **indirect** costs because there is no direct link between these costs and the amount sold.

Variable costs

These costs *are* directly related to the number of items sold or produced. Driving instructors use more fuel if they have more clients, because they are on the road more. Print shops use more paper and ink if they are producing more posters or documents. These are also called **direct** costs because they relate directly to the amount produced or sold.

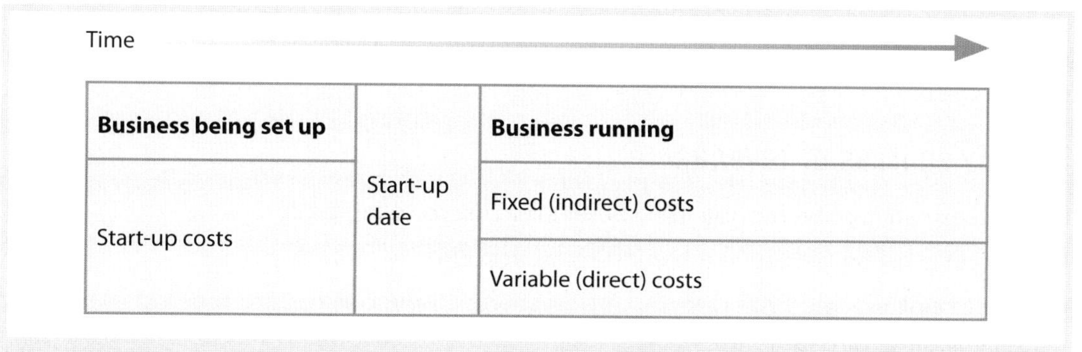

Figure 2.1 Types of business costs

Key terms

Fixed costs (or indirect costs) – expenditure on items which does not change with the number of items sold or produced.

Variable costs (or direct costs) – costs which vary according to the number of items sold or produced.

Total costs – the total amount of money spent running a business over a certain period of time (e.g. a month).

Calculate total costs

The **total costs** of running a business are found by adding the fixed and variable costs. This is shown in the formula below.

total costs = fixed costs + variable costs

Remember

You must know the difference between fixed and variable costs and remember this formula in the assessment.

Activity Calculating your costs

1. Divide your list of running costs for the sandwich shop into fixed costs and variable costs.
2. Use the formula to calculate the total costs of the business for a year if the fixed costs per month are £1000 and the total variable cost per month is £2000.
3. In the print shop, the price of ink suddenly increases considerably. Suggest two actions the owner might take.

Understand how businesses make a profit

Getting started

What do you think small business owners should do with the profit they make? Buy a house or new car, go on holiday or spend it on improving the business? Discuss your ideas as a group.

Introduction

Businesses make a profit by generating revenue through selling their products or services. If this revenue is greater than the cost of making or obtaining the items, and running the business, then the owner(s) makes a profit. After paying tax, the owner(s) can choose what to do with the profit they have made.

In this topic, you will learn more about revenue, different types of expenditure and how to calculate profit.

Understanding revenue

Usually businesses make their revenue by selling goods and/or services to customers. There are thousands of different products on sale, ranging from chocolate bars costing less than a pound, to passenger aircraft costing millions of pounds.

Some businesses sell a service, such as hairdressers, window cleaners and fitness clubs. Some businesses sell both products and services, for example, many car dealerships operate vehicle workshops for services and repairs.

When customers pay for products and services, this produces revenue (or income) for the business.

Identify sources of revenue

Businesses can receive money from other sources, for example:

- **interest** paid on money in a bank savings account
- **investment** income from people buying shares in the business or lending it money (a bank loan, for example)
- **leasing or rental income** by renting out property or equipment that is not currently required to another business.

Did you know?

Some types of organisations have other sources of revenue. For example, charities rely on public donations while state schools are funded by the government.

Activity — Researching sources of revenue

Visit the Guide Dogs for the Blind website. You can access this by going to www.pearsonhotlinks.co.uk and searching for this title. Make a list of the different ways the organisation obtains revenue. Compare your list with a partner.

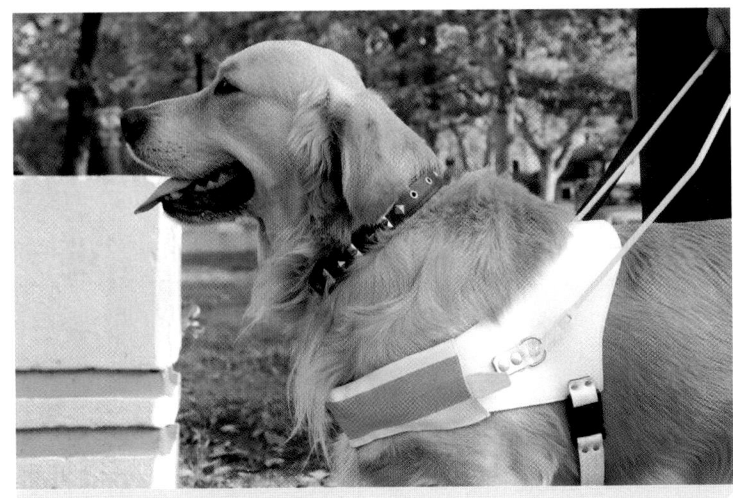

Guide Dogs for the Blind generates income in a variety of ways.

Calculate revenue

The formula used to calculate the revenue earned for each type of item sold by a business is:

$$\text{revenue} = \text{number of sales} \times \text{price per unit}$$

For example, if a business sells 1000 small boxes of chocolates at £4.00 each, the revenue will be 1000 × £4.00 = £4000

If a business sells several types of products or services, this formula is applied to each one and the totals are then added together to give the overall revenue figure.

- You must learn the formula to calculate total revenue. It will not be provided in the assessment.
- Consumable items are not the same as raw materials. Raw materials are used to make a product. Consumable items are not.

Understanding expenditure

All businesses must spend money to succeed. They have to pay the bills involved in running the enterprise on a day-to-day basis, in the same way that a family must pay the bills at home. A business needs to buy stock or pay for raw materials to produce goods, for example bread and fillings to make sandwiches, or denim, thread and fasteners to make jeans. They may want to spend money on advertising or promoting the business to increase sales and will want to employ staff who can provide excellent customer service.

Identify types of expenditure

There are many different types of business expenditure. Some examples are given in Table 2.1.

Table 2.1 Types of business expenditure and their purpose

Type of business expenditure	Purpose
Rent and business rates	To use and operate business premises
Staff wages	To pay for staff who carry out the activities needed to run the business, such as sales and office staff
Raw materials/components/packaging	To make, assemble and pack the finished products
Stock items for resale	Items purchased by retailers to sell to customers
Utility bills (gas, electric and water)	To use power, energy and water on the premises
Telecommunications links and website maintenance	To communicate and provide information to customers and potential customers
Vehicles and fuel	To obtain stock and deliver goods to customers
Consumable items	To be used and replaced regularly by the business, e.g. paper and printer cartridges in the office and soap in the washrooms
Advertising and printing costs	To promote the business to potential customers

CONTINUED ▸▸

Expenditure and overheads

The term **expenditure** relates to all the money the business pays out. Some of these will be fixed costs and some will be variable costs.

You already know that fixed costs have to be paid whether the business is busy or quiet. A newsagent near a school or college would be busier in term time than during the holidays; however, it has fixed costs to pay at all times. Another name for these is **overheads**.

Key terms

Expenditure – money that a business spends.

Overheads – the everyday running costs of the business.

Profit – occurs when revenue is more than expenditure.

Loss – occurs when expenditure is more than revenue.

Understanding profit

Revenue and expenditure

All business owners need to be constantly aware of how much revenue is being received and how much money is being paid out. You cannot run a successful business without this information because you will not know whether you have:

- made a **profit**, or
- made a **loss**.

This is obviously important as no business can make a loss for any length of time without having to close down.

Remember

- To memorise the difference between fixed and variable costs, ask the question: 'If the business sells more products, will it need more of these items?' If the answer is 'yes', the cost is variable. Otherwise it is fixed.
- Some businesses have many fixed costs, others do not. For each flight an airline has to pay airport landing fees, salaries to the crew, and fuel, maintenance and cleaning costs. The fixed costs for a painter and decorator will mainly relate to the van that is used.

What would be the overheads in a car showroom?

Definitions of profit and loss

- Profit means that revenue is more than expenditure.
- Loss means that expenditure is more than revenue.

Calculate profit

Profit or loss is calculated by using the following formula:

Profit/loss = revenue – expenditure

If the revenue of a business is £3000 and it spends £2500 in the same period, the formula gives:

Profit/loss = £3000 – £2500 = +£500

As the figure is positive, the business has made a profit of £500.

However, if the business has the same income but its expenditure is £3500, then the formula gives:

Profit/loss = £3000 – £3500 = (£500)

As the figure is negative, the business has made a loss of £500.

So the rule is: if the result of applying the formula is a positive figure, then the business is in **profit**. If the figure is negative, it is making a **loss**.

Remember

You must learn the formula to calculate profit. It will not be provided in the assessment.

Did you know?

A negative figure may be shown with a minus sign, i.e. –£500, but is often shown in brackets in business documents, i.e. (£500).

Activity — Calculating costs, revenue and profit

Write down the answers to the following questions, then check them with your teacher/tutor.

1 Which one of the following items is a source of revenue for a hairdressing business?
a) advertising, **b)** selling shampoo and conditioning products, **c)** staff wages, **d)** electricity bill

2 Asiya's expenditure in her first three months of trading was £5000 and her revenue £6250. Use the appropriate formula to calculate her profit or loss.

3 Tom runs a small business selling costume jewellery online. He estimates that he will sell 200 items next month which will cost him an average of £20 each. He thinks that his overheads will amount to £2000.

a) Copy the table below and complete it to calculate his total costs for the month.

Variable costs	200 × ______ =
Fixed costs	
Total costs	

b) Tom has two bills to pay. The first is for 40 small jewellery boxes. The second is for his internet connection. Which of these is a variable cost and which is a fixed cost?

TOPIC B.1

Understand the planning tools businesses use to predict when they will start making a profit

Getting started

The manufacturer of London's black cabs reckons that they must sell 1500 a year to break even. Cabs sell for about £30,000. What is the business's revenue at this level of sales? And if this revenue enables the business to break even, how much must the business spend each year?

Introduction

You have learned that when revenue is greater than expenditure, the business makes a profit, but if revenue is less than expenditure it makes a loss. Between these two situations, there is a point called breakeven where income and expenditure are equal.

Often, when a business starts up, it makes a loss for a short time before it starts to make a profit. The point at which this occurs (the break-even point) is an important milestone in the progress of the business.

Defining breakeven

Breakeven occurs when a business has made enough money through product sales to cover the cost of making them. There is no profit and no loss.

There are two ways of calculating the break-even point. The first is using a formula and the second is creating a chart.

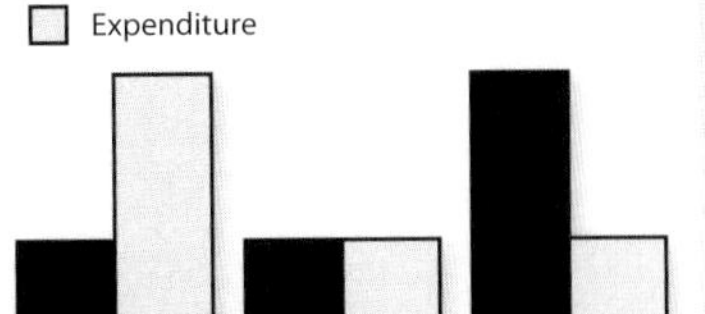
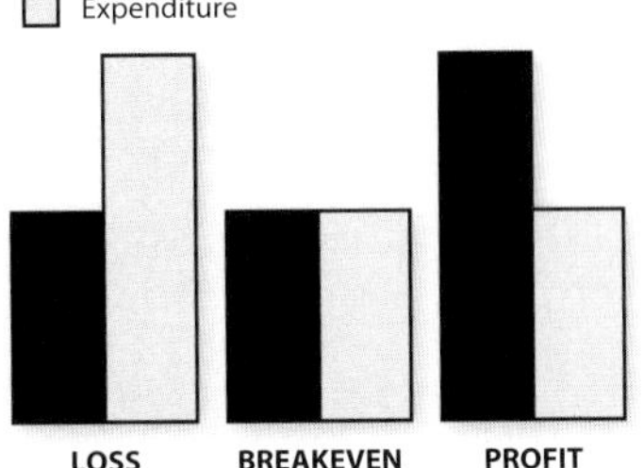

Figure 2.2 Loss, breakeven and profit

Calculating break-even point using a formula

The formula used to calculate the break-even point is:

$$\text{break-even point} = \frac{\text{fixed costs}}{\text{selling price per unit} - \text{variable cost per unit}}$$

You can see how the formula works in this example.

Tom is considering starting a mobile hot dog van business. He reckons that his fixed costs (for example, insurance and tax for the van) would average at £100 per week and the variable cost for each hot dog would be 80p. He aims to sell the hot dogs for £1.30 and wants to find out how many he would need to sell in a week before he would start to make a profit. He therefore applies the formula:

$$\text{break-even point} = \frac{£100}{£1.30 - 80\text{p}} = \frac{£100}{50\text{p}} = 200 \text{ hot dogs}$$

Remember

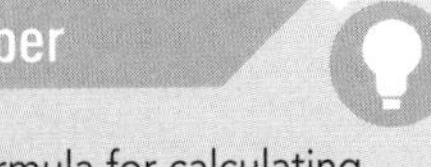

- The formula for calculating the break-even point will be provided in the assessment, but you must be able to use it.
- The meaning of fixed and variable cost is given earlier in the unit. If you are not sure, go back and check.

Activity: Calculating break-even point

If a product sells for £5, the variable cost is £3 and the fixed cost is £300, what is the break-even point? Use the formula to calculate it.

Break-even charts

The break-even point can be identified by drawing a chart. Carry out the next activity so that you understand how the chart has been created.

Activity: Working through the chart

Study the break-even chart in Figure 2.3 and read through the list of features in the table below. Do this several times if necessary. Ask your teacher/tutor if there is anything you do not understand.

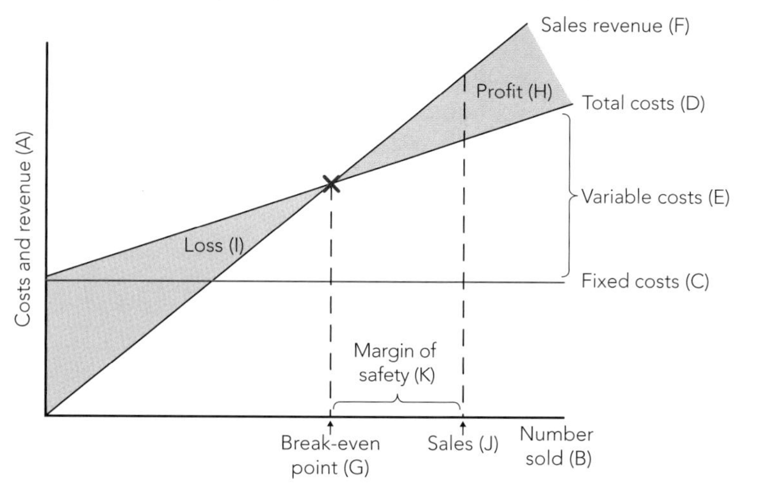

Figure 2.3 A break-even chart where 'X' marks the break-even point

Remember

You may be asked to identify and mark the break-even point in the assessment. In Figure 2.3 its position is shown by the red 'X'.

Table 2.2 Features of a break-even chart

Feature	Explanation
A – Costs and revenue	The vertical axis shows the amount of money spent as costs and received as revenue.
B – Number sold	The horizontal axis shows the number of products which could be sold.
C – Fixed costs	This line is horizontal because the fixed costs never change no matter how many products are sold.
D – Total costs	This line shows the fixed costs plus the variable costs. It starts at the left-hand side where the fixed cost line meets the vertical axis. At this point, there are no sales so the variable costs are zero. The line is then drawn to show how variable costs increase in direct proportion to the number of items sold. It then shows the total cost for each level of sales.
E – Variable costs	The difference between the fixed costs line and the total costs line is the variable costs. This gap widens as the level of sales increases.
F – Sales revenue	This line starts at the zero point since no sales means that no income is being earned. The sales revenue is calculated by multiplying the price charged by the number of items sold.
G – Break-even point	This is the point where the sales revenue line crosses the total cost line and shows the number of sales needed for the business to break even.
H – Profit	To the right of the break-even line sales revenue is greater than total costs, so the business is making a profit. The distance between the two lines shows the amount of profit for each level of sales.
I – Loss	To the left of the break-even line sales revenue is less than expenditure and the business is making a loss. The distance between the lines shows the amount of loss at each level of sales.
J – Sales	This shows that sales are higher than the number required to break even.
K – Margin of safety	This is the amount by which sales would have to fall before the break-even point is reached.

Just checking

1 **Why is the fixed cost line horizontal on a break-even chart?**
2 **Which two figures must be equal for the business to break even?**

▸▸ CONTINUED

Present break-even information graphically

The following case study shows how a break-even chart is created. Use graph paper to draw one yourself by following the step-by-step instructions. Although you will not have to do this in the assessment, this will help you to better understand break-even charts. Use the illustrations to help you if necessary.

Case study

Charlie has a three-week Christmas break from college and wants to make some money. He has been talking to a man who sells Christmas trees to different outlets and wonders if he could sell enough to make a profit.

He knows of an empty car showroom for rent and has also noted the rental terms for a van he could hire for collection and delivery. He would also need to pay two friends to help him. He jots down some figures on a notepad:

Christmas tree project

Fixed costs – van hire, staff wages,

showroom rental etc = £4000

Variable cost – price of trees, £30 each

Selling price £50

Charlie's workings

Charlie draws a break-even chart by following these steps.

Step 1: Charlie decides that the most trees he can sell is 400, so he labels his vertical axis to the maximum possible income, i.e. 400 × £50 = £20,000. The bottom (horizontal) axis shows the number of trees sold, so he labels this from 0 to 400.

Step 2: Charlie draws in the fixed cost line. This is horizontal and starts at the £4000 point on the vertical axis.

Step 3: Charlie adds the total cost line to the chart. He calculates that if he sells 400 trees, his variable costs would be £30 × 400 = £12,000. He adds this to his fixed costs of £4000 to give a total cost figure of £16,000. These would be his maximum costs if he sold all the trees.

Charlie plots this mark at the right side of his chart, above the '400' mark on the horizontal axis. He then joins this to the start of the fixed cost line on the vertical axis. This is the line he drew in step 2.

Step 4: Charlie draws the sales income line by starting at 0 (no sales, no income) and ending at the point which shows the maximum possible income if he sells 400 trees (£50 × 400 = £20,000).

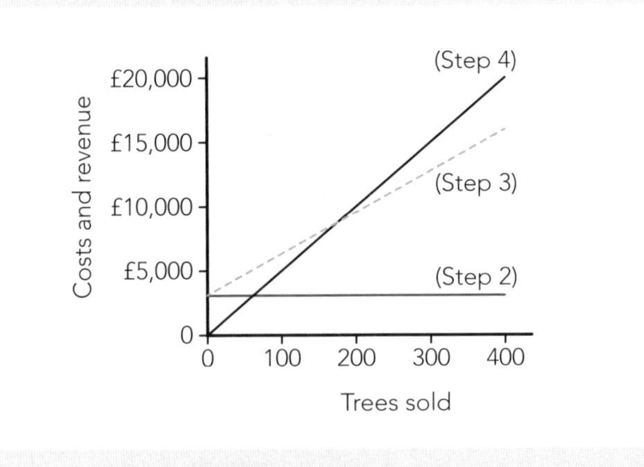

Figure 2.4 Charlie's break-even chart

Activity Labelling your chart

Show your finished chart to your teacher/tutor. If you have done it properly, the break-even point should read 200 on the horizontal scale and £10,000 on the vertical scale.

Now label all of the following features: costs and revenue axis; number sold axis; fixed cost line; total cost line; variable cost area; sales revenue line; break-even point; sales of 300 and the margin of safety for this amount; profit area; loss area.

Analyse the effect on the break-even point if the figures change

The break-even point changes if sales or costs change. For example, if Charlie has to pay more for his trees, his costs will increase. He will either have to increase his selling price (which could mean he sells fewer) or earn less money on each tree. This means he will have to sell more to break even.

Table 2.3 summarises the likely impact of different changes on the break-even point.

Table 2.3 Summary of changes in sales or costs on the break-even point

Type of change	Effect on break-even point
Increase in sales	The margin of safety increases.
Decrease in sales	The margin of safety decreases. If sales fall below the break-even level, the business could make a loss.
Increase in costs	The number of sales required to break even increases so the profit level would fall or even become a loss.
Decrease in costs	Break-even point is lower so the business makes more profit.

You can see from the table that increased sales and decreased costs are good. However, if sales fall or costs increase, then action must be taken before the business makes a loss. For example, if raw material costs increase, the business could look for a cheaper substitute or try to get the same material cheaper from another supplier.

Did you know?

In retail, the difference between the buying and selling price of goods is called the 'margin'. The higher the margin, the more potential profit, providing the goods are still priced competitively.

Discussion point

Discuss the actions a business might take if sales started to fall – ideally without adding too much to costs!

CONTINUED ▸▸

The importance of break-even analysis and risks of ignoring it

Business people need to plan to be successful. Someone starting out in business must understand the costs involved in selling a product as well as be able to predict future sales. Without knowing these, the business could stock too many items or try to sell them at too high or too low a price.

The value and importance of break-even analysis is that it could show that some business propositions would not be sensible, because the costs are too high and a profit would never be made.

A summary of the benefits of carrying out a break-even analysis, and the risks of not doing so, are summarised in Table 2.4.

Table 2.4 Benefits and risks of break-even analysis

Benefits of break-even analysis	Risks of not completing a break-even analysis
Both the fixed and variable costs are known.	Costs are unknown and/or too high.
Projected sales revenue is calculated.	The selling price is too low or too high.
The owner knows how many items must be sold to make a profit.	The owner has no idea how many items must be sold to make a profit.
The owner can make adjustments to try to make a profit sooner, e.g. reduce costs by obtaining cheaper materials or increase selling price.	The business makes a loss over a long period of time without any action being taken.
The margin of safety is known.	The margin of safety is unknown.
The best goods are stocked and sold at the optimum price so the business is successful.	Stock costs too much, is sold at the wrong price (maybe at less than cost price!) and the business fails.

Remember

Break-even analysis is one of several financial planning tools that businesses use.

Just checking

1. What costs are combined to make the total cost line on a break-even chart?
2. What is represented by the space between the total cost line and the sales income line above the break-even point?
3. Identify three benefits Charlie gains by carrying out break-even analysis.

Case study

Bridget's Bread

When Bridget Kelly left school she decided to make her own speciality bread, using an old family recipe. To keep costs down, Bridget registered her mother's kitchen so she could produce food there. Her father bought her a little second-hand car so she decided to sell at farmers' markets and to charge £1.50 a loaf. She wrote down her daily costs:

Rent for stall: £20 + travelling expenses: £10 = £30

Cost of making each loaf: = 50p

Three months later Bridget was worried. The markets were quiet due to poor weather and one week she sold only 10 loaves. Unless she made a profit, she earned no money.

Then she had a lucky break. A customer recommended her bread to the buyer at Foodies, a speciality food chain. He visited her and offered her a deal. He is prepared to buy 2000 loaves every week and pay £1 for each one.

Bridget knows that to produce 2,000 loaves a week she would need different premises and more equipment. She already knows the cost of making each loaf but needs to find out what her new fixed costs would be. This is her list.

Rent and rates: £10,000 a year

New kitchen equipment: £15,000 per year (on a 3 year credit scheme)

Van running costs: £2,000 per year

Electricity and miscellaneous office costs: £3,000

Bridget doesn't know what to do. Use your knowledge of break-even analysis to give her advice.

1 Define the term break-even for Bridget. Then calculate her break-even point, using the formula, to show why she made a loss when she only sold 10 loaves at the farmers' markets.

2 The chart below illustrates Bridget's possible new venture.

   a) Identify the meaning of each of the areas marked A – F.

   b) Identify how many loaves she must sell to break-even. Use this information to decide whether this is sensible proposition or not.

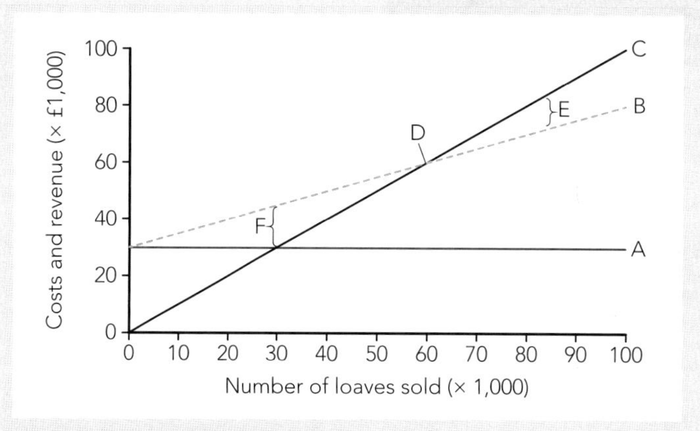

Figure 2.5 Bridget's break-even chart

3 Explain the effect on Bridget's break-even point if:

   a) she employs an assistant to help her

   b) she buys second hand kitchen equipment which is much cheaper

   c) Foodies reduce their offer to 90p a loaf

   d) she finds a cheaper flour supplier.

4 Write a brief summary of the benefits Bridget will gain by doing break-even analysis as she plans for her new business.

Understand the tools businesses use to plan for success

Getting started

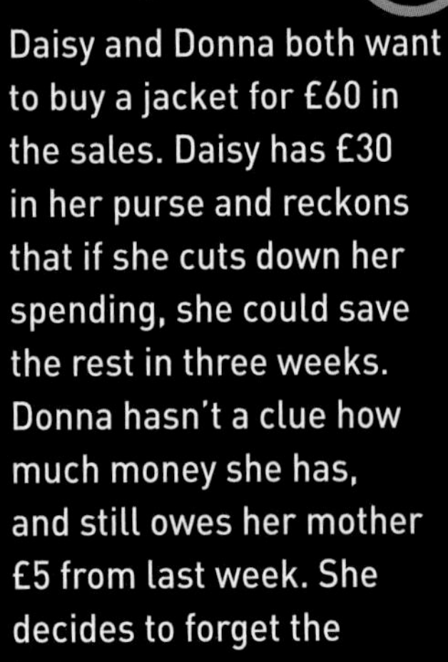

Daisy and Donna both want to buy a jacket for £60 in the sales. Daisy has £30 in her purse and reckons that if she cuts down her spending, she could save the rest in three weeks. Donna hasn't a clue how much money she has, and still owes her mother £5 from last week. She decides to forget the jacket.

Which of them understands budgeting?

The purpose of budgeting

Budgeting helps people (and businesses) to get what they want by planning. If Donna ran a business in the way she runs her private life, it would soon be in trouble.

Budgeting is a process of setting targets for spending and revenue over a future period of time. They are used in many business situations, such as:

- forecasting start-up costs for a new business
- introducing a new product or building an extension to a factory
- forecasting sales revenue.

The main purpose of budgeting is to ensure that the business is in control of its revenue and expenditure so that it makes a profit.

The budget should be set carefully, ideally using financial information from the previous year as guidance. Then any future predictions about revenue or costs must be considered, based on market trends. Ideally the budget should be realistic, achievable and challenge all the staff to do their best.

Did you know?

- In large organisations, each department has its own budget for expenditure and must keep to this. The target for sales revenue is different because the more sales a business makes, the better!
- The process of measuring performance and taking corrective action is called 'control'. A simple example is driving a car. The driver knows the speed limit (standard of performance), reads the speedometer (measuring actual performance) and uses the brakes or accelerator to adjust the speed (corrective action).

Key terms

Budgeting – planning future expenditure and revenue targets with the aim of ensuring a profit is made.

Budgetary control – the process of checking what is actually happening, comparing this with the plan and taking action if things are not correct.

Activity Talking about budget holders

The person in charge of monitoring the budget is the budget holder. Your school or college will have a budget. Ask your teacher/tutor who is the budget holder and why this person's job is so important.

Budgeting and budgetary control

Setting the budget is only the first stage. Once set, there must be a system to ensure that the targets are met. This is **budgetary control** and can be achieved by:

1. measuring actual performance regularly – normally at least once a month
2. giving this information to the budget holder who checks for any differences between the planned target and actual performance. If expenditure has been too high or sales targets have not been met, the budget holder will take action to correct this
3. if this action works, then next month the performance should be better and match the targets set.

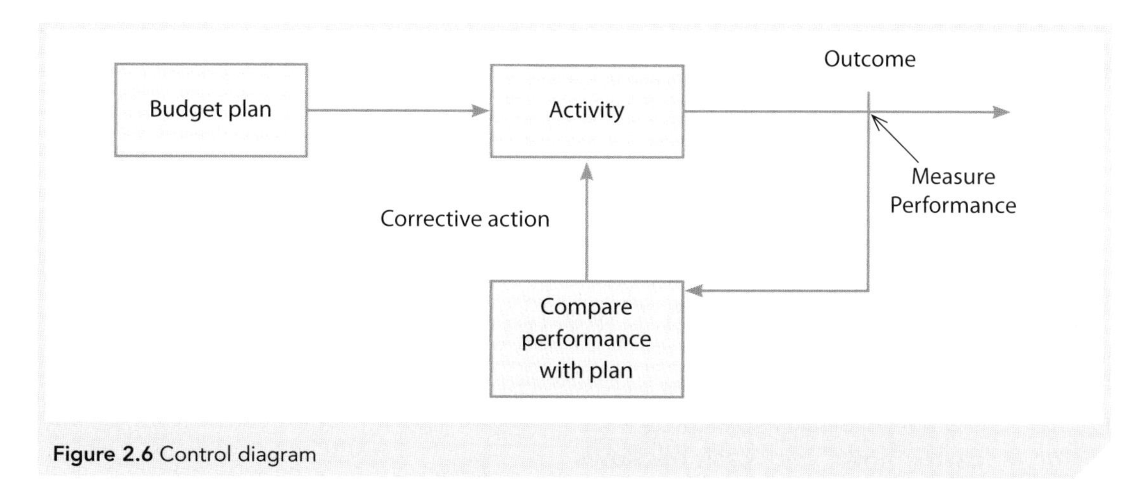

Figure 2.6 Control diagram

Activity — Thinking about budgets

1. In groups, identify two benefits of budgeting as a planning tool and two risks of not doing so. Use the information in the case study below to help you. Then compare your ideas.
2. Budgeting is usually harder for new business owners. Why do you think this is the case?

Remember

Make sure that you can explain the difference between budgeting and budgetary control.

Case study

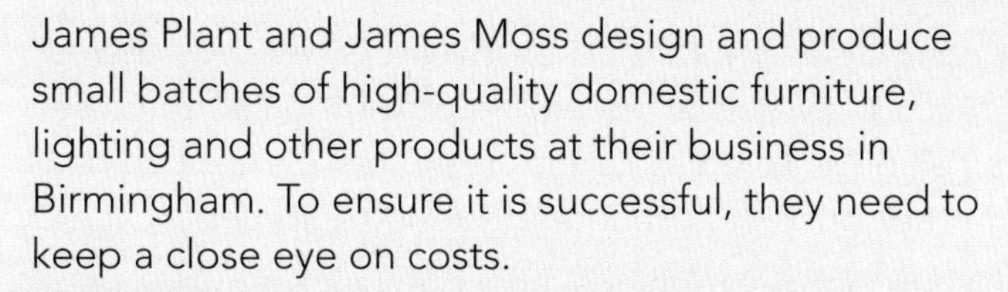

James Plant and James Moss design and produce small batches of high-quality domestic furniture, lighting and other products at their business in Birmingham. To ensure it is successful, they need to keep a close eye on costs.

When they produce their budget, they forecast the cost of making and selling an item. This includes production materials (for example, wood, metal, concrete and components such as cable), manufacturing costs, labour time and overheads. Their biggest problem is a sudden increase in costs, such as the 65 per cent price rise of stainless steel between 2009 and 2012.

James Plant says they try to minimise the problem by negotiating with other suppliers to see if they can save by ordering larger quantities and looking for different materials. However, they sometimes have to pass on the increase to customers.

Their overheads are all the costs involved in running the business, from employee salaries, to office and marketing costs. These must be paid regardless of the number of items produced, but fortunately are more predictable!

Find out more about Plant and Moss by visiting their website. You can access this by going to www.pearsonhotlinks.co.uk and searching for this title.

1. a) Explain the difference between variable costs and overheads.
   b) Give two examples of variable costs at Plant and Moss and suggest two examples of **i)** office costs and **ii)** marketing costs.
2. What actions do they take to try to minimise the problem of rising costs?
3. Explain why it is important that costs are monitored and controlled at Plant and Moss.

CONTINUED ▸▸

Cash flow forecasting

Have you ever suddenly realised that you have an important present to buy at a time when you are really short of money? Maybe you can borrow money from a relative and repay it later. In business terms, you have a cash flow problem. Businesses try to avoid this happening because they have to pay interest on any money they borrow.

The purpose of cash flow forecasting

Cash flow forecasting is concerned with predicting all the money that is expected to enter and leave a business's bank account over a given period of time. This money is known as '**cash inflows**' and '**cash outflows**'.

The purpose of doing this is to identify how much money will be left in the bank account. If this figure is positive, then the business can afford to pay its bills. However, if the cash flow forecast predicts a negative figure for the bank balance, the business could be in trouble, especially if the trend continues.

Did you know?

Cash flow forecasting is not just about cash but relates to any form of money going in and out of the business, including cheques, electronic transfers and direct debits.

Key terms

Cash inflows – the amounts of money entering a business's bank account.

Cash outflows – the amounts of money leaving a business's bank account.

Net cash flow – the difference between the cash inflow and outflow figures over a particular time period.

Cash balance – the amount of money forecast to be in the bank account after the net cash flow figure has been added or subtracted from the existing bank balance.

Cash inflows and outflows

Cash inflows

For most businesses, the main type of cash inflow is payment by customers for goods or services they have bought. However, there are other possible sources of income such as:

- **capital from investors:** larger companies are funded by investors who buy shares in the business. In return they receive dividends. As well as providing capital to set up a business, shareholders can also be asked to buy more shares if extra capital is needed, for example to buy another business or more efficient equipment.
- **loan from a bank:** many businesses borrow money from a bank either at business start-up and/or to expand a business which is doing well
- **property rental:** sometimes businesses rent out part of their building to other businesses to provide extra income.

Cash outflows

Businesses can have many forms of cash outflows. The following are the most common types:

- **staff wages:** this is probably the main form of expenditure for most businesses
- **utilities (gas, electricity, telephone):** most businesses use all three
- **materials for manufacturing:** these depend on the nature of the business. At Plant and Moss they include wood and stainless steel, whereas a jeans factory requires cloth and thread
- **insurance:** businesses insure against fire, damage to property and injury to staff or visitors
- **interest on loan:** this is charged when a business borrows money from a bank
- **dividends:** these are paid to shareholders if the business makes a profit
- **rental:** a business may rent its premises from a landlord.

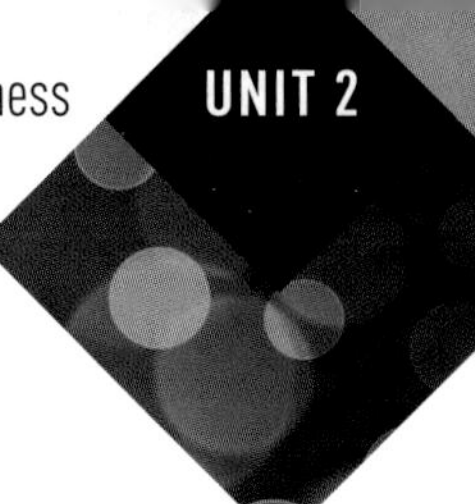

Activity Identifying cash inflows and outflows

Below is a list of cash inflows and outflows for a manufacturing business. Separate these into two columns, headed 'Cash inflows' and 'Cash outflows'.

Staff wages; consumables; sales income; utility bills (gas, electricity, etc.); window cleaning; rental on a sub-let office; production materials; loan from bank; telephone bills; ingredients for the coffee machine; cash from the coffee machine; interest on bank loan; selling shares.

The purpose of a cash flow forecast

The aim of a cash flow forecast is to identify the possible inflows and outflows, to add them together in each category and to work out the difference, which is known as the '**net cash flow**'. When the net cash flow figure is added or subtracted from the money already in the bank, the resulting figure is the '**cash balance**'.

Activity Thinking about Sophie's calculations

Sophie runs a small florist's business. On 1 June she decides to carry out a cash flow forecast for the month ahead. She does some calculations and notes the following figures:

Cash inflow £2400

Cash outflow £2100

Opening bank balance £1200

She then does the following calculations:

Net cash flow = £2400 – £2100 = £300

Closing cash balance in bank = £1200 + £300 = £1500

Study Sophie's calculations and then work out what would happen if the outflow figure was £2600 and all of the other figures remained the same.

CONTINUED ▸▸

▸▸ CONTINUED

Key term

Overdraft – this occurs if a business pays more out of its bank account than it has in credit. The bank may allow this but will make an extra charge.

Impact of timings of inflows and outflows

The actual times when money enters and leaves a business's bank account can be critical. For example, if a large payment from a customer is overdue, the bank balance could be negative and **overdraft** charges would apply.

The table below shows some of the effects of the timing of inflow and outflow payments on different types of businesses. You will learn later in this unit how varying the timing of payments can affect a business.

Table 2.5 The effects of the timing of inflow and outflow payments on different types of businesses

Type of business	Effect on cash inflow	Effect on cash outflow
Retail shop where customers pay cash, shopkeeper gets one month's credit from suppliers	Payment is received immediately goods are bought, so there are no delays receiving revenue.	Business only needs to settle bills once a month, which helps if trade is quiet during that month.
Manufacturer which supplies goods to other businesses on credit (e.g. Heinz to Tesco)	Depends on how quickly payment is received. Some customers may need chasing for payment.	Manufacturer needs to pay for raw materials but may delay payment, too. They cannot delay other payments such as staff wages.
Seasonal business, e.g. crop farm or seaside hotel	Revenue is received over a short period, e.g. when the crop is harvested or when the hotel is open or busy.	Some expenses, such as utility bills must be paid all year. Extra money may be needed for expenses out of season, e.g. the cost of seeds for planting or the cost of decorating when the hotel is closed.
Business undertaking large projects, e.g. house and road builders	Payment may only be received in one large sum when the project is complete.	Money for materials and labour is needed regularly throughout the time the project is being undertaken.

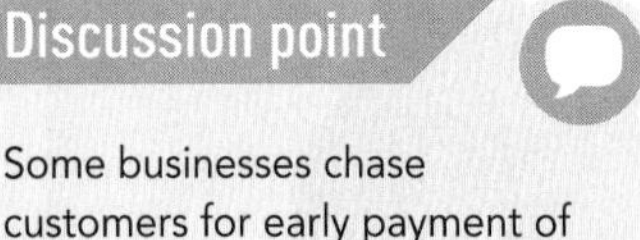

Discussion point

Some businesses chase customers for early payment of their debts, but pay their own bills from suppliers as late as possible. Can you think why? Is this good for business or bad?

The benefits of cash flow forecasts and risks of not completing them

Cash flow forecast information is another important planning tool. Creating the forecast enables the business to plan for success because if things are going well, it can ensure there are finances available to produce new goods or services, expand its activities or invest in new resources. If there is less money available, then other actions may need to be taken to save money, such as negotiating with suppliers to change payment dates or spread payments, or reducing activities. You will learn more about this when you read the WorkSpace case study at the end of the unit.

Table 2.6 shows the main benefits of using and risks of not using a cash flow forecast.

Table 2.6 Benefits and risks related to cash flow analysis

Benefits of cash flow analysis	Risks of not using cash flow analysis
The timing of all expected revenue is known (cash inflows) and reminders are sent if any is overdue.	Revenue may be received late or not at all.
The timing of all expenditure is known (cash outflows) and payment dates can be renegotiated if there is a temporary problem.	Payments are delayed and suppliers become alarmed and may refuse to trade with the business.
If there is likely to be a deficit, the owner has time to take action to delay payments or obtain a temporary loan if necessary.	The business may have to pay high interest charges on an unauthorised overdraft or emergency loan.
The owner has warning if there is a long-term problem because costs will need to be reduced or revenue increased for the business to survive.	The business cannot afford to pay its bills and eventually has to cease trading.

Completing and analysing a cash flow forecast

A cash flow forecast is completed by entering the inflows and outflows for a month, calculating the net cash flow and then working out what the closing bank balance will be at the end of that month. This is then the opening balance for the following month.

When you analyse a cash flow forecast, the most important figure is the **closing bank balance**.

- A small but positive figure means that the business can pay its bills and has little danger of going bankrupt.
- A large positive figure means that there is money available for investment or expansion, for example in new products or activities, updated equipment to improve efficiency, energy conservation.
- A small negative figure means that money may have to be borrowed, at least for a short while, so more money has to be paid out next month.
- A large negative closing balance means that the business cannot pay its way and may go bankrupt unless action is taken to increase inflows and/or reduce outflows.

Activity Completing Eleanor's cash flow forecast

Copy out and complete the cash flow forecast for Eleanor, who runs a pet ambulance service. She discovers that her van is in need of repair and will be off the road for two weeks in July.

How do you think Eleanor will react to this information? What would you advise her to do?

Eleanor's cash flow forecast

	June (£)	July (£)	August (£)
Total receipts (inflows)	1000	400	1200
Total payments (outflows)	500	1200	1500
Net cash flow			
Opening balance	200		
Closing balance			

TOPIC C.1

Understand how businesses measure success

Introduction

Businesses always plan to succeed. Break-even analysis and cash flow forecasting are two ways in which businesses can plan to be successful. However, no plan ever works perfectly and, when events have taken place, business managers need to know exactly what has happened. When they know this, they can make plans to improve performance in the future if necessary.

The two main financial analysis documents which are produced to help managers assess how successful the business has been are:

- **the income statement** (also known as the **profit and loss account**)
- **the statement of financial position** (also known as **the balance sheet**).

The income statement lists all of the business's actual income and expenditure for a year. Hopefully, the income is greater than the expenditure and the business has made a profit. The balance sheet shows how the money invested in the business (its **capital**) has been spent.

Making a profit

Cost of sales

It costs money to make any product and this amount is called the **cost of sales**. If you were making teddy bears and the raw materials for each one cost £15, this is your cost of sales. You would have to deduct this amount from the sales revenue you received to work out your **gross profit**.

The items that comprise cost of sales will vary from one business to another, depending upon what they produce. For example, the cost of sales for a building firm would include all of the components and materials used in making a house, such as bricks, sand, cement, wood for the roof supports and roof tiles.

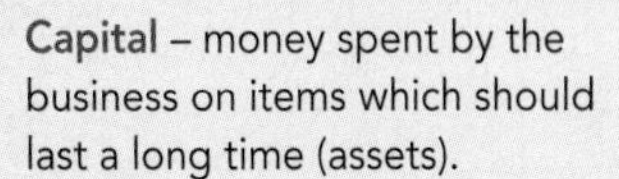

Capital – money spent by the business on items which should last a long time (assets).

Cost of sales – the cost of producing a product.

Gross profit – the money made from selling a product (the sales revenue) after the cost of producing that product (cost of sales) has been deducted.

Net profit – the money made from selling a product after all costs (expenditure) have been deducted from the gross profit.

Activity Identifying cost of sale items

You sing with a band in your spare time and you decide to produce a CD to sell at the gigs where you play. In small groups, write a list of your cost of sale items. Compare your list with other groups.

Gross profit

The formula for calculating gross profit is:

gross profit = revenue – cost of sales

Example:

A business sells £20,000 worth of goods and the total cost of sales is £4000.

Gross profit = £20,000 – £4000 = £16,000

Remember

You must know and be able to use both these formulas in the assessment.

Net profit

Net profit is the amount of money left when all the expenses other than cost of sales are deducted from the gross profit figure, for example rent, business rates, electricity and gas, telephone and wages of office staff. The formula for calculating net profit is:

net profit = gross profit – expenditure

Did you know?

The total assets less current liabilities figure is equal to the shareholders' funds figure (£2500). This is the 'balance' on the balance sheet, the two items being the same.

Activity Calculating net profit

If the gross profit of a business is £15,000 and all expenses except cost of sales amount to £11,000, what is the net profit?

The impact of positive and negative profit figures

All businesses want to have a positive profit figure because a negative profit amounts to a loss.

Table 2.7 The impact of gross profit and net profit

Gross profit and its impact	Net profit and its impact
If gross profit is positive, this means that revenue is greater than cost of sales.	If net profit is positive, this means that gross profit is also positive and expenditure is within budgeted levels.
If gross profit is low or negative, action to take is: • increase sales revenue (e.g. by increasing sales volumes or prices) • reduce cost of sales (e.g. using cheaper raw materials, bulk buying, changing supplier or negotiating better discounts).	If net profit is low or negative, this may be because gross profit is too low and/or expenses are too high. Action to take is: • increase gross profit • reduce expenses by checking overheads to see where savings can be made.
See Plant and Moss case study.	See WorkSpace case study.

Discussion point

- Businesses can try to sell more products by reducing the price, or aim to increase income by inc reasing the selling price. What are the dangers of both methods, and which one would you choose to increase income? Discuss both options as a group.
- Some people argue that you will never become rich if you don't take a few risks. They borrow as much as possible and pay their bills as late as they can. Do you agree with this approach? What are the dangers?

CONTINUED ▸▸

▸▸ CONTINUED

Link

This topic links to *Unit 1: Enterprise in the Business World.*

Looking at financial statements

Financial statements summarise the financial activities of a business and provide an immediate indication of its financial position. They are studied by a number of people because they show how well the business is being managed. The types of people who are interested in the accounts of a business are shown in Table 2.8.

Table 2.8 People who are interested in financial statements

Category of person	Reason for interest in financial statements
Shareholders	Is the money they invested safe? Will a good dividend be paid?
Managers	Is the business being managed well? Is it expanding or contracting?
Employees	Are their jobs safe? Can a wage rise be afforded?
Suppliers	Has the business enough money to pay what it owes?
Customers	Is the business sound enough to ensure that it can meet orders?
The government (HMRC)	How much corporation tax is owed?
Competitors	Are we making more or less profit than our main competitors?

Did you know?

The first part of the income statement, which gives the sales income, cost of sales and gross profit, is known as the 'trading account'.

Income statement (profit and loss account)

This statement shows how a business has performed financially over a period of time, usually a year. It shows how much revenue was received from sales of products and/or services, how much of this money was spent and how it was spent. An example is shown in Table 2.9 .

Table 2.9 Income statement (profit and loss account)

	£	£
Income from sales		50,000
Cost of sales	15,000	
Gross profit		35,000
Expenses/overheads		
Wages	25,000	
Utilities	5000	
Net profit		5000

The top three lines are the trading account.

The lower section lists the expenses.

This figure is found by subtracting the total expenses from the gross profit.

Remember

Remember that you must total the expenses before you subtract them from the gross profit figure.

Activity Checking the income statement

Work through the income statement carefully and make sure that you understand all the calculations. Ask your teacher/tutor for help if you are unsure.

Statement of financial position (balance sheet)

The purpose of a statement of financial position

All businesses have money invested in them – even a window cleaner must have a bucket and a ladder. Balance sheets show how much money is invested in the business and what it has been spent on.

Businesses normally produce a statement of financial position once a year on the last day of their **financial year**. This statement is a snapshot of the business's financial situation on that particular day. (Remember that an income statement summarises activities for the whole of the year).

What does the statement of financial position show?

The statement shows three different types of items.

- The **assets** of the business. These are all the items that the business owns, the money it has in the bank and the money it is owed by other people, for example customers who have bought on credit. These are called **debtors** (or **trade receivables**).

  Assets are divided into two types:
  - **fixed assets** are items that the business must keep to be able to trade, such as a van or a computer. They are called 'fixed' because they are here to stay
  - **current assets** are items that are changing with every transaction, such as stock, debtors and cash in the bank. Current assets can be turned into cash quickly, if necessary.
- The **liabilities** of the business. These include all the money the business owes to others, for example to suppliers or to the bank.

  Liabilities are also divided into two types:
  - **current liabilities** are money that must be paid back within a year, such as to suppliers and a bank overdraft
  - **long-term liabilities** include loans that can be repaid over a longer period.
- The capital that is put into the business. This may include:
  - **money invested** by the owner or shareholders (called **share capital**)
  - **retained profits** from previous years.

What is the purpose of a statement of financial position?

Key terms

Financial year – the trading period over which a business collects information for their annual income statement (for example, a business might have a financial year that starts on 1 May and ends on 30 April).

Assets – items that a business buys that normally last a long time, such as a van or a computer, or money it is owed.

Debtors (or trade receivables) – people who owe money to the business for goods or services they have received. Trade payables are traders to whom the business owes money because they have supplied goods or services.

Liabilities – amounts of money which a business owes.

Share capital – the amount of money invested in the business by the shareholders.

Remember

The business can be funded from internal sources, e.g. share capital and profits kept back to reinvest in the business, and from external sources, e.g. bank loans. This money enables the business to buy assets.

Did you know?

All the assets added together must always equal all the liabilities plus the capital invested in the business. This is why the statement is often referred to as a balance sheet.

CONTINUED ▸▸

▸▸ CONTINUED

Preparing a statement of financial position

Case study

Imran set up his business last month with £2500 he saved and a £500 bank overdraft. He spent £1000 on a van and £500 on a computer. He currently has £800 of stock which he has bought on credit from Tom, a friend, and has £1100 in the bank. He has sold goods worth £400 to another friend, Ashraf, who promises to settle up with him soon. What will his balance sheet look like at this point?

1 **Fixed assets:** Imran's fixed assets are his van and computer. He cannot run his business without them.

2 **Current assets:** Imran's current assets are his stock and the money in the bank. Ashraf is also an asset because he is a debtor – he owes money for the goods he bought.

3 **Current liabilities:** Tom is a creditor. He is a current liability because Imran must pay him soon. He must also repay his overdraft within a year.

4 **Working capital** (or **net current assets**): This figure represents the amount of money Imran has available to run the business every day, so it is very important. If it is too low, or becomes negative, he may not be able to pay his debts when they are due.

5 **Total assets less current liabilities:** This figure always equals the shareholders' funds if the calculations are correct.

6 **Capital:** This is the money Imran put into the business. There are no retained profits because it is Imran's first year of trading.

Key term

Working capital (or net current assets) – money the business can raise quickly which is calculated by deducting current liabilities (all current debts owed by the business) from current assets (all money owed to the business at the current time).

Table 2.10 Imran's statement of financial position (balance sheet)

Assets	£	£
Fixed assets		
Van	1000	
Computer	500	1500
Current assets		
Stock	800	
Debtors (trade receivables)	400	
Cash in bank	1100	2300
Total assets		3800
Liabilities		
Current liabilities		
Creditors (trade payables)	800	
Overdraft	500	1300
Working capital (current assets minus current liabilities)		1000
Total assets less current liabilities		**2500**
Shareholders' funds		
Share capital	**2500**	
Retained profit	0	

Activity Preparing a statement of financial position

1. Work through Imran's statement of financial position with your teacher/tutor. Make sure you understand each entry and each calculation.
2. Imran continues trading for some time, but he is rather worried. His sister suggests that he reworks his balance sheet to see what it says now.

   Imran buys a camera for £500 for taking photographs of stock for his website, and more stock for £2000. Although he sells most items for cash, he is owed £1100 by his debtors. He has increased his overdraft to £1500 and owes his creditors £1400. He has £300 in the bank.

   Copy out the balance sheet format above, enter the figures and calculate Imran's working capital. Keep your work safely as you will need it for the next activity.

Did you know?

- It is a legal requirement for many businesses to produce a balance sheet and profit and loss account each year.
- It is normally the net profit figure that tells you how well a business is being run, because the cost of overheads is more under the control of managers than raw material prices. Plant and Moss had few options when stainless steel prices dramatically increased.

Remember

When a figure in a financial report is presented in brackets, (£5000), this means that the figure is negative.

Understand how businesses can be more successful

Identify ways in which a business can increase profits

There are two main ways in which businesses can increase profits:

- by increasing income
- by reducing expenditure.

Income can be increased, for example by selling more products, increasing the selling price of products, increasing the range of products sold and encouraging customers to pay bills on time or earlier.

Expenditure can be reduced, for example by negotiating a better price for materials and utilities, looking for cheaper materials to use, reducing staffing levels, moving to cheaper premises, running machines more quickly to speed up production and delaying paying suppliers for as long as possible.

Analyse financial statements and suggest actions to take

Income statements and statements of financial position provide useful information about the financial health of a business. The main points to look for are as follows.

Income statement

- Has the firm made a healthy net profit? Has anything changed/improved since the report a year ago?
- If the business is making a loss, what can be done to improve the situation?

Statement of financial position

- Is there enough working capital to cover the amount owed to creditors? If there is not, and suppliers are not paid, they may refuse to provide goods to the business.
- Is there enough cash at the bank to cover immediate debts or emergencies?
- Is there money saved as **reserves** to increase the shareholders' funds?
- If working capital is low, this needs to be increased. The first step is to ensure there is enough money in the bank to pay suppliers and cover emergencies. Cash can be increased by selling stock and/or chasing debtors to pay their bills.
- The money raised must be used wisely. It is no use spending it all on stock again! If current liabilities are high, these should be reduced so there is less chance of the business being unable to pay its immediate debts.

Remember

Gross profit is improved by increasing sales revenue and reducing the cost of sales. Net profit is improved by increasing gross profit and reducing expenses.

Just checking

1. Which two of the following would be included in the cost of sales figure for a small printing business? Electricity; staff wages; paper; printing ink; fuel for delivery van.
2. What figure is produced when the total expenses are subtracted from the gross profit figure?
3. Which two of the following would appear as current assets on a balance sheet? Stock; trade payables; share capital; trade receivables.

Key term

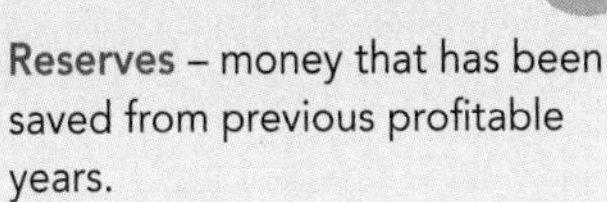

Reserves – money that has been saved from previous profitable years.

WorkSpace

Chris Reid

Managing Director, Connect Technology Group

Connect Technology Group develops and produces specialist software and hardware designed to meet the needs of childcare and security firms. Managing Director Chris Reid set up the business in 2004. His company has gone from strength to strength and now employs 14 staff.

Chris always wanted to be his own boss, but says that his main challenges have often been linked to cash flow. He says that it 'often feels that more money is going out of the business than is coming in!'

The reason for this is that many of his suppliers insist on payment within 21 days, whereas some of his customers will only pay their bills 60 or 90 days after receiving the goods. Fortunately he has a good relationship with one supplier, who allows him up to 60 days credit.

To keep costs down, the business has recently moved to cheaper premises. These are 'managed' which means Chris only has to pay one monthly bill covering rent, utilities, heating, security and maintenance. As the office equipment he uses is normally only cheap, he prefers to buy this rather than pay a monthly leasing bill.

December and January are quiet months, but Chris still has to find the money for his staff wages and overheads. To help provide a steady source of income, the company has now set up maintenance contracts on equipment it supplies that brings in a regular income every month.

Think about it

1 Why does Chris Reid prefer to operate from 'managed' premises?
2 Why is it important that Chris negotiates the longest credit terms he can with his suppliers?
3 What effect do the two quiet months a year have on Chris's cash flow, and why?
4 Why has setting up maintenance contracts been a good idea?
5 **a)** What terms would be used for i) the suppliers to whom Chris owes money and ii) the customers who still owe Chris money?
b) Which of these is a current asset and which is a current liability?

Assessment Zone

This section has been written to help you to do your best when you take the assessment test. Read through it carefully and ask your tutor if there is anything that you are still not sure about.

Hints and tips

Before the test

Remember

You do not need to bring a pen, paper or calculator.

You will improve your chances if you make sure that you have revised all the key areas that are likely to be covered. A list of these is given below. Use this as a checklist to make sure that you haven't forgotten anything!

Arrive in good time for the test, so you are not in a panic.

Listen carefully when the invigilator gives you instructions.

Key revision topics (your tutor may add to these)

- Identify start-up and running costs and state the difference between these.
- Identify fixed and variable costs and explain the difference between these.
- Define and give examples of overheads.
- List sources of revenue for a business and types of expenditure.
- Calculate revenue and calculate profit.
- Define breakeven and calculate break-even point using a given formula.
- Identify different components on a break-even chart.
- Explain the difference between budgeting and budgetary control.
- Explain the purpose of cash flow and complete a cash flow forecast.
- Explain the benefits of using different planning tools, i.e. breakeven analysis, budgeting and cash flow forecasting and explain the risks of not doing so.
- Analyse a break-even chart and a cash flow forecast.
- Calculate gross profit and net profit and explain how both can be improved.
- Identify the components of a trading account and explain its use.
- Complete and analyse an income statement (profit and loss account).
- Identify and give examples of assets (fixed and short-term), liabilities (current and long-term) and capital.
- Calculate working capital.
- Complete and analyse a statement of financial position (balance sheet).

During the test

Take a deep breath when you are told you can begin. If you have a tendency to panic, look through a few questions before you start. You can answer the questions in any order, so you might want to start with one that you find easy, to give you confidence.

Read each question carefully before you attempt an answer. Check that you are clear about what you have to do.

Remember that the number of marks relates to the number of answers you are expected to give. If you are asked to identify two variable costs, you cannot gain full marks if you only select one!

You will not lose any marks for a wrong answer, so if you are not sure, you are better to guess than to leave a blank.

On some questions you will see a 'working box' that you are invited to use. Use it! If you get part of an answer wrong, the examiner will check this box. If your workings are correct, then you may gain a mark.

Check the time regularly and use it wisely. If you complete the test early, use the rest of the time to review your answers and check that they are correct.

Most questions ask you to click a box to select an option or type your answer in a box. Others are more 'open-ended'. In this case, you may be asked to discuss or explain something and given a scrollable box in which to type your answer. These questions are worth more marks, so you need to think carefully about your response. Try to include one point for each of the allocated marks for that question.

Remember

If any question baffles you, you can 'flag' it and come back to it later.

Sample questions

On the next few pages you will find five sample questions with answers. Read these carefully and note the hints and tips that are given. Then answer the remaining six questions yourself and check your answers with your tutor.

Assessment Zone

This question is checking if you know the difference between fixed and variable costs. Variable costs are directly related to sales and you might find it easier to identify those first.

Question 1

Which two of these items are fixed costs for a florist? [2]

*Click on **two** of these boxes:*

- Staff wages ☒
- Flowers ☐
- Monthly rent ☒
- Ribbons and wrapping paper ☐

Question 2

(a) *Joanne runs her own nail bar but is not sure how to calculate her net profit. In the box below, enter the formula she should use* [1]

You may be asked to provide a formula in the assessment test.

Gross profit – expenses = net profit

(b) *Joanne would like to increase her net profit next year. Give **three** actions she could take.*

The examples show that the learner fully understands the components of gross and net profit. This answer would gain full marks.

Joanne can increase her net profit in these ways:

1. By reducing her expenses, such as her telephone bill.
2. By reducing her cost of sales, such as the cost of her nail polish. This will increase her gross profit figure.
3. By increasing her sales revenue. She could do this by attracting more clients or increasing her prices. This would also increase her gross profit figure.

[3]

Question 3

Seb works for a garden centre and his boss is thinking about building an extension to display lawnmowers for sale. The table below shows their predicted figures for the next year.

Selling price per lawnmower	*£50*
Variable cost per lawnmower	*£20*
Fixed costs	*£5000*

The formula to calculate break-even is

$$\text{Break even} = \frac{\text{fixed costs}}{\text{Selling price per unit} - \text{variable cost per unit}}$$

You should expect a question on break-even in the assessment. If this involves using the formula, it will be provided.

(a) *How many lawnmowers would the business need to sell to break-even? Put your answer in the box below.* [2]

250

You may use the working box to show your calculations.

WORKING BOX

$$\frac{5000}{50 - 30} = \frac{5000}{20} = 250$$

Using the working box shows the examiner that you know how to use the formula.

(b) *Outline what is meant by the term 'break-even point'.* [2]

The break-even point is when a business has made enough money from product sales to cover the cost of making that item. There is no profit and no loss.

Knowing this definition is useful.

Question 4

Jason runs a gardening business.

(a) *Insert the following items correctly into this extract from his statement of financial position (balance sheet) as at 31 March.* *[8]*

Stock £200	Equipment £700
Trade Payables £400	Trade Receivables £600

(b) *Complete the calculations.*

	£	£
Fixed assets		
Motor vehicle	2500	
Equipment	700	
		3200
Current assets		
Stock	200	
Trade receivables	600	
Cash	2300	
	3100	
Current liabilities		
Trade payables	400	
Overdraft	600	
	1000	
Working capital (net current assets)		2100

White spaces are left for you to complete the entries but you must know which items are fixed assets, current assets and liabilities to answer this question correctly.

Remember that working capital is current assets minus current liabilities.

(b) *Analyse the extract from Jason's balance sheet. Identify* ***two*** *ways in which he could improve his financial position.* [2]

He could pay his creditors and pay off his overdraft and still have money left in the bank. Two actions Jason could take are to pay off his overdraft, because then he will not have to pay bank charges. He could also get his debtors (trade receivables) to pay the money they owe him, particularly if some bills have been overdue for some time.

This answer shows the learner can interpret and analyse the figures correctly and can make sound business decisions based on this information.

Question 5

Alice is thinking about taking over an ice-cream kiosk in a busy shopping centre. She is concerned about possible cash-flow problems since the business is seasonal.

Discuss the benefits for Alice of using cash-flow forecasting in her business and the steps she could take to improve her cash-flow through the year. [8]

The examiner is looking for a reasoned argument here

A seasonal business is one where sales vary depending upon the time of year. Alice will probably sell more ice cream in summer than in winter because people are less likely to buy ice cream when it is cold weather. Her sales will fall at this time but she will still have her fixed costs to pay.

It is important to show you are thinking of the business example in the question. The fact the business is seasonal is important.

The forecast shows the projected inflows and outflows and when these are expected. This means Alice can plan ahead and see exactly what costs she will have to cover when sales are low. This way she can make plans to help the business survive.

This shows the learner understands the main purpose of cash flow forecasting.

Alice needs to find some way of increasing revenue during the winter months. She could find something else to offer for sale at the kiosk, such as hot drinks or umbrellas. She could close the kiosk in the winter and find a different job, for example over Christmas and during the January sales. This will lower her fixed costs. She could offer special promotions to encourage customers to return, such as giving a raffle ticket with each ice-cream purchased during the quiet period, with a weekly prize.

The learner has identified that the main action to take is to increase revenue. If this is not possible then reducing fixed costs is important. These are sensible suggestions but other realistic alternatives would be just as acceptable.

This box will keep scrolling until you have finished your answer.

Over to you!

Disclaimer: These practice questions and sample answers are not actual exam questions. They are provided as a practice aid only and should not be assumed to reflect either the format or coverage of the real external test.

Question 1

Ashraf has started his own car valeting business. Identify the following two running costs. [2]

(a) Pressure washer

(b) Car shampoo and polish

(c) Promotional leaflet

(d) Telephone bill

Question 2

Petra runs a small business making handmade photograph frames. The following figures list her projected income and expenditure for three months.

(a) Complete her cash-flow statement below by filling in the blank spaces. [3]

2012	April (£)	May (£)	June (£)
Total receipts	2000	1000	2100
Total payments	1700	1500	1600
Net cash flow			
Opening balance	1200		
Closing balance			

(b) Using the information in the cash flow, suggest one action Petra should take to manage her finances for these three months. [1]

Question 3

Misha makes children's T-shirts which she sells for £5.50 each. Last year she sold 7000 T-shirts.

(a) Calculate her total revenue. [1]

(b) Identify which one of the following expenditure items would count towards her cost of sales. [1]

Sewing machine

Cotton material

Advertising costs

Internet connection

Question 4

Jack is launching his own smoothie business and has prepared a breakeven chart.

(a) Read the chart below and label the following

(i) The fixed costs line

(ii) The total cost line

(iii) The sales revenue line [3]

(b) Identify the break-even point [1]

(c) Outline **two** benefits of carrying out a break-even analysis: [2]

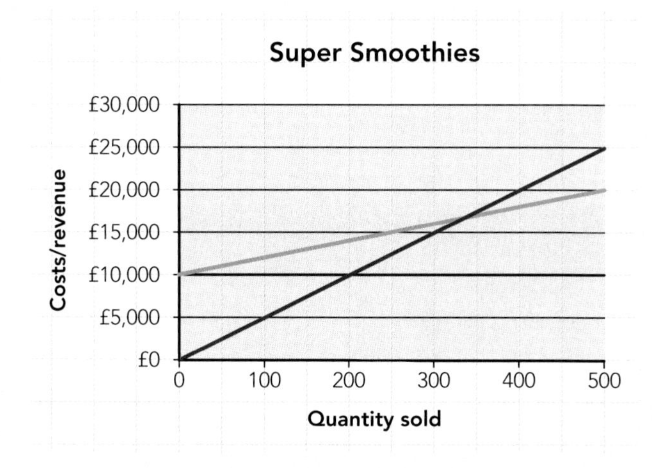

Question 5

Naseem has a sportswear shop and wants to complete his statement of financial position (balance sheet). He needs to identify which two items are short-term assets. [2]

(a) Cash register

(b) Stock

(c) Shop fitments

(d) Cash in the bank

(e) Shop safe

Question 6

Marsha has been in business for one year as a mobile hairdresser and is preparing her income statement (profit and loss account). Explain how the information it provides can help her to improve her financial position. [4]

Introduction

A brand is a way of communicating with customers. If it is done well, it makes a business unique and increases the value of a product. This unit explains how a business builds a brand and why this is important.

This unit looks at a number of promotional techniques that can be used to make people aware of your brand. You will have an opportunity to examine the differing ways that companies in business to business (B2B) and business to consumer (B2C) markets promote their brands.

You will look at the different elements that must be included in a promotional campaign, and examine ways of reviewing the success of a brand.

Finally, you will have an opportunity to use your creativity and imagination to create a unique brand for the products offered by a selected organisation.

Assessment: This unit will be assessed through a series of assignments set by your teacher/tutor.

Learning aims

In this unit you will:

A explore the use of branding and the promotional mix in business

B develop and promote a brand for a business.

My hobby is drawing so I enjoyed the creative aspect of this unit. Being able to create a brand for a product was really exciting because I got to use my imagination. It was interesting to do research into different media channels and find out how people respond to different types of promotion.

Jabez, *15-year-old Business student*

3 Promoting a Brand

This table shows you what you must do in order to achieve a **Pass**, **Merit** or **Distinction** grade, and where you can find activities in this book to help you.

Assessment criteria			
Level 1	**Level 2 Pass**	**Level 2 Merit**	**Level 2 Distinction**
Learning aim A: Explore the use of branding and the promotional mix in business			
1A.1 Describe the importance of branding for a business	**2A.P1** Explain how branding is used in two businesses **See Assessment activity 3.1, page 89**	**2A.M1** Compare the use of brand promotion in two businesses **See Assessment activity 3.1, page 89**	**2A.D1** Evaluate the effectiveness of the promotional mix for a selected branded product **See Assessment activity 3.1, page 89**
1A.2 Identify elements of the marketing mix for a selected branded product	**2A.P2** Assess the marketing mix for a selected branded product **See Assessment activity 3.1, page 89**	**2A.M2** Explain the importance of selecting an appropriate promotional mix for a selected branded product **See Assessment activity 3.1, page 89**	
1A.3 Identify elements of the promotional mix used for a selected branded product	**2A.P3** Describe the purpose of elements of the promotional mix used for a selected branded product **See Assessment activity 3.1, page 89**		
Learning aim B: Develop and promote a brand for a business			
1B.4 Outline an idea and select a target market for a brand	**2B.P4** Use branding methods and techniques to recommend a brand personality and a target market for a brand **See Assessment activity 3.2, page 94**	**2B.M3** Explain how branding methods and techniques were used to recommend a brand personality and a target market for a brand **See Assessment activity 3.2, page 94**	**2B.D2** Evaluate the effectiveness of a promotional campaign for a brand and recommend improvements **See Assessment activity 3.2, page 94**
1B.5 Outline elements of a promotional campaign for a brand	**2B.P5** English Plan a promotional campaign for a brand **See Assessment activity 3.2, page 94**	**2B.M4** Justify the choice of promotional mix for a brand **See Assessment activity 3.2, page 94**	

English Opportunity to practise English skills

How you will be assessed

This unit will be assessed by a series of internally assessed tasks. You will need to collect examples of promotional materials and label them to highlight different features. You will need to gather evidence of how well a brand has been promoted.

You will need to produce an original promotional campaign for a brand. You might produce a mail shot or a radio advert and then give a presentation on why it will appeal to a specific target market.

Your assessment could be in the form of:

- a presentation, pitching an idea for a brand to a local business
- a package of promotional materials
- a review of the use of promotion by different companies
- a podcast about the ways that different companies use branding
- a report on the appropriateness of different types of promotional material.

The importance of branding to businesses

Getting started

In 2011, Apple became the most valuable brand in the world. Research suggested that it was worth $153.3 billion. The Apple brand is known to millions of people all around the world. This has been the result of over a decade of hard work by the late Steve Jobs and his colleagues. It is the kind of success that most brands can only dream of.

What makes some mobile phones stand out from others?

What is a brand?

- **A strategy** – a long-term plan for the promotion of a company or a product.
- The **perception of a customer** – a brand is how the public sees a product or a business. It must represent everything the company stands for, for example, Innocent, the UK-based fruit drinks company, has a pure and natural brand image.
- **A logo** – part of a brand is the symbol that can be placed on a product so that people know it belongs to a particular company. The Nike 'swoosh' is a well-known example.
- **A legal instrument** – a brand is the exclusive property of its owner. This means that no one else can profit from it. Companies work hard to protect their brands.
- **A company** – for example, Virgin applies its brand to a range of different companies, each of which benefits from how well recognised the name is.
- **A personality** – customer perceptions of a brand include how they imagine a brand might behave; they see it as being almost like a person. For example, many people see Innocent as being quirky and imaginative.

Did you know?

In 2012 Apple paid China's Proview Technology $60 million to ensure it could legally use the iPad name in China.

- **A vision** – brands are often created with the intention of using them on a whole range of products, for example, the Easy brand was developed to include hotels, car rental and offices.
- **An identity** – a brand gives a company a unique identity that **differentiates** it from other companies. This might be because of the quality of the product or the way it makes the user feel. For example, Porsche drivers enjoy the luxury image of their cars.
- **An image** – each brand has its own unique associations. BMW has an image of reliability, whereas Porsche has an image of luxury.

Key terms

Perception – what a customer or consumer thinks about something.

Differentiate – make your business noticeably different from your competitors.

Brands must be careful to protect their image.

Activity Creating an image

In a group, list 10 brands. For each brand, discuss how it has created a unique image. Consider the products that it represents and the types of advertising that you are aware of. Feed back your findings to your class.

Why businesses use branding

Branding is used by businesses to create a clear image that customers can recognise. A brand shows that something is the product of a particular company, giving customers a message about what they can expect from their purchase. For McDonald's this might be value and convenience. Topshop might want its brand to represent fashion and style.

Types of branding

Businesses use different types of branding.

- **Product branding** – this brand represents a specific product, for example Jaffa Cakes.
- **Service branding** – this brand represents a specific service, for example Visa.
- **Corporate branding** – this brand represents a company and can be applied to all of their products and services, for example Kellogg's.

Adding value

The purpose of a brand is to add value to products. A good brand will differentiate a company from its competitors by making its product seem more valuable than those of unbranded competitors.

CONTINUED ▸▸

▸▸ CONTINUED

Benefits of successful branding

These are shown in Table 3.1.

Table 3.1 Benefits of successful branding

Image	A brand creates an association in peoples' minds about the image of a product. For example, Costa Coffee has an image linked to excellent customer service.
Quality	A brand tells people how good a product is.
Recognition	The golden arches of the McDonald's logo are well known throughout the world. People know what it stands for regardless of the language they speak.
Long-lasting perceptions	A well-established brand creates a lasting impression on customers. For example, Coca-Cola's 'Holidays are coming' adverts are connected with the start of Christmas in many peoples' minds.
Trust	Customers know that a product with a familiar brand will meet a certain standard. For example, a Travelodge room will be warm and comfortable anywhere in the country.
Marketing multiple products	This is called brand extension. Once a brand is successful, it can be used to promote a range of products.

Lego have extended their brand to include theme parks and video games.

Unsuccessful branding

Branding can sometimes go wrong. Negative publicity caused by unethical business practices or disasters can damage the reputation of a brand. This damages the customer perception of the brand. For example, in 2012, horsemeat found in some ready meals threatened the reputation of several well-known companies.

Promotion in businesses

Why businesses need to promote themselves

Promotion is a vital activity for all businesses. Effective promotional activity allows a business to stay ahead of its competition. This is because good promotional activity will inform customers about a company's products and persuade them that they should make a purchase from that company.

Businesses benefit from promotional activity by creating awareness of their brand. This should lead to increased sales and profits. Promotion is one of the four elements of the **marketing mix**. When it is well designed, promotion will support the other elements of the marketing mix.

Key terms

Marketing mix – the combination of product, price, place and promotion. This is often referred to as the 4 Ps.

Activities used in the marketing mix

The marketing mix consists of product, price, place and promotion. These are the four elements of a good marketing campaign.

Product

This is what a business sells to its customers. A product is a combination of features and benefits.

- **Features** are what a product does or what it is made of.
- A customer **benefits** from using a product or service. For example, subscribers to LOVEFiLM have access to exclusive films that aren't available on other websites.

What are the features of a smartphone?

Activity Identifying the 4 Ps

In pairs or small groups research how a local business uses the 4 Ps. Recommend four improvements.

CONTINUED ▸▸

▸▸ CONTINUED

Price

It is important to make the right decision about how much to charge your customers. If you charge too much, people might not want to buy your products. If you charge too little, you will not be able to make a profit.

The price that you charge will depend on the quality of your product. Better-quality products command a higher price. Demand from customers is also important. The more demand you have from potential customers, the more you can charge. It is also important to take into account your competitors. If your company charges £100 less than your rival, then customers will come to you.

Did you know?

New technology, like games consoles, have a higher price when they are first released to take advantage of customers' desire for the latest products. This is called price skimming.

Link

This topic links to *Unit 6: Introducing Retail Business.*

Key terms

Wholesaler – a company which sells goods in bulk to retail businesses.

Direct distribution – selling your product direct to the market yourself.

Place

- It is important to think about where your products will be sold. It is no good offering luxury chocolates in a discount store. Businesses must decide how to offer their goods for sale in a way that will appeal to their target market. Are shops better than catalogues? Is the internet best or should you choose door-to-door selling?
- You must also decide if you will sell directly to the market yourself or if you will use a **wholesaler**. **Direct distribution** is more profitable because you keep all the revenue, but using a wholesaler might mean your products are offered in a wider range of outlets so more customers see your product.
- Websites such as Folksy and Etsy allow small businesses to sell directly to the public anywhere in the world. This means that designers keep their profits after paying a small fee.
- Food manufacturers might use a wholesaler such as 3663 to sell their goods to small shops and restaurants. This wholesaler provides a range of goods in bulk at a discount, delivering goods to their customers.

How would the promotion of luxury products be different to that of cheaper alternatives?

Promotion

This is how a business communicates with potential customers. Once the other elements of the marketing mix have been set, promotional activities are used to create awareness of your product. For example, to promote its orange juice, Tropicana took a giant orange ball to town centres during the winter. They hung this from a crane over rows of deckchairs and gave away bottles of their juice so that people could sit under the 'sun' and enjoy a drink. Each bottle came with a money-off voucher to encourage people to buy Tropicana.

Can you think of any inventive ideas to promote a business?

Benefits of promotion to businesses

Promotion is essential for businesses to communicate with customers about their goods and services. The different methods of promotion are covered in detail later in this unit.

Take it futher

The 4 Ps version of the marketing mix has been extended to include three more Ps – People, Process and Physical Environment. Investigate this extended marketing mix. Find out what each of the Ps involves and describe some examples of how each works.

Elements of the promotional mix and their purposes

Introduction

The promotional mix refers to the different elements that a business can use to encourage customers to buy its products. Which promotional methods have you seen successful brands like Coca-Cola or Virgin use?

Advertising

Advertising is when a business pays for space in the prime media to communicate with the public about their products and services. This can be expensive and businesses must ensure that they spend their **advertising budget** carefully.

Key terms

Advertising budget – the amount of money that you make available to spend on adverts.

Message – what you want to tell your customers.

Medium – how you choose to advertise to your target market.

The purpose of advertising

There are two main purposes of advertising:

1. **To inform people.** You need to make potential customers aware of your product and its benefits. If you are advertising food, you might tell people about the nutrients it contains.
2. **To persuade people to make a purchase.** You might tell people about the great benefits that you offer or the low prices that you have set.

Different companies use adverts with one or both purposes. The NHS might use adverts to inform people about the dangers of obesity and persuade people to lose weight.

Activity — Explaining adverts

Collect 10 adverts from newspapers and magazines. Take photos of 10 adverts in public spaces such as billboards and posters. Divide the adverts up according to whether they are trying to inform or persuade. For each advert write a short explanation of how it uses words and pictures to achieve these purposes.

Message and medium

When you design an advert, you must think about what you want to tell people (the **message**) and how you will tell them (the **medium**).

Your message might be what you sell, where you sell it and how much it costs.

The medium that you use for your advertising depends on your advertising budget and the type of market that you are trying to reach. A large company such as McDonald's might use TV adverts because it has a lot of money and it wants to reach the whole country. A small independent cafe might use a local newspaper to reach its local community.

Methods of advertising

There are many different methods of advertising available to businesses, depending on the medium that they choose.

- **Moving image:** This type of advert, which is often shown on television or in cinemas, is useful where products have many features or moving parts. It allows dynamic demonstrations of products being used. These adverts can be put onto DVDs and given away at shop counters or videos can be uploaded to sites such as YouTube.

- **Print:** It is possible to pay for advertising space in newspapers and magazines. Alternatively, eye-catching billboards can be placed beside busy roads. Modern technology means that digital signs are used, allowing the advert to be changed at different times of day.
- **Ambient:** Adverts in public spaces such as the sides of buses can be effective at catching the eye of potential customers.
- **Digital:** Adverts can be placed on websites or sent to customers via a text message. Companies such as Google and Facebook have developed technology that makes adverts appear when people type in certain key words.
- **Audio:** Radio adverts provide an opportunity to talk to customers about your product. For a relatively low cost, you can tell people about the features of your product and where they can buy it. Sometimes these adverts feature famous voices to give them extra credibility.

> **Did you know?**
>
> Adverts printed on the odd-numbered pages (right-hand side) of a newspaper or magazine cost more than those printed on the even pages (left-hand side). This is because people see the right-hand side of the paper first when they are turning the pages.

Why is this type of advertising so effective?

Activity — Choosing methods of advertising

The type of product or service that you are promoting will influence your choice of advertising method. For each of the following businesses, suggest a type of advert and explain why you think it is appropriate.

1 A local car dealer
2 An online retailer
3 A national chain of coffee shops
4 An office cleaning company.

CONTINUED ▸▸

▸▸ CONTINUED

Sales promotion

Sales promotions are used to encourage customers to purchase your products or for distribution channels to stock your goods. This involves offering an incentive to make it more attractive to make a purchase.

Sales promotion methods include:

- **Price promotion:** This could be a simple discount on a product (e.g. 25p off), a multi-buy offer (e.g. buy one get one free) or a larger package for the same price (e.g. 25 per cent extra free). Price promotions are useful in **B2B markets** because they help businesses to negotiate with **distribution channels** by offering a lower price for a larger order.
- **Coupons:** This is a small paper or card token, offering customers a discount or free gift when they buy something.
- **Competitions:** This is when customers win a prize when they buy a product. This might include an 'instant win' offer where a prize is in a package.
- **Money refunds:** Some companies offer a cash back scheme. When a customer makes a purchase, a portion of the cost is refunded over a period of time such as a year. This is popular for products such as cars or mobile phones.

  Another type of refund promotion is offered by some supermarkets. If a customer is able to buy products cheaper in a competitor's store, the supermarket will refund the difference between its price and its competitor's price.
- **Loyalty incentives:** Loyalty schemes are offered by many companies. Caffè Nero uses a simple scheme where it gives customers a card on which they can collect stamps. When their card is full, they can exchange this card for a free drink.

Key terms

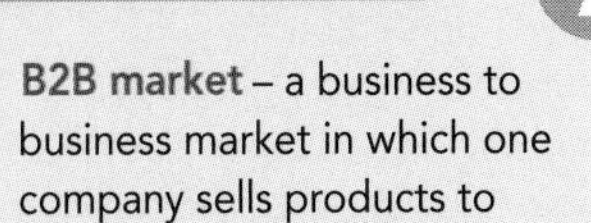

B2B market – a business to business market in which one company sells products to another.

Distribution channels – the route that a product or service takes to get to the market, e.g. manufacturer to wholesaler to retailer.

Interpersonal skills – being able to speak to customers and read their body language.

B2C market – a business to consumer market in which companies sell products directly to the public.

Pitch – the proposal made by a salesperson to sell their products to a potential customer.

Discussion point

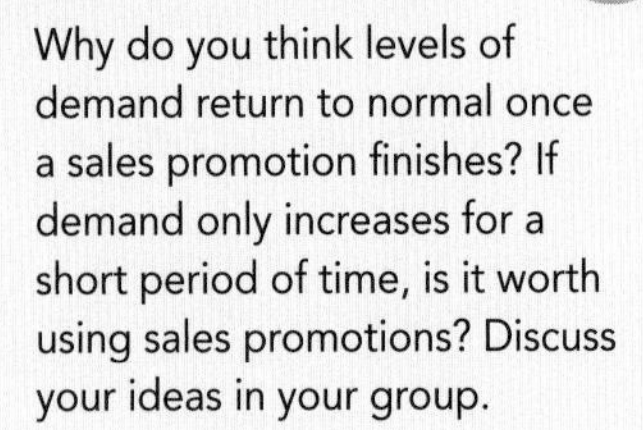

Why do you think levels of demand return to normal once a sales promotion finishes? If demand only increases for a short period of time, is it worth using sales promotions? Discuss your ideas in your group.

Personal selling

This is where a representative of a company interacts directly with a potential customer. The salesperson uses their **interpersonal skills** to try to persuade the potential customer to make a purchase. This is called 'closing a sale'.

This can be a much more appropriate method than advertising if products or services are complicated. The salesperson is able to explain the features to the customer and answer any questions that they might have.

Computer shops are a good example of personal selling in a business to consumer market (**B2C market**). Sales staff can explain technical information in terms that the customer understands.

Link

This topic links to *Unit 5: Sales and Personal Selling.*

Activity — Investigating trunk shows

Stella and Dot moved to the UK in 2011. They use a modern twist on direct selling called a trunk show. Visit their website to find out more about their business. You can access this by going to www.pearsonhotlinks.co.uk and searching for this title.

1 What is a trunk show?
2 Why do you think Stella and Dot employ stylists rather than salespeople?

There are a number of methods of personal selling.

- **Face to face:** The salesperson watches the customer's body language and listens to the tone of their voice to assess how interested they are in making a purchase. This allows them to adapt their sales **pitch**.
- **Telephone:** This method does not allow the salesperson to read the customer's body language. However, a good salesperson can still hear a lot from the tone of the customer's voice and the words that they use.
- **Email:** Deals can be discussed over a period of time. The salesperson can send their customer attachments containing details of their product or links to relevant websites.
- **Video or web conferencing:** The use of a webcam allows the salesperson to see the customer wherever they are in the world. They can demonstrate products on camera as well as sending the customer files or links to relevant websites.

Activity — Selling mobile phones

Imagine you are a salesperson for a mobile phone company.

1 Which method of personal selling would you choose? Why?
2 What steps would you take to make sure that your customer bought a phone?

The customer and the salesperson meet.

Did you know?

Energy companies and banks have been criticised because their salespeople have given customers misleading information to make sales. This is because their salespeople are paid money for each sale that they make.

CONTINUED ▸▸

▸▸ CONTINUED

Public relations activities

Public relations are the activities a business carries out to place information in the media without paying for it directly. If this is successful, then the time gained on television or presence in the press can be worth thousands of pounds.

A potential problem is that the message you are trying to give the public might not be transmitted exactly as you intended. With television or print advertising, you have some control over what is published. When you send public relations material out to the press, you no longer have any control over it.

Public relations activities include:

- **Exhibitions:** An exhibition is when one or more companies present and display their products. These are often large events, such as 'Clothes Show Live' where many different stalls are set up to highlight the latest and most exciting new products on offer.
- **Sponsorship:** This is when you pay to display your brand at an event such as a music concert or on a television programme; for example, McCain Foods sponsor films on Channel 4. Some companies use sponsorship to create a positive image for their company. BP sponsors a number of art galleries in the UK. Unfortunately, this has attracted negative publicity for the art galleries, with climate change groups protesting outside some galleries.
- **Press releases:** Issuing a press release involves writing a statement which can be used by journalists as part of a news story. Journalists get many press releases each day, so it is important to highlight something interesting in your press release to get their attention.

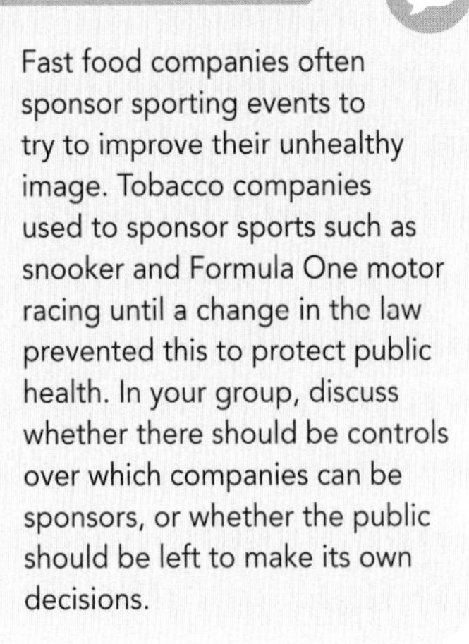

Discussion point

Fast food companies often sponsor sporting events to try to improve their unhealthy image. Tobacco companies used to sponsor sports such as snooker and Formula One motor racing until a change in the law prevented this to protect public health. In your group, discuss whether there should be controls over which companies can be sponsors, or whether the public should be left to make its own decisions.

Activity — Writing a press release

Think about a recent success at your school or college. It might be the triumph of a sports team or it might be a visit that you have made to a local business. Write a press release that could be sent to your local newspaper to promote this achievement.

Did you know?

One of the biggest exhibitions held in the UK is called Spring Fair. Over 70,000 people visit the event over a week in February to see stalls set up by three thousand exhibitors. You can find out more by going to www.pearsonhotlinks.co.uk and searching for this title.

Why are exhibitions a good way of promoting new products?

Direct marketing

Direct marketing is when a business communicates directly with a customer, establishing an individual relationship between the business and the customer.

While adverts are shown to everyone in a specific area, direct marketing material is aimed at a specific customer and can be tailored according to the individual or group to whom it is sent. According to the mail preference survey, postal sales in the UK are worth £25 billion a year, but the public often call these mailshots 'junk mail'. Why do you think this is?

Direct marketing techniques include the following:

- **Direct mail:** Letters posted to customers give them information about new products or special offers.
- **Mail order catalogues:** Sending customers a catalogue containing photographs and details of different products allows them to look at your products in the comfort of their home. Sometimes these catalogues are distributed by agents who take and deliver orders, for example Avon.

Activity Researching direct marketing

Customers sometimes find forms of direct marketing such as junkmail and cold calls unpleasant and frustrating.

You can find websites to learn more about the mail preference service and the telephone preference service by visiting www.pearsonhotlinks.co.uk and searching for this title.

Magazines: Some companies produce short magazines which can be sent out to the people on their mailing list. These often contain pictures and short descriptions to inform customers about new products.

Activity Analysing magazines

Topman produces a monthly magazine called *Generation* about music, clothes and celebrities. Read a copy of this magazine online. You can access this by going to www.pearsonhotlinks.co.uk and searching for this title.

1. How does the magazine support Topman in promoting its brand?
2. Compare the features in the magazine to the products in a branch of Topman. Would reading the magazine make you more likely to make a purchase from the store? Explain your answer.
3. Find examples of magazines produced by five contrasting businesses. Compare the contents and features, suggesting reasons for any similarities or differences.
4. Rank the magazines in order from most effective to least effective at promoting that company's products. Explain your decisions.

- **Telemarketing:** This is when a phone call is made to a customer to tell them about your latest product and invite them to make a purchase. Telemarketers sometimes make uninvited calls to customers. This is called cold calling.

TOPIC A.4

Promotional activities in business

Introduction

Promotional activity can be expensive so it is important to carefully plan how you will spend your budget. The first step is to consider what type of market you will target.

Discussion point

B2B markets are worth a great deal more money than B2C markets. The value of all of the goods and services bought by businesses is far greater than those bought by consumers.

In groups, discuss Starbucks. Think about everything that is involved in attracting a customer to buy a cup of coffee. How many opportunities can you think of to sell goods and services to this company?

Types of market

To create an effective promotional campaign, businesses must identify which customers they want to target with their promotions.

Business to business (B2B) markets

When a company sells goods or services to other companies it is targeting a B2B market. Companies such as Heinz are part of these markets. Its customers are companies such as the supermarket chain Morrisons, which buys cans of beans and soup, for example.

Companies in B2B markets often use a 'push and pull' strategy when choosing their promotional mix; they use methods such as advertising to create demand from consumers and personal selling to sell their products to shops.

Business to consumer (B2C) markets

Consumers are the people who use goods and services. There is a range of products available in B2C markets, including phones, clothes, food, toys and many other items.

In a B2C market, the purpose of promotion is to gain sales from the public. A company might use loyalty cards to encourage people to come back to its store or adverts to create awareness of its latest product.

B2C companies also use 'push and pull' strategies. Companies might push their products to people on Facebook who have 'liked' them, and pull customers in by encouraging them to click a link with the promise of a discount.

Activity: Choosing promotional methods

For each of the following products, suggest which promotional methods you would use to sell it in a B2B market and a B2C market:

1 Laptop computer
2 Frozen chips
3 Flight to America
4 BTEC Business Student Book

Give a reason for each of your choices.

Key terms

Segment – to identify and divide customers into groups sharing certain characteristics.

Fairtrade – products which pay a fair wage to the producer.

Market segmentation

Dividing a market up into groups of people allows money to be spent more efficiently. The process of identifying and targeting a group of people with similar interests is called segmentation. Markets can be **segmented** in a number of different ways.

How could a shopping centre segment its customers?

Age

People have different needs at different stages in their lives. Teenagers might be interested in mobile phones and the latest fashion. The elderly, those over the age of 80, might be more interested in excursions and theatre offers.

Family status

People have different needs depending on whether they are married or single and whether they have children. Walt Disney World® promote holidays for younger families with children.

Gender

Goods such as hair care and deodorant are promoted differently to men and women. Arcadia has different brands of clothes to appeal to men (Topman, Burton) and women (Topshop, Dorothy Perkins).

Income

Consumers can be divided up according to how much they earn. People with different incomes have different needs and wants. Supermarkets aim their premium products at wealthier customers while providing a value range for the less well off. For example, Sainsbury's has a 'Taste the Difference' range of premium goods and a 'Basics' range of simpler, more affordable items.

Attitudes

People buy different products according to how they see the world. Some people are interested in ethical products, such as **Fairtrade** goods. Newspapers such as *The Times* are targeted at people with conservative views, while *The Guardian* is aimed at those with more liberal ideas.

Lifestyle

Markets can be segmented according to people's hobbies, interests and the way that they live their lives. Some services appeal specifically to people who are busy with their career, such as shirt-ironing services.

Activity

Comparing promotional materials

Compare the promotional materials for Lynx, which is aimed at men, and Impulse, which is aimed at women.

How do the messages in the adverts differ to appeal to each group?

Activity

Explaining market segmentation

Car manufacturers often segment their markets according to the income of their customers. Companies such as Ford and Toyota produce a range of cars at different prices. Explain why you think it is important for these companies to appeal to customers with different incomes.

CONTINUED ▸▸

The use of promotional activities in business

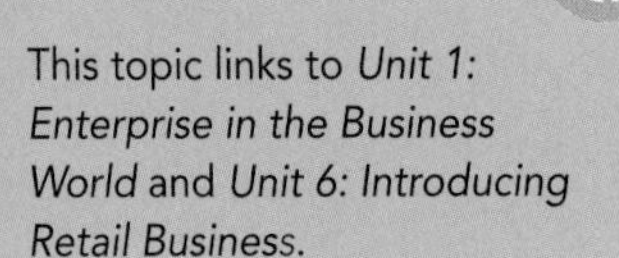

Link

This topic links to *Unit 1: Enterprise in the Business World* and *Unit 6: Introducing Retail Business.*

Setting objectives

There is no point spending time designing your promotional mix if you don't know what you want to achieve. When you are planning promotional activity, it is important to set appropriate SMART objectives.

Table 3.2 SMART objectives

Specific	What do you want to gain from the promotional activity? More customers? Extra revenue?
Measurable	How many customers do you want to attract? How much market share do you want to gain?
Achievable	Is it possible to meet the objective? Are there enough customers in the market?
Realistic	Do you have the capacity to meet the objective? Can you manufacture enough products?
Time-related	When do you want to achieve the objective by? In a month? A year?

Activity Setting objectives

Imagine you are the marketing director for a new soft drink brand. You are launching your new product in three months' time. Write three suitable SMART objectives for your new product.

How appropriate is your promotional mix?

The type of promotional activities that you select will depend on the type of product you sell and the market you are aiming at. If you want to sell to a B2B market, then cinema adverts might not be appropriate. If you wish to sell to a large consumer market, selecting an appropriate promotional mix based on personal selling might be far too expensive.

The appropriateness of your promotional mix will also depend on your target segment. For example, digital advertising might be more appropriate for younger consumers. Audio channels such as radio might be more appropriate for older age groups.

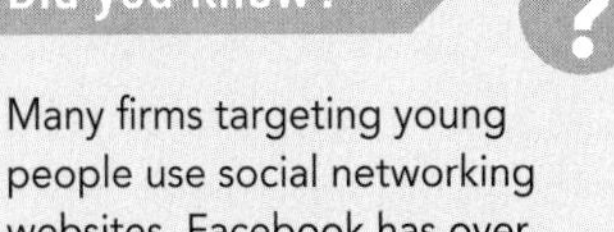

Did you know?

Many firms targeting young people use social networking websites. Facebook has over 1 billion active users, 50 per cent of whom log in every day. Facebook's advertising revenue was over $5 billion in 2012.

Benefits of selecting an appropriate promotional mix

Selecting an appropriate promotional mix means that money is spent efficiently. Otherwise money is wasted on activities that attract few customers. Well-planned promotional activities will also make a business more competitive. Staying ahead of competitors is an important business aim. If your competitors are more effective at promotion than your business is, they will win more customers than you.

The AIDA model

AIDA stands for awareness/attention, interest, desire, action. It describes the stages that a customer goes through when looking at well-designed promotional material. This model can be used to evaluate the quality of the different elements of your promotional mix.

Awareness/attention

Good promotional material attracts people's attention. Eye-catching slogans or striking images make people notice your message.

Interest

The features of your product should be communicated to your customer in a way that they will find interesting. It is important to understand the needs of your market segment. If you are selling a mobile phone, teenagers might want to know how many songs it can store. Their parents might be more interested in security features.

What methods are being used to attract people's attention?

Desire

Having gained your customer's interest, you have to persuade them to buy from you. Highlighting the price and any special offers might be enough to achieve this.

Action

Once you have created the desire for your product, you must give your customer an opportunity to buy it. This could mean telling them where they can make a purchase, for example by stating where it is for sale. If you are using a digital advert in an email or on a website you might provide a link to an online shop. Alternatively, you might provide a phone number so that your customer can call your telesales staff.

Assessment activity 3.1

2A.P1 | 2A.P2 | 2A.P3 | 2A.M1 | 2A.M2 | 2A.D1

Colin is leaving school next year and he wants to set up a bookshop. He has been advised that he should create a brand to make his business stand out from its competitors. He thinks that this will be an important part of the marketing mix for his business.

Colin thinks that his main competitors will be high street retailers such as Waterstones and online retailers such as Amazon. He is particularly interested in understanding how successful companies plan their marketing mix.

His own knowledge is limited to the work experience he did with the Red Cross whilst he was doing his BTEC and he is therefore interested in looking at some of the branded products of market leaders.

1. Investigate how branding is used by both Innocent Smoothies® and the Red Cross and why it is important for each company. Then find out more about Innocent by visiting a retailer selling their products and viewing the company website. Collect examples of the company's promotional material and other relevant evidence. Consider how well Innocent have designed their marketing mix before assessing how well they apply each of the 4 Ps of the marketing mix and how they have used each element of their promotional mix.
2. Write a report for Colin summarising your findings. Include a section which evaluates the promotional mix used by Innocent. Explain to Colin how important each element is and whether or not it is being used effectively.

Activity

Comparing adverts

Collect 10 adverts for different products. Compare the different features of the adverts. How do they gain attention or create interest and desire to buy? Which adverts are most effective? Explain your decisions.

Branding methods and techniques

Introduction

An effective brand combines a number of different elements to represent an appropriate image for a business. A successful brand may combine several elements:

- **Logos:** A logo is a symbol that represents a company, for example the golden arches of McDonald's. It can be used in adverts and on packaging to tell people that a product belongs to that company.
- **Straplines:** These are short phrases that make people think of a particular product. One of the most famous examples is Nike's 'Just Do It' slogan. While this does not refer directly to its products, it creates an active image for the company.

Discussion point

Tiger Woods and Wayne Rooney both endorsed a number of products until allegations about their private lives were reported in the press. In your group, discuss why it is important to carry out thorough research into a celebrity's background before asking them to endorse your products.

Activity — Designing a logo

Design a new logo and write a strapline that your school and college could use on its promotional materials. Explain why it is appropriate to the image of the institution.

- **Celebrity endorsements:** If a celebrity who appeals to your target market is seen to use your product, it can encourage people to use it themselves. Nintendo used a major advertising campaign featuring numerous celebrities such as Jamie Oliver and Louise Redknapp to promote their Wii™ and DS™ consoles.

Have you ever been influenced by celebrity endorsements?

Planning ideas for a brand for a business

When you are planning a brand for a business, the first thing to consider is what type of brand you want to create.

- **Concept brands –** these are often used by charities or political parties to sell an idea to the public, for example 'New Labour' or 'Keep Britain Tidy'.
- **Commodity brands –** this is when a brand is placed on a company or a product. It creates a unique identity which differentiates the product from its competitors.

You must take a number of different factors into account to ensure that your brand is suitable for your target market. These are listed in Table 3.3.

Table 3.3 Factors you must consider to ensure your brand is suitable

Factor	Implications	Example
Race/nationality	The culture of different countries is important. Tastes vary in different areas.	Germans prefer to rent houses rather than buy them with a mortgage.
Religion	It is important not to offend any religious groups with your brand.	Tesco stores stock ranges of kosher foods in areas with a Jewish population.
Children	If your brand is appealing to children, it should not be used on products that are unsuitable for them.	Alcopop brands have been criticised for appealing to children.
Disabilities	Your brand should be sensitive to people with physical or mental disabilities.	Use a clear font in your logo so people with poor sight can see it clearly.
Environmental	Some brands benefit from being linked to environmentally friendly practices.	Ikea only uses wood from sustainable sources.

Did you know?

The term 'branding' comes from the practice of farmers stamping a symbol onto their animals to show who owns it. The purpose of a brand is to show that a product has come from a specific organisation.

The Red Cross is also known as the Red Crescent in countries that aren't traditionally Christian so that people do not think it is a religious organisation.

▸▸ CONTINUED

Activity Researching brands

In groups, research two brands that appeal to different age groups. Each member of the group should interview six people of different ages about what they think of the brand. Discuss your findings and present them to your class.

Brand personality

Some businesses try to give their brand a personality to appeal to the target market. This helps customers relate to the product. It might be the language in the adverts or the type of images used on the packaging. Peperami is well known for being 'a bit of an animal', which is reinforced by eye-catching adverts featuring an animated sausage.

Discussion point

Find out which major company now owns Innocent. To what extent does this alter your perception of the brand? Discuss your ideas.

How have Innocent created a brand personality?

Brand objectives

It is important to decide what you want to achieve when you create your brand. Objectives might include brand awareness (how many people know about your brand) or brand value (how much your brand is worth to the public).

Target market

Your brand must meet the needs of your target market. You should ensure that the promotional methods you choose are relevant to your audience and that the brand personality is appropriate.

Promoting a brand

Promoting a brand image

The way that you promote your brand makes a big difference to how customers perceive it. The type of media that you use will influence their views. More people will see an advert on television because it has greater reach, but an advert in a magazine might be more relevant to your target market because a magazine is more specialised.

Activity Investigating brand promotion

Different types of media influence the way people see a brand. For example, brands wanting to be seen as modern and innovative might use web-based media. If a brand wants to look cool, they might use guerrilla advertising methods. Investigate five brands with different images. Explain how they use different forms of promotion to create their brand image. Suggest why certain forms of promotion create a different image.

Planning a promotional campaign

When you plan a promotional campaign, there are several stages that you must go through:

1 **Setting promotional objectives**

Table 3.4 Types of promotional objective

Raise awareness	Make the public aware of the product or service that you are offering.
Remind	Jog the public's memory about the product or service that you are offering.
Differentiate	Create a unique image for your brand so you stand out from your competitors.
Persuade or inform	Do you want to let people know about the features and benefits of your product or convince them to buy it? Many promotions aim to achieve both.
Create market presence	To win sales, customers must be aware that your product is available.
Increase market share	You must persuade people to buy your product.

▸▸ CONTINUED

2 **Developing the most appropriate promotional mix**
Once you have set your objectives, you must choose promotional activities that will help you achieve them. For example, if you want to create brand awareness, you might choose a national television advert.

3 **Justifying the choice of promotional mix**
You must be able to explain why the promotional activities you choose are appropriate for your target market.

4 **Designing promotional activities**
This involves thinking about the message that you want to deliver and the purpose of your activities. Do you want to persuade or inform? Colours and images must be carefully selected to fit your brand personality.

Assessment activity 3.2 *English*

2B.P4 | 2B.P5 | 2B.M3 | 2B.M4 | 2B.D2

Colin is opening his bookshop next month. He has asked you to design a brand and to plan a campaign to promote it. You need to investigate the market for bookshops and prepare a presentation of an idea for a brand that is targeted at a specific target market.

Based on this you must produce suitable promotional materials and prepare a presentation in which you explain your choices to him. Your presentation should include:

- The brand personality and target market you recommend for Colin's bookshop. Support your recommendations by providing information about the branding methods and techniques you used.
- The promotional campaign you have planned for the bookshop, including examples of promotional materials and information about the promotional mix you consider would be best.
- Your own evaluation of the promotional campaign that you have created for Colin. Recommend improvements that could be made to your work before it is launched to the public.

WorkSpace

Paul Birch

Managing Director, Revolver World

After running a record company for 30 years, Paul Birch wanted to put something back into the community. He became interested in the principles of fair trade, because he wanted to give a fair deal to farmers in poorer countries. This interest led him to extend his existing brand into a new market.

After carrying out some research, Paul found some suppliers of fair trade coffee in Africa and Colombia. The next step was to create a brand personality. He created characters to use on the packaging to represent the farmers who grow the coffee. Paul decided to make the packaging yellow because potential customers thought that this looked fresh and bright.

Paul uses personal selling to encourage stores to sell his coffee. When a store stocks his products, he sends his staff to run free tasting sessions to encourage people to buy the product. This creates sales for the retailer and helps Paul to create brand awareness. The other target market for the coffee is 18–35-year-olds. He uses discount vouchers to encourage them to try the coffee. Paul has a website to inform people about the brand and his other fair trade products.

Think about it

1. Which elements of the promotional mix does Paul use to sell his coffee?
2. Is Paul's promotional mix appropriate to his target market? What improvements would you recommend?
3. What objectives would you suggest that Paul should set for his brand? How will this help him to evaluate the success of his new brand?

Introduction

Customer service is one of the most important aspects of running a business, because customers are vital to the success of every business. Making sure customers come back to the business again and again helps the business to grow, and it costs less to keep existing customers than to find new ones.

Anticipating customer needs is a key factor in business, but so are meeting and exceeding customer expectations. If customers leave your business feeling satisfied (their experience of your business has been good), they are more likely to return and more likely to tell their friends about your product or service.

This unit introduces you to the different types of customers that businesses come into contact with, and how to deal with them to ensure that their expectations are met. You will demonstrate the interpersonal skills required in customer service situations and identify the key skills required to offer a professional and efficient service.

Assessment: This unit will be assessed through a series of assignments set by your teacher/tutor.

Learning aims

In this unit you will:

A understand how businesses provide customer service

B demonstrate appropriate customer service skills in different situations.

I work part-time in a shop, so this unit really helps me to understand how what I do affects the business. When I help customers, they form an impression of the shop based on their impression of me. Fortunately customers come back time and again, so I must be doing something right!

Marcus, *16-year-old Business student*

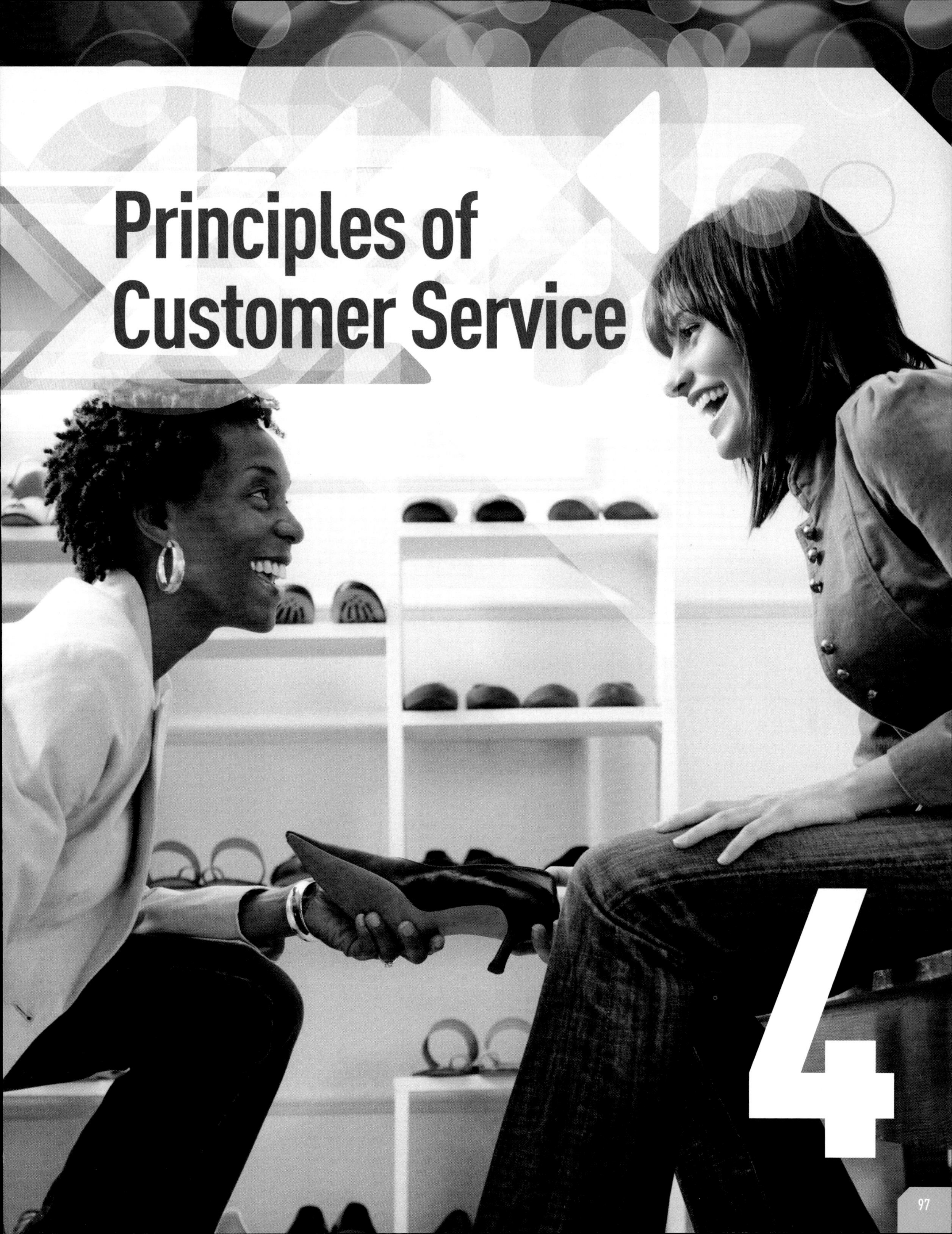

4 Principles of Customer Service

This table shows you what you must do in order to achieve a **Pass**, **Merit** or **Distinction** grade, and where you can find activities in this book to help you.

Assessment criteria			
Level 1	**Level 2 Pass**	**Level 2 Merit**	**Level 2 Distinction**
Learning aim A: Understand how businesses provide customer service			
1A.1 Define customer service, giving an example of a customer service role in a selected business	**2A.P1** Describe the different types of customer service provided by two selected businesses **See Assessment activity 4.1, page 109**	**2A.M1** Compare how two selected businesses satisfy customers **See Assessment activity 4.1, page 109**	**2A.D1** Assess the effect of providing consistent and reliable customer service on the reputation of a selected business **See Assessment activity 4.1, page 109**
1A.2 Identify features of consistent and reliable customer service	**2A.P2** Describe the characteristics of consistent and reliable customer service **See Assessment activity 4.1, page 109**	**2A.M2** Explain how a selected business attempts to exceed customer expectations **See Assessment activity 4.1, page 109**	
1A.3 Identify how organisational procedures contribute to consistent and reliable customer service	**2A.P3** Explain how organisational procedures and legislation contribute to consistent and reliable customer service **See Assessment activity 4.1, page 109**	**2A.M3** Compare the impact of legislative and regulatory requirements affecting customer service on a selected business **See Assessment activity 4.1, page 109**	
1A.4 Outline how legislative and regulatory requirements affect customer service in a selected business	**2A.P4** Explain how legislative and regulatory requirements affect customer service in a selected business **See Assessment activity 4.1, page 109**		

Assessment criteria			
Level 1	**Level 2 Pass**	**Level 2 Merit**	**Level 2 Distinction**
Learning aim B: Demonstrate appropriate customer service skills in different situations			
1B.5 Identify different types of internal and external customer in a selected business, giving an example for each type	**2B.P5** Describe how a selected business meets the needs and expectations of three different types of customer **See Assessment activity 4.2, page 118**	**2B.M4 English** Demonstrate effective communication skills when responding to customer problems and complaints in three customer service situations **See Assessment activity 4.2, page 118**	**2B.D2 English** Evaluate the effectiveness of own customer service skills, justifying areas for improvement **See Assessment activity 4.2, page 118**
1B.6 Identify when it is necessary to refer a customer service problem to someone in authority	**2B.P6** Describe, using examples, the limits of authority that would apply when delivering customer service **See Assessment activity 4.2, page 118**		
1B.7 English Demonstrate appropriate communication skills in three customer service situations	**2B.P7 English** Demonstrate effective communication skills to meet customer needs when dealing with three different customer types in customer service situations **See Assessment activity 4.2, page 118**		

English Opportunity to practise English skills

How you will be assessed

This unit will be assessed by a series of internally assessed tasks. You will be expected to research two different businesses to show that you understand how good customer service impacts on a business, and ways in which a business can exceed customer expectations. You will also demonstrate a range of different customer service skills in a real or simulated work environment.

Your assessment could be in the form of:

- a written account, display or presentation of your research
- video role-play evidence of customer service skills
- a personal statement reflecting on your demonstration of customer service skills
- observation records from your tutor.

TOPIC A.1 A.2 A3

Customer service in business

Getting started

Many businesses aim to provide excellent customer service. Why do you think that customer service is so important?

Key terms

Service deliverer – a member of staff who delivers customer service.

Front-line customer service staff – those people who are a customer's first point of contact with the business.

Face-to-face customer service – when the customer receives service in front of a member of staff.

Remote customer service – when a business offers customer service by telephone or online.

Did you know?

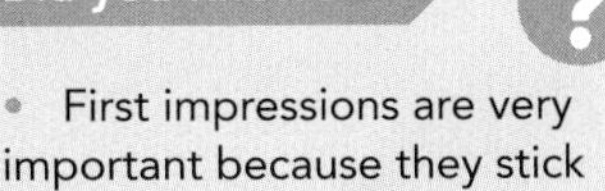

- First impressions are very important because they stick in our memory and colour our judgement. Can you remember your first day at school or college? What other 'firsts' can you remember?
- It can cost around five times more to bring a new customer into a business than it costs to keep an existing customer.

The meaning of customer service

Customer service can be defined as 'all the ways in which a business meets customer expectations to satisfy customers'. This may include:

- greeting customers
- having products in stock and available to buy
- providing information about products and services
- staff completing sales, wrapping goods, assisting customers using self-service checkouts, etc.
- after-sales support, such as a customer helpline.

Different customer service roles in a business

In business, employees can be involved in many different customer service roles. They can be involved directly with the customer, or indirectly:

- Roles that are *directly* involved with customers include receptionists, contact centre workers, shop assistants, delivery drivers, etc. These roles normally involve direct contact with customers.
- Roles that are *indirectly* involved with customers include cleaners, gardeners, engineers, etc. Although these staff are usually in the background, they contribute to the business by providing a good experience for its customers.

The different types of customer service businesses have

Businesses offer different types of customer service. This depends on the industry and the needs of the customers, so a vehicle repair garage may offer customers a courtesy car, whereas a retail store will help with packing or providing a gift-wrapping service.

Service deliverer

The person providing customer service is known as the **service deliverer**. They are often the first person a customer comes into contact with in a business. As service deliverers are the 'face' of the business, there are usually set standards and guidelines they must follow. This allows all **front-line customer service staff** to provide a consistent level of service.

Why are service deliverers so important?

Face-to-face customer service

Face-to-face customer service is delivered in many businesses, for example:

- in a hotel, face-to-face customer service is provided by the receptionist
- in a restaurant, face-to-face customer service is provided by the waiter
- in a leisure centre, face-to-face customer service is provided by personal trainers and pool attendants.

Activity Identifying customer service roles

In groups, identify two staff at your school/college who are directly involved with the customer and two who are not. Then do the same for a hospital and a retail store. Compare your ideas.

Remote customer service

Many businesses provide **remote customer service** so that customers can contact them without visiting the premises. Remote customer service is essential for businesses that sell only online, such as Ticketmaster. This type of customer service includes:

- call centres, which may be based in the UK or overseas
- online options for contacting customer service staff, such as an online form, email, or 'call me' website button. Some international businesses, such as British Airways, use Skype so that customers can make video or voice calls over the internet.

Customer service teamwork

Providing good customer service requires teamwork. If a customer has a complaint or a complex query, it may be necessary to liaise with another member of the team or the team leader to find the answer and provide excellent customer service.

Table 4.1 shows when teamwork is essential.

Table 4.1 Customer service teamwork

Cooperation is essential between...	When...
Departments	... a receptionist in a business needs to direct customers, or visitors from other businesses, to different departments.
Individuals	... a customer has a query that you cannot answer, you may need to ask a colleague who will be able to tell you the answer.
Businesses	... a customer returns a faulty product or has a problem with a product, the business needs to contact the manufacturer (if the product was made by another business) to report the problem and suggest a solution.

Activity Comparing customer service experiences

Think of a time when you received good customer service, and a time when you received bad customer service. What made the customer service good or bad? How did this affect the way you thought about the business? Compare your ideas.

Providing customer service

Customer satisfaction

Providing **consistent** and reliable customer service is vital in business. If customers are not satisfied, they do not return.

What is customer satisfaction?

Customers are satisfied when they receive the service they expect. Customer satisfaction may relate to:

- **Confidence in the service:** Customers know they can trust the business to keep its promises.
- **Value for money:** Customers feel that the quality, features and benefits they gain are worth paying for.
- **Repeat custom:** Satisfied customers are more likely to make future purchases.
- **Word-of-mouth reputation:** Satisfied customers often share their experiences with others, which enhances a company's reputation effectively and cheaply.
- **Loyalty:** When customers are loyal to a business, they are likely to buy more and spend more.

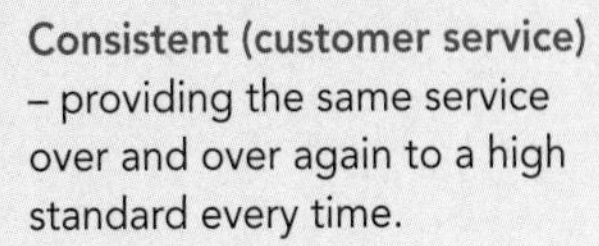

Key terms

Consistent (customer service) – providing the same service over and over again to a high standard every time.

Value for money – belief that the price paid is fair.

Word of mouth reputation – customers tell their friends, family and colleagues about their experiences with an organisation.

How businesses can satisfy customers

The techniques a business chooses need to be matched to the products and services that the company provides. Many popular techniques are shown in Figure 4.1.

Discussion point

What is the difference between 'cheap' and 'value for money'? Does this mean that all sale items must be a good deal? Discuss your ideas as a group.

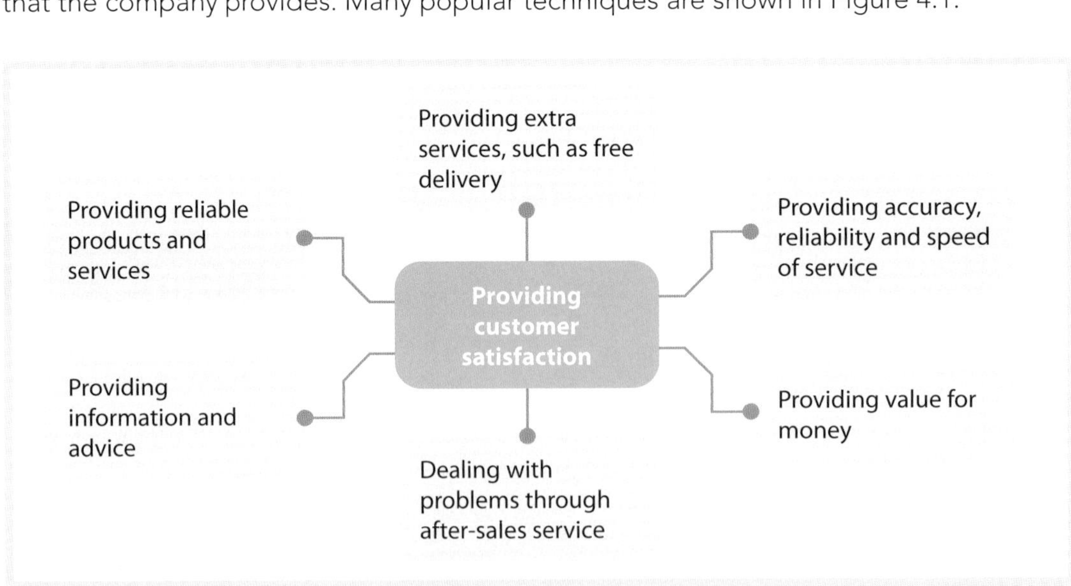

Figure 4.1 How businesses can satisfy customers

Activity Identifying examples of techniques

Look at the techniques for providing customer satisfaction in Figure 4.1. Can you identify an example of each technique in businesses in your area?

Consistent and reliable customer service

Consistent and reliable customer service means that customers can rely on good service no matter how or when they contact the business. This is achieved in the following ways.

- **Staff knowledge of products and services:** Customers may have several queries before they are ready to make a purchase. Businesses should provide regular training so staff product knowledge is up to date.
- **Staff knowledge of scope of their job role:** Staff should know the limits of their authority and when to refer a query or problem to their team leader or manager.
- **Staff attitude and behaviour:** Businesses may have procedures for how customer service staff should address and respond to customers. This may include answering phone calls within a set number of rings and making sure that someone is always available to help a customer.
- **Meeting specific customer needs:** Customers have different needs which affect the product, service or advice they need. They may have a technical query or want to report a fault. They may need help choosing accessories or seek advice on a personal issue. The aim should be to assist all customers, no matter what their needs.
- **Working under pressure:** Even when the business is busy, customer service staff must remain calm and deal with each customer as quickly as possible while keeping the same high standard of customer service.
- **Confirming service meets needs and expectations:** Customer-focused organisations may follow up a purchase with a short phone call or online questionnaire to check customers are happy with their purchase and the service provided.
- **Dealing with problems:** Businesses often have specific return periods (for example a 28-day money-back guarantee) and helplines so that customers can check what to do if they have a problem. Dealing with a problem promptly and effectively builds trust and restores a customer's faith in the business.

Did you know?

- Portakabin, the company that provides high-quality permanent and temporary buildings, has the motto 'Quality this time, next time, every time' to ensure the customer service it delivers is consistently excellent.
- Fitness First promises that all its gym staff and personal trainers are fully qualified so that customers can have confidence in the knowledge and experience of the staff.
- Christmas Day is the busiest day of the year for Orange call centre workers. This is because many people receive mobile phones as presents and they don't know how to use them.

Activity — Providing consistent customer service

In groups, select one organisation from the following list:

a) a leisure centre
b) a call centre
c) a large hotel
d) a cafe.

Identify how each organisation can provide consistent customer service. Then exchange ideas with another group.

Just checking

1. Suggest three ways in which an organisation can achieve consistent and reliable customer service.
2. Describe what is meant by a 'service deliverer'.
3. What is the difference between 'remote' and 'face-to-face' customer service?

TOPIC A.6 A.7

Good customer service and customer expectations

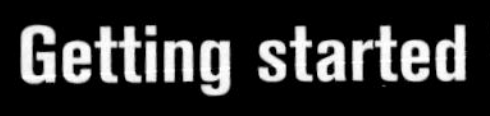

Getting started

Many people trust their friends more than adverts or websites, such as TripAdvisor. Are you impressed by someone else's opinion, or do you prefer to make up your own mind?

Did you know?

Businesses use social media such as Facebook and Twitter to monitor what is said about their business. This means they can respond to problems quickly and try to ensure that customers recommend them to their friends or followers.

The effect of good customer service

There are many benefits to providing good customer service:

- **building a good reputation** by providing:
  - quality products – Dyson and Apple are renowned for these
  - value for money – John Lewis guarantees they are 'never knowingly undersold'. To keep this promise, they lower their price if a competitor is selling the same item more cheaply
  - consistency – Pizza Express guarantees to provide the same service, quality and menu at each restaurant
  - a reliable and trustworthy service
- **increased sales** through effective selling of related products and services, and attracting new customers through a strong reputation
- **increased profit** as the business may need to spend less on promotional activities and will gain through customer loyalty
- **retention of existing customers**, which means the business may need to spend less on advertising
- **new customers** who are attracted to the business when they hear about its reputation, possibly through word of mouth.
- **competitive advantage,** which means that customers consider the business offers the best value for money or provides a better service than its competitors
- **staff job satisfaction and motivation** because staff who feel they are giving customers a positive experience are more likely to be happy in their jobs. This helps to keep staff and reduces the costs involved in recruitment and training

Activity — Identifying ways to save money

Excellent customer service can save businesses money. In groups, identify three ways in which businesses can gain these financial benefits.

What elements of customer service can you identify in this photo?

Different ways of exceeding customer expectations

Exceeding customer expectations improves the reputation of the business. The aim is to 'delight' customers, rather than merely 'satisfy' them.

Table 4.2 Exceeding customer expectations

Exceeding customer expectations by ...	How this exceeds expectations
... providing value for money	Value for money is important to most customers, so retailers may offer a price-matching service to build customers' trust, e.g. John Lewis.
... providing information and advice quickly	Some queries are easy to answer, but others may be complicated. Making the effort to find out additional information or to answer a difficult enquiry will impress a customer.
... providing additional help and assistance	Additional help may be helping a customer to their car with purchases, checking when an item will be in stock or pointing out discounts and special offers. Dealing promptly with problems, offering additional products or services and giving information about the company's returns policy are ways to provide extra assistance.
... providing exceptional help and assistance for customers with special requirements	Some customers may have special requirements, e.g. they may have physical disabilities or English may not be their first language. Exceptional help may be providing leaflets in relevant languages, a large print version, an accessible website (with a user-friendly design that takes into account colour blindness) and an induction loop system at customer service counters for anyone with hearing difficulties.

Assessment activity 4.1 *Introduction*

Your boss is training new business entrepreneurs in the importance of customer service. She asks you to produce a leaflet that summarises excellent customer service and gives examples of good practice. Choose two different businesses to investigate, such as a retailer, delivery firm, fitness centre or other service provider. Research the types of customer service both businesses provide, and the ways in which they aim to satisfy customers and exceed their expectations.

1 a) Start your leaflet with a clear definition of customer service, and describe the different types of customer service provided by each business.
   b) Describe the characteristics of consistent and reliable customer service, and compare how your two selected businesses satisfy their customers.
   c) Select one business and explain how it aims to exceed customer expectations.

2 Make notes for a report on the link between providing good, consistent and reliable customer service and the reputation of a business. Do this by identifying examples to illustrate how the reputation of your selected business has been affected by different aspects of its customer service. Keep your notes safely as you will complete this task in later in the unit.

TOPIC A.8

Providing effective customer service

Introduction

Organisational procedures are instructions that tell staff how to carry out specific tasks, such as responding to a complaint or giving a refund. These help to ensure that all customers are dealt with fairly and correctly and according to their legal rights.

Key terms

Organisational procedures – step-by-step instructions issued to staff to ensure consistent standards.

Code of practice – a set of guidelines that set standards of service customers can expect.

Organisational procedures

Businesses can provide effective customer service by:

- monitoring customer service, often through customer feedback (from questionnaires or feedback forms) or through 'mystery shoppers'
- following **codes of practice** that set out certain standards:
  - Industry codes relate to a particular type of business, such as the mobile phone industry which has codes of practice about mobile phone content.
  - Organisational/business codes are set by the business itself. In the public sector these are often called customer charters – or student charters in a college or university.
  - Professional codes set out minimum standards for professionals such as doctors, solicitors and accountants, and are often drawn up by a professional body on behalf of its members.
- meeting legal and regulatory requirements, which is essential for all organisations.
- having ethical standards, which means having strong principles and, in business, not compromising these to make a profit: for example, never misleading customers or trying to withhold a valid refund.

Activity Investigating mystery shoppers

Many agencies advertise online for mystery shoppers to visit businesses and check the standards of service. Find out more about these jobs by searching online.

Ensuring that correct procedures are followed

It is important that all staff follow the correct procedures. These may include:

- when to refer to someone in authority – the procedures may tell you to do this if there is a serious complaint, if a decision is outside your area of authority or if you are asked a question that you cannot answer
- dealing with a refund, which may require a supervisor's approval if the item is damaged, was purchased some time ago or if the customer has lost the receipt
- treating customers equally, which is a legal requirement.

Did you know?

Once a customer query has been dealt with, your team leader may check to see if you have followed the correct procedure.

Minimising hazards and risks

All businesses have a legal responsibility to minimise hazards and risks. (See also the following topic). The first step is to identify where customers could be injured and then take steps to minimise the risk. Examples are given in Table 4.3.

Table 4.3 Minimising hazards and risks

Action to take	How the risk is minimised
Informing people about dangers	Display safety or warning signs if there is a danger. For example, if the floor has just been cleaned, a 'Wet floor' sign should be in place until it is dry.
Complying with fire regulations	Fire exits should be clearly indicated and staff should know the location of fire extinguishers. Fire drills should take place regularly so that staff know the evacuation procedure and meeting points.
Dealing with security alerts	During a security alert, all staff must react appropriately. Any messages received must be passed promptly to management, and the correct evacuation procedures followed.

Remember

Procedures help to ensure that all customers are treated fairly and equally (see also next topic).

What other signs help to prevent accidents in the workplace?

The purpose of organisational procedures

Organisational procedures contribute to consistent and reliable customer service in several ways.

Meeting or exceeding customer service offered by rivals

Businesses offering similar products or services may compete on price, but many aim to offer a better service. If customers know they will get excellent service every time, this gives the business a competitive edge.

Following company mission/vision statements

A mission or vision statement explains the main purpose of the business and may define the brand for its customers. If the procedures are based on this statement, the business shows it is striving to achieve this aim.

Meeting external quality benchmarks

Benchmarks are set by independent organisations to denote a level of quality in an area. For example, the Crystal Mark, awarded by the Plain English Campaign to businesses, sets a standard for documents in clear everyday English. This gives customers confidence that they will understand the information provided by the business.

Activity Investigating procedures at your school or college

Find out how visitors to your school/college are dealt with when they come in for the first time. Do the reception staff follow a procedure? What information are visitors given on evacuation procedures in the case of an emergency?

Discussion point

McDonald's mission statement is: 'Our mission is to be our customers' favourite place and way to eat'. Discuss how excellent customer service can help McDonald's to achieve this aim.

TOPIC A.9

Customer service requirements

Introduction

All businesses are subject to different forms of legislation and regulatory requirements. Customer service staff must know those that directly affect customers.

Key terms

Legislation – relates to the laws of the land which everyone must obey.

Regulations – these interpret the law and state simply what people have to do to abide by the law.

Complying with legislative and regulatory requirements

Health and safety

The Health and Safety at Work Act is the main law relating to health and safety. Additional **regulations** apply to areas such as noise and the use of work equipment. The aim is to ensure the safety of employees, customers, suppliers and anyone visiting a business premises.

To comply with the law, businesses carry out risk assessments to identify hazards. If these cannot be eliminated, then precautions must be taken, such as limiting access to hazardous areas, putting up safety signs and issuing protective equipment such as hard hats. All businesses must have an emergency evacuation procedure which is known to all staff.

Did you know?

- You have a legal responsibility to cooperate with your employer on health and safety matters. Anyone who ignores the Health and Safety at Work Act and is negligent can face criminal prosecution.
- There are regulations that protect customers when they make a purchase on credit, online or in their own home.

Activity — Researching health and safety

1. Find out more about the Health and Safety at Work Act by visiting the HSE website. You can access this by going to www.pearsonhotlinks.co.uk and searching for this title.
2. Find out how visitors to your school/college are warned about hazards. What procedures exist to ensure the safety of any wheelchair users in an emergency evacuation?

Sale of goods

The Sale of Goods Act is the main law that regulates sales transactions. It states that all goods, whether new or second-hand, must be:

- as described, e.g. leather shoes must be made of leather
- of satisfactory quality, given the price, description and age of the item
- fit for the purpose for which they are intended.

If these conditions are not met, then the buyer can reject the item and insist on a refund.

The Supply of Goods and Services Act covers buyers of services, such as dry cleaning, and states that these should be carried out for a reasonable charge, within a reasonable time, with reasonable care and skill and using satisfactory materials.

Data protection

The Data Protection Act covers personal information collected, stored, processed and distributed by business organisations. It includes information held on employees, customers, potential customers and suppliers. Anyone who has data held on them can formally request to see it to check that it is up to date and accurate. Breaching customer or employee confidence by selling or buying personal data is a serious offence, with an unlimited fine.

All staff who handle or have access to personal data, such as contact details, medical records or bank details, must store this securely and must never disclose it to any unauthorised person.

Discussion point

Discuss why police records are not covered by the Data Protection Act.

Equal opportunities

Many laws and regulations aim to ensure that employees and customers are treated fairly and equally. Discrimination (treating someone differently) is unlawful on many grounds, for example age, gender, race, sexual orientation, disability, gender reassignment, religion and belief. **The Equality Act** states that all disabled people must receive the same service as able-bodied customers. Unfavourable treatment may result in the business having to pay compensation.

What other adaptations can be made to businesses to make them accessible to those with disabilities?

Activity: Investigating equality

British banks have been criticised for ignoring the needs of disabled people. In the USA, blind users can plug headphones into a cash machine that 'talks' to them.

How good is a) your centre and b) your selected business at providing access to services for anyone with special requirements? Investigate both of these.

Assessment activity 4.1

2A.P1 | 2A.P2 | 2A.P3 | 2A.P4 | 2A.M1 | 2A.M2 | 2A.M3 | 2A.D1

For the training event for new entrepreneurs, you are asked to produce a display which shows the impact of organisational procedures and legislation/regulations on customer service.

1. Obtain specific examples of organisational procedures, such as how refunds are processed, and explain how these have contributed to consistent and reliable customer service. Remember to show a clear link between the procedures and their contribution to consistency and reliability.
2. For one of the businesses you selected in the introduction to this activity, explain how legislative and regulatory requirements have affected its customer service.
3. Compare the impact of the different legislative and regulatory requirements on your selected business by identifying the different effects each one has had and explaining the similarities and differences.
4. Add to the report notes you made in the introduction to this activity by identifying examples that show how the procedures in place at your selected business, and its response to its legislative and regulatory responsibilities, have contributed towards providing excellent and consistent customer service.
5. Then write a report in which you assess the effect of providing consistent and reliable customer service on the reputation of that business.

Tip

Ensure you evaluate how much each aspect of customer service has contributed towards the reputation of the business.

Who are your customers?

Getting started

You have a part-time job in a store selling office products. Who are your external customers? Are your delivery driver and the office administrator also your customers?

Customers

Types of customer

- **Internal customers** are those people who work in the same organisation, including managers, colleagues in your own team or other departments, supervisors and other staff.
- **External customers** are existing and new customers. They include individuals, groups, members of the public and other businesses who need the goods and services provided by your organisation.

Table 4.4 The main differences between internal and external customers

Internal customers	External customers
• They work in the same organisation as you. • They may need information about a customer or order you have dealt with. • They may need your assistance to deal with their own external customers effectively. • They rely on you for prompt cooperation to do their job properly.	• They are not part of the same business as you. • They may contact the business with an enquiry, to make a purchase or to return a faulty item. • They can choose to go somewhere else if dissatisfied. • They may complain or tell others if they are unhappy with the product or service provided.

Key terms

Internal customers – colleagues who work in the same organisation and need you to do something.

External customers – outside businesses and individuals who want to make a purchase.

Customers with special requirements include:

- **Non-English speaking:** You should talk relatively slowly and use simple words and short sentences. Writing something down may help. Know which colleagues speak other languages and ask for help.
- **Different ages:** Businesses that deal with various age groups often aim to meet their varying needs, for example by providing toys in a hospital waiting area and seating in a store for older customers. Elderly customers vary just as much as young ones but many dislike making quick decisions.
- **Different cultures:** Cultural differences affect what we wear, what we eat and drink and our expectations. You should know the main cultural differences of your usual customers. If you are uncertain, ask a more senior colleague for advice and remember what you are told.

Why is it important to recognize cultural differences and ask a colleague if you are unsure how to pronounce a name?

- **Gender:** Research shows that men and women shop very differently. Women like to browse and look at goods over a longer period of time, whereas men are usually more direct, tend to buy the targeted item as quickly as possible and then leave the shop.
- **Families:** Many businesses that deal with families offer group booking discounts and facilities for everyone, such as a soft-play area and teashop at a visitor attraction.
- **Customers with special needs:** Customers with visual, hearing or mobility disabilities may need extra support such as Braille leaflets, hearing aid induction loops, or ramps and lifts within the business.

Factors that impact on different customer service expectations

Factors that may affect a customer's expectations include:

- **The customer's age or culture:** These factors may affect the speed or type of service a customer expects. Young customers may want to browse for a while, whereas older customers may be less patient and want instant attention.
- **The public image of the business or owner:** Customers who are attracted to a business because it has a good reputation or because they are told the owner provides a high level of personal service will have high expectations.
- **The customer's disposable income:** A customer buying a premium product will expect a better level of service.

Activity — Listing your expectations

You have won a competition and will stay in a luxury hotel in Paris for three days. In groups, list the ways in which you would expect the service and facilities to be better than in a standard hotel.

Assessment activity 4.2 — *Introduction*

Your group will be helping with events at your school or college involving outside guests. These include parents' evenings, open evenings and social events. You will be involved in several different customer service situations as follows.

Before the event, you will assist prospective visitors who telephone or email asking for information.

During the event, you will greet guests, show them round if appropriate, run the enquiry desk, keep records and provide information and literature

Prepare for this by identifying the different types of internal and external customers that may visit the premises. Then find out how your school or college aims to meet the needs and expectation of three different types of customer. Write notes that will help you describe this to your tutor. Keep these safely because you will need them when you carry out the assessment activity later in the unit.

Tip

Remember that you must identify the needs and expectations of each of your three types of customer before you can describe how your school or college meets these.

Did you know?

- In some Asian countries (e.g. Japan, Korea and Thailand) it is considered rude to make continuous eye contact during a conversation. Children are taught from a young age to avert their eyes and avoid direct eye contact.
- In the USA, families visiting a restaurant expect instant, friendly service, scrupulously clean tables, and crayons and activity sheets for young children!

Where can you find this type of information?

Customer service skills

Getting started

What skills do you think are needed to deliver excellent customer service? Can anyone do it? Is it a gift, or do you need training?

Discussion point

Most large retail stores issue an employee handbook that stresses the importance of personal appearance. How do you think a team leader should deal with a member of staff who disregards this?

Skills required to deliver consistent and reliable customer service

Creating a good impression

Professional customer service staff have the skills required to create a good impression. These include the following.

- **Good manners:** Being polite to customers at all times is essential. Many organisations train staff to use a specific greeting.
- **Appropriate dress:** Many businesses require their employees to wear a uniform, e.g. airlines, travel agents. If there is no uniform available, there may be a dress code which sets specific rules about jewellery, hairstyles, makeup and style of clothes.
- **Using appropriate language:** When you are dealing with different customers, you may need to vary the language that you use. For example, it is not appropriate to use technical language to someone buying a computer unless you know they are computer literate.
- **Good posture/body language:** Greeting a customer with a smile and looking them in the eye (not staring) will create a much better impression than appearing bored and not making eye contact.
- **Tidy work area:** An untidy work area may give a customer the impression that you are disorganised. It is your duty as an employee to ensure that your work area is kept tidy and does not present a health and safety hazard to customers and colleagues.

How is this doorman creating a good impression?

Positive attitude

Having a positive attitude will give a good impression to customers and will also help develop relationships with your fellow colleagues. For example:

- **good timekeeping** – always being on time for work, or being in the right place at the agreed time, is important and shows that you care about your job and your customers
- **being conscientious** about your role gives customers confidence in your ability because they know you will take care to do your best
- **being motivated** means that you are keen to help a customer and enthusiastic about your business's products and services. This impresses a customer and inspires trust in the business.

Effective communication with customers

Communicating effectively is vital to customer service. This involves both **verbal communication** (what you say and how you say it) and **non-verbal communication** (what you do).

Key terms

Verbal communication – what you say and how you say it.

Non-verbal communication – the process of communication through body language, facial expressions, gestures, eye contact and tone of voice.

Table 4.5 Essential factors for effective communication with customers

Verbal communication	Non-verbal communication
Give an appropriate greeting, such as 'Good morning' or 'How may I help you?' Speak clearly using language that the customer will understand and try to avoid jargon. Use an appropriate tone of voice. Make sure you don't speak too loudly, but also make sure you can be heard. Adjust the language you use and the speed you speak at if customers do not speak English as their first language.	Smile at the customer and appear friendly and approachable. Make eye contact with customers and look at them when you're talking to them. Use open body language, i.e. don't cross your arms or put your hands in your pockets. Your facial expression must make you approachable, and look as though you want to help the customer.

Activity Demonstrating body language

In small groups, research positive and negative body language online. Then devise a customer service role play that will demonstrate both. Two people should enact the roles of customer and employee. The rest of the group should observe and identify how body language affects the customer's experience.

Completing communication with the customer

The way you end a conversation is important. Make sure that you don't leave the customer wondering what will happen next.

- Thank the customer, whether they have bought anything or not.
- Use an appropriate tone of voice.
- Use positive body language.
- Use an appropriate form of address. If you are unsure of the customer's name, use 'Sir' or 'Madam'.
- Use the customer's name if you know it, but don't be overfamiliar (for example, use 'Mr Smith' not 'John').
- Offer further assistance by asking if there is anything else you can do such as packing goods, carrying items to their car or telling them when an item is in stock.
- Check the customer is happy with the service they received by following up with a telephone call or questionnaire.

Discussion point

In some stores, staff are trained to ask customers when they are paying for goods whether they have forgotten anything. Is this annoying or helpful? How would you feel if you were in a long queue and in a hurry?

Customer service skills

Getting started

How do customer service skills vary between people who work in a shop and a call centre? Or are they all the same?

Developing customer service skills

If you work in customer service, you have to respond to customers in different ways. The skills you need to communicate effectively are shown in Table 4.6.

Table 4.6 Effective customer service skills

Type of communication	Presentation skills	Personal skills	Communication skills
Face to face	Keep a professional appearance at all times. Your body language tells people your manner and attitude.	Greet customers appropriately, and be friendly and keen to meet their needs.	Speak clearly and use an appropriate tone of voice. Avoid jargon and slang.
Telephone	Smile during a conversation – your voice will let the caller know you are friendly.	Greet the caller. Show your concern by your response and tone of voice.	A clear voice and appropriate pace are essential as gestures cannot be seen.
Writing	Write neatly and use a clear layout. Check your spelling and grammar. Always proofread your work.	All written communications should be courteous and tactful, and the wording appropriate for the situation.	The degree of formality depends on who you are writing to, and why you are writing.
Email	The style and layout of your message must follow a business format.		Business emails must follow organisational rules and standards.

Remember

It is just as important to use the right tone when you are dealing with internal customers over the telephone as it is with external customers.

Dealing with customer queries

How you deal with customer queries will decide how they feel afterwards. You should always:

- **be polite** – no matter how difficult the customer may be
- **show empathy** – this means showing you really understand how the customer feels about a problem
- **keep customers informed** – if you are dealing with a query and arrange to contact the customer again later, make sure that you do this. Even if you still don't have the answer, contacting the customer gives them reassurance that you are still doing all you can to help them
- **don't disagree** – even if you think the customer is wrong. Being tactful is important. Focus on the topic rather than an opinion. If the situation becomes very difficult, ask for assistance. After all, the customer may be right!
- **use appropriate body language**, including making eye contact – this gives the customer positive signals that you are interested in helping them.

Activity Answering queries

In small groups, select four difficult, but realistic, queries that you might receive in a store that sells beauty products and medicines, such as Boots or Superdrug. Pass your questions to another group to decide on appropriate answers. Then vote for the best responses. You can extend this and gain further practice by changing the store to one that sells stationery, toys, DVDs, or any other type of product you choose!

Dealing with customer problems and complaints

Customers usually complain for a reason. The first rule is to listen carefully so that you understand the problem and what the customer wants you to do to put it right. This will usually mean:

- offering an alternative if a product is currently unavailable
- offering an exchange or a refund if the original is faulty
- immediately telling your supervisor or manager if the customer problem or complaint is very serious or outside the limit of your authority (see below).

Did you know?

The 'grey pound' is worth over £100 billion a year. This is the amount spent by UK customers who are over 50 years of age. Remember this next time you are tempted to ignore or rush someone who is much older than you!

Customer types

You may come into contact with many different types of customers. Table 4.7 gives guidelines about how to deal with them.

Table 4.7 Dealing with different customer types

Type of customer	Do ...	Do not ...
Difficult customers	• be patient • listen to what the customer is saying • remain positive • seek help if required from a more senior colleague.	• lose your temper • be impatient • argue or contradict them.
Abusive customers	• stay calm • get help in a face-to-face situation if the customer does not calm down • inform the customer that if the abuse continues you will end the call (if on the telephone).	• shout back at the customer or get angry • let the situation get out of hand • get upset or distressed.
Customers with disabilities	• focus on the person, not the disability.	• treat them any differently from any other customer.
Elderly customers	• be patient • listen to their needs • speak clearly • show respect.	• be impatient • dismiss their needs • try to get rid of them too quickly.
Customers needing technical information	• be patient • explain clearly • seek help (if required) from a more experienced colleague.	• use lots of jargon/technical language • assume that the customer knows what you are talking about • guess what they want.

CONTINUED ▸▸

▸▸ CONTINUED

Did you know?

Marks & Spencer offers a 'no quibble' exchange or refund on most purchases within a stated period. The final date is printed on the receipt. This policy enables all sales staff to deal promptly with undamaged returned goods and keep the customer happy.

Different customer service situations

Customer service staff may have to deal with a range of different situations:

- **providing information about products and/or services:** to do this competently you must be familiar with the range of items available, their features and prices. This means having any relevant information leaflets or catalogues to hand and being familiar with the content
- **promoting additional products and/or services that may meet the customer's needs**, for example underlay for a carpet or upholstery protection for a car or sofa
- **giving advice** to help the customer to make the best decision in their particular circumstances
- **taking and relaying messages**, which means being able to identify and record the key facts accurately, and ensuring the message is promptly passed to the correct person.

Activity — Identifying skills and knowledge

You need a new blind in your bedroom. You have no idea what types are available, how they are fitted or how much they cost. What skills and knowledge would the person who handles your enquiry need to help you?

Case study: Other customer service skills

Why does Carl need additional customer service skills?

Carl has a part-time job driving a van to deliver groceries ordered online. He must keep an accurate record of the deliveries he makes and any incidents that occur. For example, if a product has been substituted and is rejected by the customer, he can process a refund. If a product is damaged, he may be able to let the customer keep it without charge. If he is delayed for any reason, he must phone ahead to warn the customer that he might be late. If he breaks down, he must call the depot immediately.

As a service deliverer for the store, Carl is the 'face' of the business to online customers. In addition to being polite and helpful, he needs to demonstrate other skills.

CONTINUED ▸▸

Case study: Continued

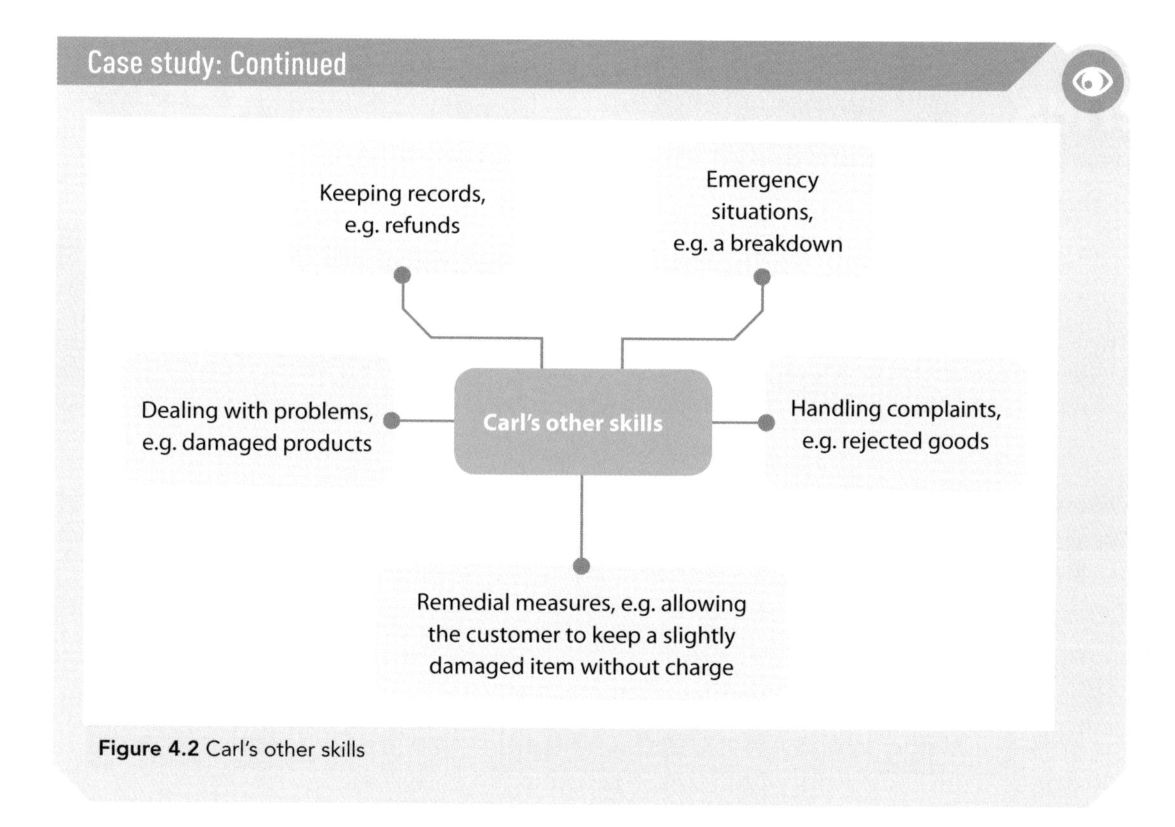

Figure 4.2 Carl's other skills

Complying with organisational procedures/policies

It is important to comply with the procedures and policies that are in place in a business. These may include:

- **A complaints procedure** which gives details about the information that must be obtained, the actions that can be taken by each level of staff and the senior person who is responsible for resolving serious problems.
- **A disclaimer**, which is a statement that denies responsibility. For example, many retail stores disclaim responsibility for damage to cars in their car park. Note that a business can never disclaim responsibility for personal injury to customers on its premises.
- **Service specification statements**, which are also known as service level agreements and tell customers the level of service they can expect to receive when they are dealing with the organisation.

Discussion point

A shop owner decides he will put up a notice that disclaims all responsibility for any faulty products he sells. Can he do this? Discuss your ideas as a group.

Key term

Service specification statement – issued by an organisation giving details of the level of service to be expected.

Just checking

1 What specific skills are needed to talk to customers on the telephone rather than face to face?
2 What is 'empathy' and how can you demonstrate it?
3 A customer is opinionated and argumentative. What skills are required to deal with this person?
4 Suggest two reasons for recording complaints that are received.

Limits of authority and customer queries

Remember

Never make a promise to a customer that you may not be able to honour, and never guess information that you don't know!

Introduction

In any job role there are decisions and actions you are allowed to take and those you must refer to someone more senior. This is good, because it prevents junior employees from making serious errors that could have major consequences. In customer service, the usual authority levels are as shown in Table 4.8.

Table 4.8 Limits of authority

Role	Limit of authority
Service deliverer, e.g. shop assistant, receptionist, call centre operator	• has limited authority on refunds – if the refund is over a certain amount or the item is damaged, a supervisor may need to authorise the transaction • has limited authority to offer free products. Staff can usually only do this if there is a special promotion. In other situations, staff must check with their line manager.
Line manager/ supervisor	• has greater authority to authorise refunds and may be able to authorise discounts or free goods. They must work within the organisational guidelines • has supervisory or line management responsibilities for junior members of staff • ensures that all policies and procedures are carried out by their staff.
Management	• may be a branch manager and have control of a branch • is able to authorise exceptional changes to policies and procedures, and make decisions where unusual or difficult issues arise.

Assessment activity 4.2

2B.P5 | 2B.P6 | 2B.P7 | 2B.M4 | 2B.D2

You will now be helping with events at your centre involving outside guests.

- Before each event, identify your own job role and the limits of your authority by preparing a summary sheet on which you list and describe actions you can take and situations where you must notify a tutor.
- On your own, discuss your summary sheet with your tutor and also describe how your school or college meets the needs and expectations of three different types of customer using the notes you made in the introduction to this assessment activity.
- In groups, discuss the request and enquiries you will receive, the types of customers you will meet and how to cope with any problems and complaints. Practise your skills by role playing typical scenarios for your tutor.
- At each event, your tutor will conduct individual observations and record your performance to identify whether you were able to demonstrate effective communication skills when you were dealing with different customers in different situations and responding to problems and complaints.
- After each event, evaluate your own performance. Think about the skills where you would receive a high customer feedback score, and those areas where you would not. Take into account your tutor's feedback and write your own report in which you identify areas for improvement and justify each of your choices.

Tips

If you deal with customers on other occasions, such as when working in a school or college shop, in a part-time job or on work experience, then you can also use evidence in the form of witness statements to help you achieve this unit. Discuss with your teacher/tutor the evidence that you will need to produce.

WorkSpace

Janet McGregor

Customer Service Representative

Janet is a customer service representative for a large mobile phone company. She is a member of a team in the retentions section of a contact centre in the North East of England.

Janet's main role is to ensure that customers who call her section are retained. They may call because they have received a large bill or are unhappy with the coverage on their phone. Or they may have problems using their phone or be unhappy about roaming charges. Janet has to ensure that they remain with the company by resolving their issues.

She does this by often upgrading their phone and trying to get them the best deal on calls and texts. Janet can only upgrade to a certain level of cost to the company. Beyond that, she must involve her team leader.

Janet knows that excellent customer service is vital. She always makes sure that she keeps in regular contact with the customer if she has to put them on hold to investigate an issue. She wants them to know that she is still dealing with the problem and hasn't left them holding on.

After the call, the customer receives an automatic text message asking them to grade the service they have received. Each representative receives a grade between 1 and 10 (10 being brilliant) and these scores form part of the staff targets each month.

Janet is very busy at times, especially at Christmas, but really enjoys her job. She likes interacting with customers and helping to solve their problems, and gets a buzz when she hits targets!

Think about it

1 How can Janet ensure she makes a good impression when she receives a call?

2 Identify five additional skills that Janet needs to do her job successfully.

3 **a)** Why does Janet have to refer some phone upgrades to her team leader?
b) Suggest two other occasions when she would involve her team leader.

4 Suggest two reasons why the phone company asks callers to grade the service they have just received.

Introduction

Can you think of a business that does not involve selling? Selling is a vital business skill and jobs in sales are vibrant and exciting with good promotion prospects. Nowadays many of us shop online, but most of us still prefer personal selling where we talk to a salesperson face to face or over the telephone. We like the personal attention and it is good to get a quick response to our questions and help finding the right product.

If you want to work in sales, your main job will be to promote and sell products. You need to be knowledgeable about the products and able to communicate well with customers. If you are ambitious, quick-thinking and able to create a positive first impression, you will go far.

This unit explores the role of sales staff and will help you to demonstrate personal selling skills and processes.

Assessment: This unit will be assessed through a series of assignments set by your teacher/tutor.

Learning aims

In this unit you will:

A explore the role of sales staff

B demonstrate personal selling skills and processes.

Before studying this unit, it never occurred to me how important I was to the business and I didn't realise that there were so many things that I could do to increase sales. I now get quite a buzz from making a sale and keeping my customers happy.

Chloe, *16-year-old Business student and part-time sales assistant*

Sales and Personal Selling

5

This table shows you what you must do in order to achieve a **Pass**, **Merit** or **Distinction** grade, and where you can find activities in this book to help you.

Assessment criteria			
Level 1	**Level 2 Pass**	**Level 2 Merit**	**Level 2 Distinction**
Learning aim A: Explore the role of sales staff			
1A.1 Identify two functions of sales staff in a selected business	**2A.P1** Describe, using examples, four functions of sales staff in a selected business **See Assessment activity 5.1, page 133**	**2A.M1** Compare the functions of the sales staff and the different sales skills used in two selected businesses **See Assessment activity 5.1, page 133**	**2A.D1** Assess the effectiveness of sales skills and knowledge used by sales staff in two selected businesses **See Assessment activity 5.1, page 133**
1A.2 Identify the sales skills used by sales staff in a selected business	**2A.P2** Describe the sales skills used by sales staff in three different selling situations **See Assessment activity 5.1, page 133**		
1A.3 Outline the importance of product knowledge when making sales	**2A.P3** Explain the knowledge and skills needed to sell two selected products **See Assessment activity 5.1, page 133**		
1A.4 Outline legislation which affects personal selling in a selected business	**2A.P4** Explain the legislation which affects personal selling in a selected business **See Assessment activity 5.1, page 133**	**2A.M2** Assess the importance of complying with the legal requirements for customer care and selling products in a selected business **See Assessment activity 5.1, page 133**	

Assessment criteria			
Level 1	Level 2 Pass	Level 2 Merit	Level 2 Distinction
Learning aim B: Demonstrate personal selling skills and processes			
1B.5 Identify product knowledge required to make personal sales	**2B.P5** Prepare for the sales process for making personal sales to two different types of customer **See Assessment activity 5.2, page 143**	**2B.M3** English Demonstrate handling a customer problem or complaint **See Assessment activity 5.2, page 143**	**2B.D2** English Demonstrate the confident use of personal selling skills when making sales in at least three different personal sales situations **See Assessment activity 5.2, page 143**
1B.6 English Answer two routine customer enquiries in a personal sales situation	**2B.P6** English Demonstrate handling two different types of customer enquiry **See Assessment activity 5.2, page 143**	**2B.M4** Assess the effectiveness of the selling skills and processes used in two different situations **See Assessment activity 5.2, page 143**	**2B.D3** Evaluate the preparation, skills and processes used in two different personal sales situations and recommend improvements **See Assessment activity 5.2, page 143**
1B.7 English Use selling skills in two personal sales situations	**2B.P7** English Demonstrate effective customer care skills in two personal sales situations **See Assessment activity 5.2, page 143**		

English Opportunity to practise English skills

How you will be assessed

The unit will be assessed by a series of internally assessed tasks. You will be expected to explore the role of sales staff by investigating selected businesses and selling situations. You will also complete tasks that require you to demonstrate and provide evidence of your own personal selling skills and processes in a simulated or real-work environment.

Your assessment could be in the form of:

- a written account or presentation detailing your investigations
- video role-play evidence of personal selling skills
- log or sales diary evidence of personal selling skills
- a personal statement reflecting your own selling skills.

TOPIC A.1

The role of sales staff

Getting started

Think of one good experience and one bad experience you have had as a customer with a salesperson. In a group, discuss what made you form these opinions and how your impressions of the sales staff have affected your opinion of the product/service they were representing.

Introduction

Sales staff work in a wide range of businesses. You often see sales staff at work on the high street or in out-of-town shopping centres, selling anything from clothes and beauty products to electrical goods and mobile phones. You may have been stopped in the street by a salesperson who has tried to sell you a raffle ticket for charity, and sales staff may have telephoned you at home to offer you a deal on your mobile phone contract.

The principal job of all sales staff is to make a sale. To be successful, a salesperson has to be knowledgeable about the product they are selling and skilful in the way they make a sale.

Sales staff are crucial to the success of many businesses. They are the public face of an organisation and are very influential in the customer's decision as to whether or not to make a purchase.

Selling

Selling is the most important part of the salesperson's job. Sales staff around the world sell millions of different things, but what they sell normally fits into the following categories:

- goods – physical products, e.g. clothes, food, cars, houses
- services, benefits or experiences offered by a business, e.g. cleaning, hairdressing and dog walking
- product surrounds – the features and benefits related to a product or service, e.g. brand name, company's reputation, reliability.

Did you know?

Sometimes when you make a purchase, you get a product, a service and a product surround.

Table 5.1 Examples of products, services and product surrounds

Product	Service	Product surround
Xbox®	A subscription to their online gaming community	Microsoft's backing
Micro scooter®	A spares and repairs service	The reputation of the maker
Kindle™	Access to over 900,000 books, magazines and newspapers	The Amazon brand

As well as making a sale, the salesperson has a number of other roles.

Providing information

Sales staff give information to the customer about the product. They must communicate in a way that the customer will understand. A person selling laptops needs to be able to simplify the features of a laptop so that a customer with little knowledge of IT can understand what they are buying. They should be able to adapt their approach and use more technical language for the more IT-literate customer.

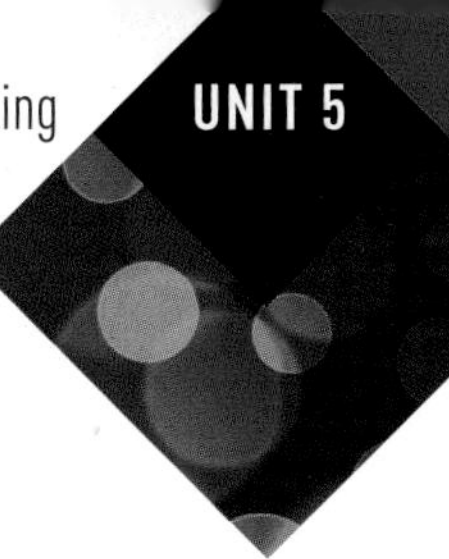

Dealing with routine enquiries

Customers may have many questions including questions about the product itself, the range of products offered, the shop's opening hours, the company's policy on exchanging goods and whether the company sells online.

Customers are not impressed if a salesperson is unable to answer their questions, as this gives a poor impression of the business.

Did you know?

Holland and Barrett, the well-known retailer of vitamins, minerals and herbal supplements insist that all their sales staff complete a staff training programme to teach them about their products. This ongoing training programme enables their staff to recommend appropriate products based on the customer's requirements.

Representing the organisation

Sales staff represent the business and the product. They are often the first person the customer comes into contact with when they see the product, and many customers judge the product on their impression of the sales staff. It is essential that sales staff make a good impression by dressing and behaving appropriately and by being informative.

How important is the appearance of sales staff?

Remember

It only takes a few seconds for somebody to judge you when they first come into contact with you. People use your appearance, body language and mannerisms to form an impression of you and this happens every time you meet somebody new. Sales staff should aim to make great first impressions and never forget that they are the public face of the business.

Just checking

1. What is the primary objective of sales staff?
2. What are three other functions of sales staff?
3. What is the difference between goods and services?
4. What is a product surround?

Knowledge and skills

Getting started

Who do you think would be the most successful salesperson: someone who is shy but hard-working, or someone who is outgoing but not particularly conscientious?

The answer is probably neither of them. A shy person might struggle to deal with people, but the outgoing person who is not very hard-working might not be motivated enough to learn the additional knowledge and practise the necessary skills to become effective in their job.

What knowledge and skills do sales people need?

Product knowledge

Sales staff must know enough about a product and how it works to match the customer with the appropriate product. Sales staff should know the following:

- **Stock availability** – what is normally available and when out-of-stock items will become available
- **Price information** – the prices of the products and how these compare with other available products
- **Store information** – location of products in the shop and the delivery/collection arrangements
- **Product care** – how to look after the product and what after-sales service is available such as warranties, servicing and repair
- **Key information** – how to demonstrate how the product works. The main features, uses and what variations in colour, size etc. are available.

Activity Demonstrating product knowledge

You have received two emails from friends who have job interviews next week for part-time sales jobs. One friend has an interview at a pet shop and the other has an interview at a mobile phone shop. Both of them are very excited, but worried that they do not know enough about what the shop sells. Choose one friend to help and send them an email giving them advice on what you think they should know about the products sold in the shop. Also, advise them about where they can find the information they need.

Sales motivation

Motivation is the driving force that enables people to achieve their goals. Successful sales staff are highly motivated individuals who are eager to make a sale. They are often seen using inventive techniques such as **cross-selling** and **up-selling** to increase sales.

Motivated sales staff are ambitious, hard-working and enthusiastic people who set themselves high targets. They appear to be passionate about the product they are selling, and their desire to succeed motivates them to try hard to match their products to their customer's needs.

Activity Role-playing sales situations

In pairs, role-play a number of sales situations where a salesperson uses cross-selling to suggest a related item to the customer.

Understanding potential customers

Being able to identify potential customers and understand their requirements is vital to being able to recommend the right product to the customer. This also helps sales staff to communicate with customers appropriately.

Some people are naturally more intuitive and have better interpersonal skills, but salespeople who carefully listen and ask the right questions can learn more about the potential customer.

Sales preparation skills

The physical sales environment, that is the shop, the market stall, the car showroom or the exhibition hall, is very important in enticing customers to make purchases. The **sales environment** should be welcoming, clean and tidy and products should be clearly displayed and be accessible to everyone.

The design of the sales environment should reflect the business's image. Sales staff are often involved in the preparation of the sales environment, and depending on their position in the company and the size of the business, they may be involved in designing, setting up and maintaining displays and exhibition stands.

Some interesting tactics are used to increase sales:

- Fast music can be used to encourage customers to purchase more quickly. This is useful during busy periods in a fast food outlet. Slow music can be used to encourage customers to take their time when buying expensive products such as jewellery.
- Some supermarkets pump the smell of fresh bread near the entrance of their store to give the impression that bread is available all day. Some coffee shops do the same with fresh coffee.

What is attractive about this **sales environment**?

Key terms

Cross-selling – suggesting a related product to a customer to increase the overall sale, for example a hairspray to go with a haircut.

Up-selling – promoting a more profitable alternative to increase the value of the sale.

Sales environment – the place where sales are made.

Did you know?

Businesses attempt to increase their sales staff's motivation by paying them a sum of money, known as commission, based on the value of what they sell. This means that top salespeople can earn a lot of money. However, some jobs are paid commission only, which means that the salesperson only earns money if they make a sale.

CONTINUED ▸▸

▸▸ CONTINUED

Sales techniques

Here are some of the sales techniques used by businesses in personal selling:

- **Cold calling:** This sales technique involves contacting a stranger unexpectedly, usually by telephone. It is 'cold' because they have shown no prior interest in the product. You need to be patient and resilient to use this technique because you are likely to get many refusals and some hostility. Cold calling is sometimes used to sell double glazing and insurance.
- **Face to face:** This is when the salesperson talks to the customer in person, and this is usually the most effective way of selling a product. This technique is used by sales staff in shops, door-to-door salespeople and by street sellers.
- **Drop-in visits:** This is when salespeople visit potential customers, which are usually businesses rather than individuals. Drug companies employ sales representatives who make drop-in visits to doctors' surgeries to promote their products.
- **Telemarketing:** Also known as telesales, this technique involves contacting prospective customers usually by telephone and delivering a sales pitch. Calls are either pre-recorded messages or made from people in call centres.

  This is different from cold calling because the people who have been called have been selected through a system that has identified them as being a potential customer. A holiday company selling clubbing holidays may use telemarketing by contacting young adults who have been identified as enjoying clubbing through having previously been on a clubbing holiday.

What are the advantages and disadvantages of telemarketing?

Discussion

In a group, discuss your experiences of aggressive, high-pressure selling, known as hard selling. Do you think that it encourages people to buy? When can its use be criticised?

Activity Evaluating sales techniques

Discuss the strengths and weaknesses of the different sales techniques. Include in your answer information about the effectiveness, the benefits and the likely problems with each of the methods.

Closing a sale

Sales staff can spend hours over many days carefully negotiating and persuading the customer to make a purchase. Knowing how and when to close the sale is a skill which many good salespeople find challenging.

Legislation and organisational policies

Table 5.2 demonstrates how legislation, aimed at protecting the customer, affects personal selling. Organisational policies offer additional benefits to the customer but do not affect the customer's legal rights.

Table 5.2 Legislation aimed at protecting the customer

Legislation	Effects on personal selling
Sale of Goods Act 1979 (amended in 1994, 1995 and 2002)	
Items purchased must be: • of satisfactory quality – given the price, description and age of item • fit for the purpose for which they are intended • as described – match the description on the packaging or the one given by the seller.	The after-sales service should provide a refund, repair or replacement for problems and complaints about a purchased item that does not meet these rights. Customers may be entitled to additional rights beyond that stated in the guarantee.
Supply of Goods and Services Act 1982	
Services purchased must be carried out with reasonable care and skill, at a reasonable price that reflects the skills of the provider and within a reasonable time.	Poor workmanship is unacceptable. Businesses cannot charge excessively for services – a builder cannot charge a day's work for changing a light bulb.
The Consumer Protection from Unfair Trading Regulations 2008 (CPRs)	
It an offence to treat customers unfairly through misleading actions such as lying, exaggeration or making inaccurate claims/discounts/offers. This act also stops sellers missing out key information and behaving aggressively.	Shops cannot have closing down sales that last for months, they cannot have discounts and special offers, such as price-matching policies that do not exist, and they cannot be too forceful in their sales techniques.

Did you know?

- If you do not want to receive marketing and unsolicited sales calls you can register your telephone number with the Telephone Preference Service and companies will no longer be able to legally contact you.
- When you buy something from private sellers, for example on eBay, you have fewer rights. The goods only have to be as described and theirs to sell.

Discussion point

The television programme *Watchdog* has a feature called 'Rogue Traders' that investigates complaints from customers about services they have received. Read through some of the cases on their website and identify a trader that you think is particularly bad. Give reasons for your opinion.

▸▸ CONTINUED

Organisational policies

Many organisations have policies that offer the customer additional benefits beyond their legal requirements. These policies benefit the business because they encourage customers to make impulse buys even if some are returned at a later date.

Table 5.3 Organisational policies

Organisational policy	Features
Price matching	Some businesses offer to match the cheaper price of a competitor for the same product. This sometimes excludes online purchases.
Discounting	Discounts may be given to customers who make repeat purchases, who spend over a certain amount or who are trade customers.
Guarantees	Some businesses offer extended guarantees well beyond their legal requirements.
After-sales service	Some organisations offer additional services after the purchase of the product, such as free delivery, order tracking, spare parts and a repair service.
Customer care	Additional services and facilities are sometimes available to help the customer, for example gift-wrapping and children's play areas.
Dealing with problems and complaints	To help the customer, some organisations have special policies for handling problems and complaints, e.g. giving the customer the name and direct line of the person dealing with their complaint.

Did you know?

In 2011 the supermarket Asda introduced its own price guarantee policy that promises to refund the difference if they are not 10 per cent cheaper on comparable grocery shopping. Customers can check this themselves using Asda's website.

Reflective practice

Good sales staff think carefully about why they did not make a sale to improve their skills. This is known as reflective practice. Professor Graham Gibbs put together a method of reflecting on your performance called the cycle of reflection and this is illustrated in figure 5.1.

You can use Gibbs's cycle to reflect on your performance in the unsuccessful encounters you have with people. It will help you to learn from your mistakes by making sense of what happened.

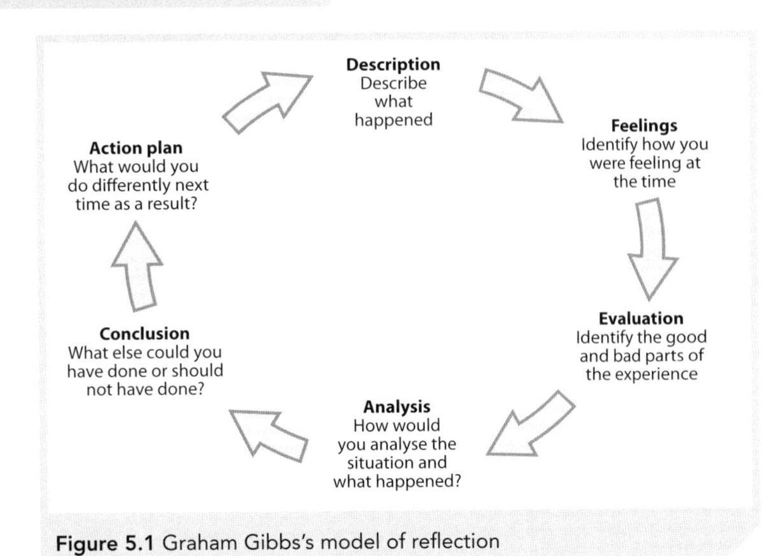

Figure 5.1 Graham Gibbs's model of reflection

Activity — Reflecting on your own performance

1. Think of an encounter you have had with someone that did not go well. If possible, use a selling situation.
2. Reflect on your own performance by using each element of Graham Gibbs's model of reflection.

WorkSpace

Ben Moss

Estate Agent – R A Bennett & Partners

Buying your own home may be the biggest purchase you will ever make and one that you will not enter into lightly. Therefore, estate agents need extensive knowledge and skills and the ability to communicate well.

Ben Moss is the manager of the Winchcombe branch of the estate agent R A Bennett & Partners. He built up his expertise from a sales career that started with door-to-door selling of gas and electricity and telemarketing of advertising space before quickly progressing up the career ladder as an estate agent.

Ben believes that when promoting a property it is important to highlight the features that match the buyer's needs. He reminds us that your views on what is a positive feature might not be the same as the customer's. After all, not everyone likes a big garden.

Ben emphasises the importance of knowing your product. Before promoting a house, Ben makes sure that he and his team have an in-depth knowledge of the property by making an initial visit.

To establish potential buyers' needs, Ben asks questions to discover more about their requirements and listens carefully to people's responses. For instance, if someone says that a double garage is a must-have, Ben will find out why. If it is for an artist's studio, a property with no garage but alternative space may still be an appropriate match.

Estate agents need to be able to solve problems and they must be skilful at negotiating to satisfy the different goals of both the buyer and the seller.

Ben thinks that the personality of a salesperson is important. Good estate agents have confidence both in the service that they are selling and in dealing with people from different backgrounds. They are persistent and do not give up easily. They are intuitive and understand that buying and selling property can be stressful.

Ben stresses that if someone is inviting you (a stranger) into their home it is important to look professional and he recommends wearing a traditional business suit.

Finally, Ben targets and evaluates every part of the selling process on a regular basis. Knowledge of what you have done and what you want to do leads to improvement and better results for customers.

Think about it

1. Why do you think it is important for estate agents to have a good knowledge of the properties they are selling?
2. Identify both the products and the service that estate agents sell.
3. What communication skills do you think have been important to Ben in his sales career?
4. Why does Ben think that reflective practice is important?

TOPIC A.4

The process of personal selling

Introduction

Personal selling is important for most businesses and it offers a number of benefits.

Helping businesses remain competitive

There is likely to be fierce competition from other businesses, so you must be able to stand out from the crowd. This can be achieved through the following:

- providing special facilities, for example, toys to entertain children
- extra services, for example, gift-wrapping and free delivery
- excellent customer service
- sales promotions, for example, price reductions.

Activity Identifying how businesses compete

In small groups, choose three shops that you are all familiar with and discuss what you think they are doing to remain competitive.

Establishing customer requirements

Effective sales staff identify their customers' requirements and match them to appropriate products.

Matching goods/services to customer requirements

All sales staff must listen carefully to the requirements of their customers or clients. For example, estate agents know that house buyers do not appreciate being contacted with details of properties that are in the wrong area, too expensive or not suitable.

Remember

If you admit that you do not have a suitable product/service and advise the customer where to find it, you will create a good impression of the business and the customer may return in the future.

Complying with the law

Sales staff must follow the law. See Table 5.2 for details about how the law governs products sold, pricing and customer care.

Developing customer care and building relationships

You must look after your customers from your very first encounter, throughout the whole buying process and in any aftercare you provide.

Customers want to be treated well. You must handle their queries efficiently and deal with complaints in a professional manner.

Did you know?

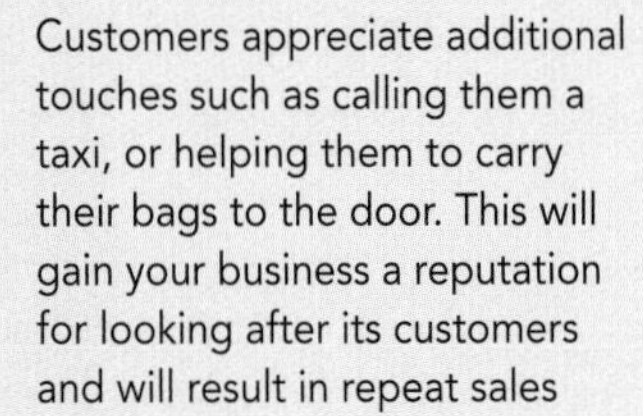

Customers appreciate additional touches such as calling them a taxi, or helping them to carry their bags to the door. This will gain your business a reputation for looking after its customers and will result in repeat sales through customer loyalty.

Gathering feedback

Feedback is important to businesses in order to make improvements. This is done through informal questions or questionnaires; for example, holidaymakers are often asked to complete questionnaires on their experience.

First point of contact

If a customer walks into your sales environment and sees a messy display or feels ignored, they may walk out and never return.

Activity Observing first point of contact

Note which of the following happens next time you are shopping.

- The salesperson acknowledges your presence with a polite hello and a quick comment that they are available if you need them.
- They leave you alone to browse, but stay close enough to help if required.
- They approach you to see if you need assistance.

Promoting the product

Sales staff are trained to promote the product by:

- informing the customer of the features and benefits
- reminding and/or persuading them using the features and benefits.

To do this they have to appear passionate about the product.

Assessment activity 5.1 2A.P1 | 2A.P2 | 2A.P3 | 2A.P4 | 2A.M1 | 2A.M2 | 2A.D1

Your school/college is holding a careers fair and they have asked you to put together some information on jobs in retail. To do this, you can use your own observations as a customer and job descriptions that can be found online on relevant companies' websites.

1. Describe, using examples, four functions of sales staff working in a supermarket.
2. Now select a business selling bicycles as a comparison, and compare the functions of sales staff and the different sales skills used in the two selected businesses.
3. Describe the sales skills used by sales staff working in each of the following scenarios: a) an online bookshop, b) a call centre selling flights, c) a florist.
4. Explain the knowledge and skills needed to sell a pair of children's shoes and a laptop.
5. Explain the legislation which affects personal selling in a business selling double glazing.
6. Assess the importance of complying with the legal requirements for customer care and selling products in a car sales garage.
7. Visit two different shops. Observe the sales staff in order to assess the effectiveness of sales skills and the knowledge used by sales staff in two selected businesses.

Tips

- Think about how the sales skills needed would differ in each scenario because of the different selling methods used.
- Think about specialist knowledge that would be needed and whether any special skills would be needed for working with small children.
- Ensure you have to identify the sales skills used and knowledge demonstrated and then judge how effective they are in making a sale.

Remember

The features of a product/service are its attributes or its characteristics, whereas the benefits are why the feature is important to someone, for example it saves them time or money, is convenient, fun or has a good image.

Demonstrate personal selling skills

Introduction

If you want to become a top salesperson, ask yourself the following questions:

Personal selling skills: Are you ready to make a sale? Are your appearance and attitude right? Do you know how to communicate with the customer? Can you close a sale?

The selling process: Do you understand what you have to do to make a sale? Are you able to manage other sales-related tasks such as handling customer complaints?

Sales staff continually learn and improve their skills throughout their careers, but if you want to get ahead, preparation and practice are the key to success.

Preparing for the sales process

Before you meet any customers, you must make sure that you have the appropriate product information, that you can identify the features and the benefits of the product and that you know how to present this information to customers.

When you are new to a job, this can be more difficult and you may have to carry out extra research in your own time about the products you are selling. If you do this, you will feel more confident when meeting customers and you are much more likely to be able to answer their questions and help them to find what they are looking for.

Activity Preparing for a sale

Try to persuade a friend to buy membership to a sports club/leisure centre. To do this, select a local club and if necessary look at their website, making sure that you are aware of the features and benefits of membership. Use this information to persuade your friend to join.

Maintaining an appropriate appearance

Sales personnel should be clean and tidy. Customers will be unimpressed if you have muddy shoes and scruffy hair.

- **Personal hygiene:** You need to be pleasant to be around, so you should be fussy about personal hygiene. Remember that body odour, stale breath and dirty fingernails are big turn-offs.
- **Dress:** You may be given a uniform to wear and it is important that you wear it correctly. Some businesses allow you to wear your own clothes, but have a dress code. You need to be disciplined about keeping to the dress code and ensure that you have enough appropriate clothes in your wardrobe. Where there is no dress code or uniform, you must dress appropriately according to the business and the product you are selling. It may be appropriate to wear a tracksuit if you work in a sports shop, but it will not be appropriate in a car showroom.

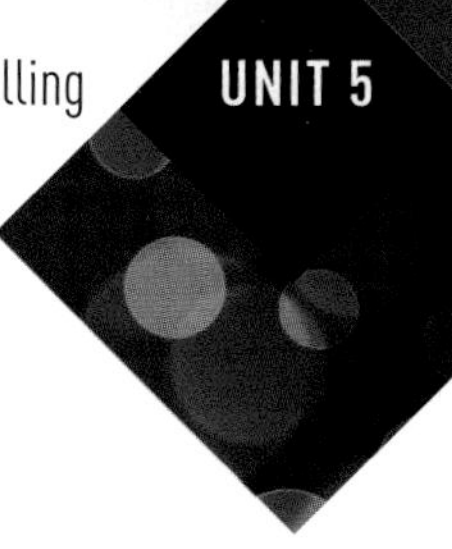

Maintaining an appropriate attitude

Do you prefer to deal with an enthusiastic person or a negative, resentful one? Employers and customers like dealing with people with a good attitude. In maintaining an appropriate attitude at work, you should be aware of the following:

- **Good manners** show respect and include saying please and thank you, holding the door open for customers, not swearing or using offensive language, not spreading gossip and not interrupting people when they are talking.
- **Courtesy and consideration** means putting other people first and being polite at all times. You should always appear interested in the customer and have excellent manners.
- **Language** is important. You need to speak in a more formal way than you are probably used to. Avoid starting sentences with 'um' or 'er', and instead of using the phrases 'like' or 'you know', you should say 'such as'. Addressing customers as 'Sir' or 'Madam' makes them feel valued and respected.
- **Positivity** is all about showing optimism and enthusiasm, which are both important in making sales. Avoid the negative, focus on the positive, smile and forget your own worries.

Did you know?

The popular high street retailer Topshop likes their staff to wear the clothes that they are selling, so they give their retail staff a clothing allowance of up to £1500 a year and a 25 per cent discount off all their merchandise.

Remember

It is rude to use your mobile when talking to a customer, and if you really have to answer your mobile, you should apologise and walk away from the customer.

Just checking

1. What can you do to prepare for the selling process?
2. What is an appropriate appearance and attitude for a salesperson?
3. Why do sales staff need excellent communication skills?

How is this sales assistant meeting the customers' expectations?

▶▶ CONTINUED

Link

This topic links to *Unit 4: Principles of Customer Service.*

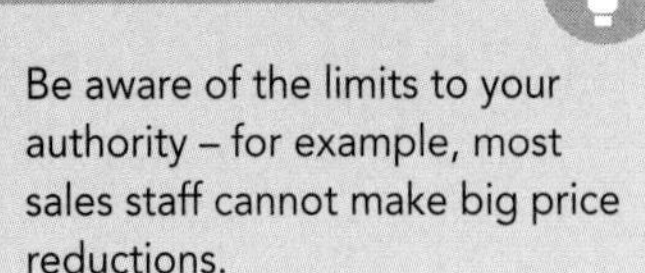

Remember

Be aware of the limits to your authority – for example, most sales staff cannot make big price reductions.

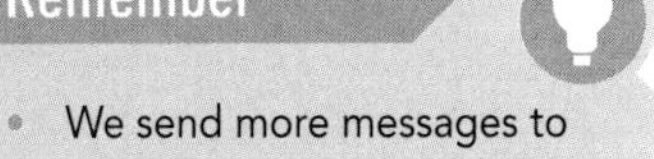

Remember

- We send more messages to other people using non-verbal communication than verbal communication.
- Non-verbal communication often gives away our true feelings and is hard to fake.

Key terms

Non-verbal communication – the process of communication through body language, facial expressions, gestures, eye contact and tone of voice.

Body language – the messages communicated through facial expressions, gestures and posture.

Dealing with different types of customers

Sales staff must know how to help different types of customers, for example:

- Customers for whom English is not a first language – it may help to speak relatively slowly using simple words in short sentences.
- Customers with physical disabilities – inform them of appropriate special facilities.
- Families with young children – offer appropriate facilities such as toys, books to read or colouring pens and paper to keep children occupied.

Communicating with customers

In most selling situations, communications are face to face and your speaking, listening and **non-verbal communication** skills are crucial.

However, technology such as email and call-me buttons on websites mean that sales can be made remotely. Here a different set of skills are important. You need good listening skills to establish over the telephone what a customer wants and you need good written skills if you have to promote something on a website.

All salespeople have to answer customers' questions and this requires a range of good communication skills and product knowledge.

Table 5.4 Tips for communicating with customers

Type of communication	Tips
Spoken	Speak clearly, not too quickly or too loudly, and use words the customer will understand.
Written	Write clearly, use spell check and use words that the customer will understand.
Listening	Think about what the customer is saying and do not interrupt.
Non-verbal	Convey the right impression with a firm handshake, stand upright, avoid slouching and show you are interested by smiling and nodding.
Face to Face	Make sure your **body language** is right and that you are clean and tidy and dressed appropriately.
Eye contact	Show that you are interested in your customer by making regular eye contact, but do not hold their gaze for too long.
Remote	Speak clearly and slowly as connections are not always good. Sit near the microphone, ask for confirmation and speak one at a time. Be precise and concise as time/space may be limited.
Limits of authority	Never overstep your own job role and do not make promises you cannot keep. Ask colleagues for advice if you are unsure what to do.

Different types of communication

- **Greeting:** It is disrespectful to shout 'Hiya!' across the shop, even if this is how you normally say hello. Instead, a polite and unthreatening 'Good morning, let me know if I can help you' is more suitable and creates a good impression.
- **Introductions:** Telling customers your name will help you to build a relationship with them.
- **Attracting customers' attention and interest:** Reassure the customer that you have what they are looking for, and give the impression that you are knowledgeable about the product range. Mentioning benefits that they might not be aware of heightens their interest in the product.
- **Identifying and meeting customers' needs:** Avoid talking too much. Instead, listen to the customer and ask the right questions to establish their requirements, and then use your extensive product knowledge to recommend the most suitable product/service.
- **Presenting products/product information:** Clearly and succinctly outline the main features of the product in appropriate language that your customer will understand.

Remember

Think of your customer having an invisible bubble around them that you are not allowed to enter. Research has shown that if you get too close to people, they will feel uncomfortable and are likely to move away from you. This could mean that they walk out of your shop and you do not make a sale.

Closing techniques

You will find out about closing techniques in Table 5.5.

Preparing the sales area

Sales staff must prepare the sales area so that it is a healthy and safe environment for customers and staff. Make sure that spilt liquids are correctly cleaned up, and walkways are kept clear by removing obstacles such as bags and boxes. The main legislation that protects people at work is the **Health and Safety at Work Act of 1974**. Sales staff must prepare the sales area so that it complies with this legislation, which states that those who create health and safety risks in the workplace are responsible for managing those risks as far as reasonably possible.

Did you know?

The majority of major injuries in 2010–11 involved sales and retail assistants. Previous data has shown that most accidents occur from slips and trips and more than half involve people working in supermarkets and food stores.

Awareness of personal space

Personal space is the area around a person's body that they feel belongs to them. You should be aware of this space and avoid overcrowding people by standing too close to them. Customers often want time alone to chat to each other or to browse.

In some retail jobs it may be necessary to enter the customer's personal space. What can you do to put the customer at ease?

TOPIC B.2

Demonstrate personal selling processes

Introduction

The sales process can be split into three stages: initiate the sale, make the sale and close the sale.

Greeting and introduction ▶ Attracting customers' attention and interest ▶ Presenting product information ▶ Persuading customers to buy.

Figure 5.2 The sales process

Remember

Recording information means it is easy to contact the customer again.

Recording information

After you have closed the sale, it is good practice to record the following information:

- **customer information** – their name, title, address, telephone number and email address and, where relevant, the business's name, type of business, size of business and the buyer's name, title and position in the company
- **transaction information** – the name of the salesperson, item purchased, amount paid, method of payment, any discounts or offers and the date.

This information is useful for accurate marketing that targets the right people, and it can be helpful if a customer returns with a complaint or query.

Closing techniques

Table 5.5 Different types of closing technique

Closing technique	Method
Direct close	This is using a straightforward question to close a sale, e.g. 'How would you like to pay?' Beware – it can be risky if you get your timing wrong.
Silent close	Ask a closing question and then keep quiet. This can be awkward if the customer does not respond.
Alternative close	Offer the customer two choices as your closing question, e.g. 'Would you like it delivered or would you like to take it away now?'
Presumptive close	Close the sale by making a statement that shows that you have assumed that they have decided to buy, e.g. 'You are going to really enjoy this holiday.'

Is being able to close a sale the most important sales skill?

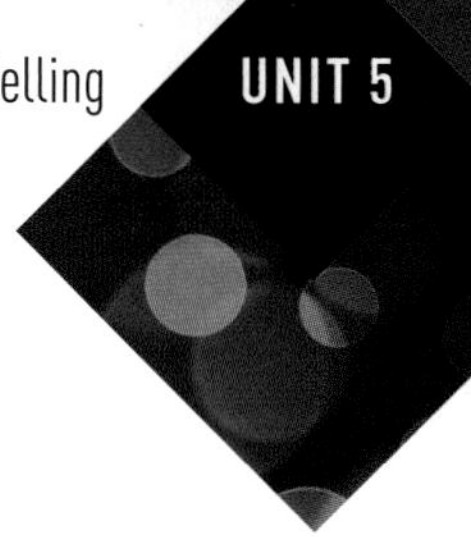

Activity Closing a sale

Practise the following closing techniques through role-playing a selling scenario with a partner: direct close, silent close, alternative close and presumptive close. Then discuss how each closing technique felt. Finally, research alternative closing techniques online.

Did you know?

Warranties are different from guarantees. Guarantees are a free declaration that if a product breaks, it will be repaired free of charge for a limited period of time, usually a year. Warranties have to be paid for, they provide additional cover beyond the guarantee period and may include other cover such as accidental cover.

Customer care and after-sales services

- **Delivery:** Sales staff often arrange the delivery of the product. Delivery may be free of charge and may be made to alternative addresses.
- **Warranty:** Sales staff often try to sell customers a warranty once they have made a purchase.
- **Satisfaction:** Sales staff may check that customers are happy and they have received the service they expect. Only satisfied customers make repeat purchases and recommendations.
- **Follow up:** Sales staff sometimes check that individual customers are satisfied by contacting them a few days after they have received the product.
- **Feedback:** Sales staff occasionally gather feedback through questionnaires.

Dealing with enquiries

Customers often telephone or visit several businesses to ask questions about a product or service before they decide where to purchase the product.

If you get your response right, you are much more likely to see the customer return. Customers will expect you to be approachable and knowledgeable. Ideally, you should try to give the customer a quick but accurate response.

Before answering customers' questions, you need to work out exactly what they want by carefully listening to them and asking further questions.

Handling complaints or problems

It is inevitable that there will be situations where things go wrong from the customer's point of view. Handling complaints can be difficult especially when faced with angry or dissatisfied customers. You must:

- know the company's procedures for recording and reporting a complaint and follow these procedures correctly
- stay calm and establish the details of the complaint by sympathetically listening to the customer
- know which problems you can handle yourself and which you have to pass on to a manager/supervisor
- know the appropriate way to rectify the problem (refund, repair or replacement).

Remember

Try to see complaints as an opportunity to improve things for future customers, and remember that if you handle the complaint well, you could build a rapport with the customer and increase your chances of repeat sales.

CONTINUED ▸▸

Overcoming barriers to closing the sale

If you can see that the customer is hesitating to close the sale, it is likely that they have some objections that you must overcome first. These objections are known as barriers to closing a sale. They can be overcome by reinforcing the features and benefits of what you are selling and by adapting behaviour to audience requirements. Showing respect for your customer and empathising with their views will also help.

Table 5.6 gives examples of different types of objections with suggestions of how to overcome these barriers.

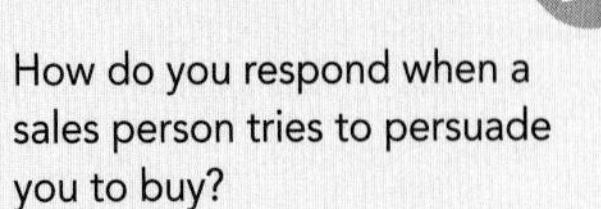

How do you respond when a sales person tries to persuade you to buy?

What excuses do you give to justify a refusal? Compare your ideas as a class.

Table 5.6 Barriers to closing a sale

Type of objection	Example	How to overcome these barriers
Price	'It is too expensive.'	Reinforce the benefits of the product, e.g. 'This is cheap to run.'
Item	'I'm worried about parking a car of this size.'	Reinforce the features of the product, e.g. 'It has parking sensors.'
Competition	'I'm going to look online to see if I can find it cheaper elsewhere.'	Point out the benefits of buying the product from your business, e.g. 'All of our cars come with a one-year guarantee against any type of mechanical problem.'
Timing	'I don't need it yet.'	Adapt your behaviour to audience requirements by creating a sense of urgency, e.g. 'I can offer you a 10 per cent discount today.'
The brand	'I had one of these before and it kept breaking down.'	Empathise with their views, e.g. 'The products are much more reliable today than when they first appeared on the market.'

Activity Closing a sale

Work with a partner to practice closing a sale. First identify an item to sell, such as a mobile phone or T-shirt. The 'buyer' should express interest and the 'seller' should then point out the main benefits and features of the item before trying to close the sale. It is the seller's task to overcome any (valid) objections raised by the 'buyer'. Then change places.

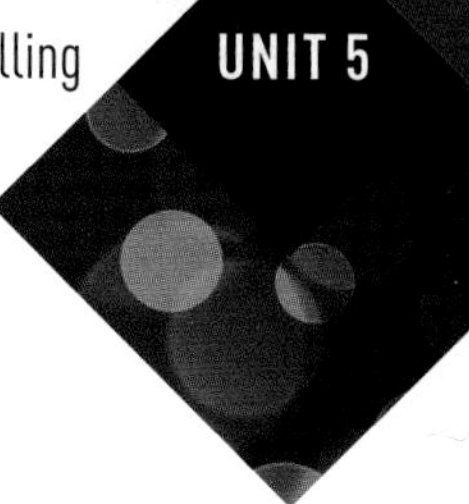

Repeat sales

If you have treated your customer well and kept them happy, they are much more likely to return and make a repeat purchase. For that reason it is sensible to maintain contact by email, phone and mail-shots so that you can point out new products or special offers that may be of interest.

Did you know?

Many businesses make repeat sales through using social networking sites such as Facebook and Twitter to inform customers about their new products/offers and services.

Up-selling

Sales staff can increase overall sales by using up-selling. This is when you recommend your customer a more expensive, upgraded product. This can be done as part of the sales process, or at a later date you could contact the customer to alert them of a new upgrade that has just become available.

Why is this an example of up-selling?

Remember

Up-selling happens all the time and applies to cheap items as well as expensive ones. Cinemas make higher profits because they promote bargain buckets of popcorn and giant size drinks. Fast-food outlets will offer you 'large fries' or a 'family meal' rather than a smaller size. Because it costs very little to give you a larger portion, but the price is higher, profits are also higher.

Activity Researching upselling and cross-selling

As a class, research both upselling and cross-selling and find five examples of each. Then identify how many occasions you are 'upsold' in the next week and compare your findings. Identify how a small business of your choice could benefit from this strategy and share your ideas.

Just checking

1 Describe three barriers to closing a sale.
2 How could you overcome these barriers?

CONTINUED ▸▸

Liaison with other departments

Sales staff work as part of a team and they must liaise with other departments such as:

- **Customer collection:** Customer collection points are usually found in larger stores and they enable customers to collect their shopping at leisure. This is useful for customers who want to continue shopping without carrying heavy bags. The customer is given a receipt to hand over at the collection point to claim the goods.
- **Despatch:** The despatch department is responsible for getting the product to the customers. The customer either collects the product from the despatch department or the despatch department sends the customer the product. Sales staff need to liaise with the despatch department and the customer to organise this process.
- **Accounts:** This department stores information about money paid, received, borrowed or owed to the business. Sales staff liaise with accounts when dealing with financial matters such as setting up credit arrangements, or when they need information about a previous sale.
- **Service:** Technical services support both customers and sales staff in situations where specialist knowledge and skills are needed, such as engineering or IT. Customer services, however, are primarily concerned with customer welfare. Customers contact this department with a complaint and they may liaise with sales staff to help them to deal with that complaint.

Methods of recording

It is important to keep records of sales in an organised and concise manner. Some organisations rank customers by profile and spending patterns so that they can target customers who are most likely to make large repeat purchases. The Pareto effect means that 20 per cent of customers are likely to provide 80 per cent of sales income. A good ranking system will enable you to target this top 20 per cent so that you can invite/send them to special functions or send them brochures or emails to inform them of new products and discounts.

Why is the organisation of records so important in a despatch department?

Assessment activity 5.2 *English* 2B.P5 | 2B.P6 | 2B.P7 | 2B.M3 | 2B.M4 | 2B.D2 | 2B.D3

As a whole class activity, set up a college or school shop selling products and/or services that learners will find useful, for example second-hand uniform, books, stationery and snacks. It is important that everybody in the class takes part in the activity. Working in the shop will give you the opportunity to demonstrate your own personal selling skills and processes. You will need to provide evidence through keeping a personal log or sales diary detailing that you have completed a number of tasks, and your teacher/tutor will observe you and assess your individual performance and provide an individual written observation record.

You must complete the following:

1. Make necessary preparations to sell, including preparing the shop, self-preparation and ensuring you have the necessary product knowledge.
2. Demonstrate that you can process personal sales to two different types of customer and respond to two different types of customer enquiry.
3. Demonstrate good customer care skills in two different situations.
4. Demonstrate that you can show good customer care in handling a customer complaint or problem.
5. Assess the effectiveness of your selling skills and processes in two personal sales situations.
6. Demonstrate confidence in selling goods and services in at least three different situations.
7. Evaluate your own preparation skills and processes used in two different personal sales situations and recommend improvements.

Tips

- You need to help set up the sales environment, dress appropriately and conduct some research on what you are selling.
- If you do not get any complaints/problems, ask a friend to pretend to be a customer with a complaint so that you get the opportunity to demonstrate your response.
- You need to reflect on your own performance in a written statement.

If you find that you do not have the opportunity to demonstrate all of these skills and processes, you could ask your teacher/tutor to observe you role-playing these situations.

Introduction

The retail sector employs over three million people in the UK alone. Britain's biggest private sector employer is a retail business. London is one of the world's leading cities for retail sales. It has over 26,000 shops and an annual non-food turnover of more than £64.2 billion. This emphasises the importance of retail to the British economy.

This unit looks at the structure and organisation of the retail sector in the UK. You will learn about the different types of retail organisation in the UK and the type of employment opportunities they offer.

You will consider the place of retail within the economy and the wider community, looking at how developments such as retail parks can have a positive and negative impact. You will also think about online retail which is growing steadily.

Finally, you will look at the issues that retailers face when they expand abroad, and explore the issues faced by retail managers who want to operate in a foreign country.

Assessment: This unit will be assessed through a series of assignments set by your teacher/tutor.

Learning aims

In this unit you will:

A explore the structure and organisation of retail business

B investigate the relationship between retail business and the external environment.

I always wanted a job in retail, it seemed like an exciting environment where I could interact with a lot of different people. This unit helped me to learn about the different career paths that are available in this sector so that I could make an informed decision about which job to apply for.

Summa, *15-year-old Business student*

Introducing Retail Business

6

This table shows you what you must do in order to achieve a **Pass**, **Merit** or **Distinction** grade, and where you can find activities in this book to help you.

Assessment criteria			
Level 1	**Level 2 Pass**	**Level 2 Merit**	**Level 2 Distinction**
Learning aim A: Explore the structure and organisation of retail business			
1A.1 Identify the sub-sector, channels, format, size and location of a retail business	**2A.P1** Describe the sub-sector, channels, format, size, ownership and location of two retail businesses operating in different sub-sectors **See Assessment activity 6.1, page 159**	**2A.M1** Assess two different types of ownership of selected retail businesses **See Assessment activity 6.1, page 159**	**2A.D1** Evaluate how two retail businesses operating in different sub-sectors measure their performance, with reference to Key Performance Indicators (KPIs) **See Assessment activity 6.1, page 159**
1A.2 Outline the functions of two job roles in store operations	**2A.P2** Describe the functions of two job roles in store operations and their progression routes **See Assessment activity 6.1, page 159**	**2A.M2** Explain how and why two retail businesses operating in different sub-sectors use aims and objectives **See Assessment activity 6.1, page 159**	
1A.3 Identify two types of business that support retail businesses	**2A.P3** Explain, using examples, the role of two businesses that support retail businesses **See Assessment activity 6.1, page 159**		
1A.4 Identify types of non-outlet retailing used by two retail businesses	**2A.P4** Describe how two retail businesses operating in different sub-sectors make use of non-outlet retailing **See Assessment activity 6.1, page 159**		
1A.5 Outline one aim and one objective of a retail business	**2A.P5** Describe the aims and objectives of two retail businesses operating in different sub-sectors **See Assessment activity 6.1, page 159**		

Assessment criteria			
Level 1	**Level 2 Pass**	**Level 2 Merit**	**Level 2 Distinction**
Learning aim B: Investigate the relationship between retail business and the external environment			
1B.6 Outline two issues of concern and two benefits that can arise from two retail developments in the UK	**2B.P6** Explain, using examples, two issues of concern and two benefits that can arise from retail developments in the UK **See Assessment activity 6.2, page 164**	**2B.M3** Assess the benefits for the local community of a retail development in the UK **See Assessment activity 6.2, page 164**	**2B.D2** Evaluate the impact of a retail development in the UK on the local community **See Assessment activity 6.2, page 164**
1B.7 Identify three issues UK businesses must consider when they decide to operate in another country	**2B.P7** Explain, using examples, three issues facing UK retail businesses when they decide to operate in another country **See Assessment activity 6.2, page 164**		

How you will be assessed

This unit will be assessed by a series of internally assessed tasks and you will be expected to show an understanding of the retail business in your local area. The tasks will be based on a scenario where you provide advice to the owner of a local retail business or promote opportunities in the retail sector in your area.

Your assessment could be in the form of:

- a map, showing details of different retail outlets in your local area
- training materials for retail businesses such as leaflets and posters
- a website providing advice to the owners of retail businesses in your area.

TOPIC A.1

The nature of retailing

Getting started

Retail is the biggest private sector employer in the UK. According to the British Retail Consortium, over three million people work in this sector in the UK. What type of jobs do they do? Can you suggest six different ones?

What is retail?

We all participate in retail and go shopping for items such as food, clothes and magazines. Some of us shop using the internet to buy groceries, books, clothes and music downloads or apps for our mobile phones.

Retail can be defined as selling products to the public in small quantities. **Retailers** buy goods in bulk from **wholesalers** or **manufacturers** and then sell them in smaller quantities to the public.

Retail is the final stage in the **chain of production** where products are sold to the public. At every stage in the **supply chain** the amount of profit that can be made by the retailer is reduced because each business wants to earn some money.

Discussion point

Think about Sunday dinner. How many different businesses are involved in getting a roast from the farm to your plate? Why do you think big retailers might prefer to deal directly with farmers?

Wholesalers and manufacturers

Small manufacturers make products and they need help to get them on the shelves in your local shop. A wholesaler will sell products to a retailer in bulk at a discount. Some large manufacturers deal directly with retailers so that they don't have to split their profits with anyone else.

The supply chain

The supply chain is the series of stages that a product goes through to reach a customer, for example wholesaler to manufacturer to retailer.

Some large retailers have cut out the middlemen in the supply chain. This allows them to make more money on each sale.

Why does it benefit supermarkets such as Asda to buy directly from suppliers and transport goods to stores using their own lorries?

Key terms

Retailer – a business which sells goods directly to the public.

Wholesaler – a business which sells large quantities of goods to other businesses.

Manufacturer – a business which transforms raw materials into finished goods, ready to be sold.

Chain of production – the steps taken to turn raw materials into a finished product.

Supply chain – the stages that goods pass through between the producer that makes them and the retailer that sells them.

Retail channels

A retail channel is the method that a retailer chooses to sell their products or services to the market. A retailer might use only one channel or a number of channels; for example, Sainsbury's uses a number of different retail channels to reach the market including shops, e-tailing and catalogues. Table 6.1 shows the different types of retail channel.

Table 6.1 The different types of retail channel

Shops and stores	Shops and stores take a variety of forms. Corner shops have limited selling space, whereas hypermarkets have a very large selling space. In shops, customers handle and select products themselves, taking their purchases to counters or tills to pay for them.
Showrooms	A showroom is a large space where products can be set up, allowing customers to try out their features. An example is Euronics, an electronics retailer, where people can look at different items and measure goods such as fridges to make sure that they will fit in their houses.
E-tailing	A website contains details of the goods or services offered by a business, allowing customers to make a purchase using a credit card or a payment service such as PayPal.
Mobile technology	Devices such as e-book readers and smartphones can link to online shops via the internet, allowing people to buy content directly for their device. It is possible to buy books on your Kindle or music and film on your iPad. iPod, iPad and iPhone customers can buy apps from the App Store and other items from online stores on their device.
Catalogues	A catalogue can be a short booklet or a longer hardback book. Businesses produce catalogues of their products giving details such as sizes, colours and features. Customers can find out about products in the comfort of their own home and then place an order by phone or post.
Home shopping	This is where customers watch television channels such as QVC which broadcast information about products. Customers can then make purchases on the phone or the internet.
Market stalls	Market stalls can be indoors or outdoors. They tend to have a low rent which makes them popular with entrepreneurs who want to try out an idea for a new business with less risk than a shop.

Did you know?

- In 2010, there were 286,680 retail businesses in the UK with total sales of over £293 billion. More than a third of this was spent in shops.
- Apple and Amazon integrate their own e-tailing channel into their digital devices. iPod Touch, iPad and iPhone devices allow customers to buy content directly from iTunes. Kindle users can buy books and newspapers on the internet through their device. Therefore once a customer has bought a product, they continue to generate money for the company by passing sales through their store using that product.

Activity – Researching a retail chain

Research a major retail chain such as Sports Direct.

1. Which retail channels does your chosen retailer use?
2. Why do you think that it operates in these retail channels?
3. Suggest one way that it will benefit from operating in more than one retail channel.

Just checking

1. Can you name all of the retail channels used by HMV?
2. Produce a diagram of the supply chain for a corner shop.
3. Explain the difference between a wholesaler and a manufacturer.

Remember

Many retailers will operate in more than one retail channel so that they can make the most of their opportunities to sell products to the public.

Sub-sectors and ownership

Introduction

Retail is a broad sector of the economy, covering the sale of a very wide range of goods. Similarly, the businesses in the retail sector range from very small to very large, with different types of business ownership.

Retail sub-sectors

The retail sector can be divided up into a number of **sub-sectors** according to the types of products that they sell. Table 6.2 shows these sub-sectors.

Table 6.2 Retail sub-sectors

Sub-sector	Description	Example
Automotive	Sellers of vehicles and related products such as oil or stereo equipment	Halfords, Carcraft
Clothing	Sellers of clothes and related products such as sewing equipment	H&M, Topshop, Next
Food and grocery	Companies which specialise in a specific type of food (for example frozen or fresh) or sell a range of products	Iceland, Londis, The Co-operative
Footwear	Shops which sell shoes and provide related services such as repairing heels	Footlocker, Clarks
DIY	Shops which sell products such as tools and wood for people who wish to improve their homes	B&Q, Homebase
Electrical goods	Shops which sell a wide range of products from fridges to PCs, and MP3 players to ovens	Currys, PC World
Homeware	Retailers which focus on selling products for the home. This might include furniture, carpets or ornaments	Ikea, Utility
Music and video	Shops which sell music and films in physical formats such as CD and DVD or as downloads such as MP3 files	HMV, iTunes Store
Specialised stores	Stores which specialise in selling a specific type of product or service. These are often unique goods that are not sold in general retailers	Holland and Barrett, Hotel Chocolat
Personal care	Retailers which sell goods and services for personal hygiene. These stores might sell products such as soap or services such as manicures	Boots, Lush
Second-hand goods	Companies which sell products that have been owned by someone else previously	Cash Converters, CEX

Activity Carrying out a survey

Carry out a survey of the different retail sub-sectors on a shopping street or retail park near your school or college. How many of the sub-sectors are represented?

Retail business ownership

The most appropriate type of business ownership for a retail business will vary according to the size of the business and the retail sub-sector in which it operates.

Sole trader

Small retail businesses such as local corner shops or food kiosks on busy high streets tend to operate as sole traders. Many market stalls are run by sole traders. An example is Richard Branson's first business which was a stall selling records.

Partnership

One of the most well-known partnerships is the John Lewis Partnership. Every member of staff owns a part of the business and receives a share in the profits. Some specialist retailers such as opticians set up as a partnership to share skills with people who have experience of customer service.

Private limited company (Ltd)

Family-run retailers often choose this form of ownership so that they can benefit from the security of limited liability but still have control of their business. Some retailers such as the Arcadia Group, owned by Philip Green, stay private as they want to operate without the pressure of having to satisfy shareholders.

Public limited company (plc)

Large retail chains such as Tesco raise money from selling shares to expand across the UK and the world. Expanding a public limited company (plc) is risky; if new stores fail, this can be expensive and therefore the protection of limited liability is important.

Franchise

When a retailer wants to expand quickly, they can sell franchises, allowing them to share the costs with potential investors. The cost of a franchise varies depending on the brand. A United Carpets franchise costs £30,000 compared with a Shell franchise at £100,000, but the franchisee will still have to pay the start-up costs for the business.

Activity Starting up a franchise

If you choose to open a retail franchise, in addition to paying for the rights to use the brand name, you will have to pay all of the start-up costs and operating costs for the business.

1. What start-up costs would you have to pay to open a retail outlet? List as many as you can.
2. Considering all of the costs involved in setting up a new retail store, do you think it would be better to be a sole trader or a franchisee? Explain your answer.

Link

This topic links to *Unit 1: Enterprise in the Business World.*

Key terms

Economy – the system by which a country's money and goods are produced and used.

Retail sector – the section of the national economy made up of retail businesses.

Sub-sector – a specific category of products or services offered by a retailer.

Did you know?

Both public and private limited companies benefit from limited liability, which means that if the business fails, its owners will only lose what they have invested in the company.

Remember

A franchisee can be a sole trader, partnership or private limited company. The term 'franchise' actually refers to the legal contract between the franchisor and franchisee, not the type of ownership.

Retail outlets

Link

This topic links to *Unit 1: Enterprise in the Business World.*

Organising retailers by size

The size of a retail business depends on the number of staff they employ.

Table 6.3 The size of retail businesses

Size	Micro	Small	Medium	Large
Number of employees	Up to 9	10–49	50–249	250 +

As retail businesses get bigger, they gain a number of benefits. Larger retailers can buy goods in bulk for lower prices. This helps them to earn more profits. Larger retailers can also invest in hiring specialist staff such as accountants or marketing specialists.

Activity Judging business size

The number of employees is not always the best way to assess the size of retail businesses. For example, a market stall and an art gallery might both employ five people, but their earnings might be significantly different. In groups, discuss other ways that you could judge the size of businesses.

How many different types of retail outlet can you see on this high street?

Types of retail outlet

Independent trader

These are small firms that are not part of a bigger company. They are often family businesses. They tend to be sole traders.

Convenience store

These are small shops, often located on busy streets. They normally sell a range of food and beverages, newspapers and magazines. Convenience stores account for over £30 million of sales in the UK each year.

Symbol group

This is where small retailers join an organisation that allows them to make purchases in bulk and to use a well-known brand name on their store. An example of a symbol group is SPAR. They provide advice and support to their network of independent grocers as well as specialist services like advertising. Other examples include Londis and Costcutter.

Specialist outlet

These outlets vary in size and ownership. They focus on selling a specific type of product or service. The Apple store is a specialist outlet.

Market stall

Market stalls can be indoors or outdoors. They often have low rents and short notice periods which allow entrepreneurs to try out new ideas with little risk. The goods and services offered can be varied, for example fruit and vegetables, clothes or electronics.

Kiosk

This is a small booth, often seen at bus or train stations. They do not normally have a large amount of space to display goods and a member of staff supplies goods to their customers over a counter.

Multiple/chain store

This is where one company has 10 or more stores which operate under the same brand. These stores can be any size and they normally operate as a plc with a high degree of centralised control. For example, Timpson is a small multiple while Currys and PC World are large chain stores.

Discount store

These retailers focus on selling goods at a reduced price. Companies like Poundland buy branded goods and sell them for one pound. In recent years, chains such as Home Bargains and 99p Stores were among the fastest growing chains on the high street, opening branches in stores once occupied by Woolworths.

Cooperative

A cooperative is a business owned by its customers, suppliers and/or workers. Many of these companies focus on ethical products such as fair trade products. Chains such as the Co-operative Group and Southern Co-ops account for over £10 billion of grocery sales in the UK each year.

Franchising

This could be a shop or store such as Costa Coffee or a concession in a larger store such as a branch of McDonald's within an Asda store. Selling franchises helps retailers to expand quickly at a lower cost.

Superstore

Normally, these stores are more than 20,000 square feet in size and sell a range of goods. These stores are owned by major chains such as Asda, but there are some independent supermarkets such as Stan's in St Martin's, Shropshire, which is run by the family of the original owner.

Hypermarket

These are some of the biggest retail outlets, normally over 100,000 square feet in size. They might sell a range of goods (for example, Tesco Extra) or focus on a specific type of goods (for example, Ikea).

Department store

A large shop that is divided into separate departments, each selling a different type of goods. An example is Debenhams. Department stores will often contain small units called concessions, each of which is a small version of a shop. These are often operated by well-known brands such as Ted Baker or Miss Selfridge.

Discussion point

Are our high streets all becoming the same? Some people argue that multiple chains are taking over the main shopping areas in every town and that it is better to have small independent retailers to add variety to the high street. As a group, discuss whether it is good to have a shopping area full of chain stores or whether it's better to have independent stores as well.

Activity Researching cooperatives

Read about The Co-operative. You can access their website by going to www.pearsonhotlinks.co.uk and searching for this title.

1 What are the similarities and differences between a cooperative and a chain store?
2 What are the benefits of being part of a cooperative?

TOPIC A.5 A.6

Aspects of retailing

Non-outlet retailing

This type of retailer might not have any physical premises that customers can visit.

Mail order/catalogues

This is when a customer responds to an advert in a newspaper or magazine, for example a Brennan MP3 player. Customers simply see an advert in a newspaper, post the company an order and then wait to receive their MP3 player in the post.

Alternatively, customers read about products in a catalogue before placing an order; for example Boden, Lands' End, The Book People and Great Little Trading Co. Once goods have been ordered, they are either sent through the post or by a courier service.

Activity Analysing forms of retailing

Many retailers combine outlet and non-outlet forms of retailing. As a group, identify the advantages of combining both forms of retail and of focusing on just one.

Discussion point

Each year, Christmas Day and Boxing Day shoppers have spent more time and money buying goods online. Why do you think this was?

E-tailing

Selling products online through a website has grown in popularity over the last 10 years. Companies such as Amazon can sell through their website and through apps on smartphones or tablet PCs. E-tailers sell a mixture of digital content which customers download to their PC and physical goods which are sent through the post.

Telephone selling

Some goods can be purchased over the telephone. This involves phoning a retailer and placing an order for goods or services which are then delivered to the customer's home, for example fast-food takeaways. Customers phone a restaurant, place an order and they can pay the driver when the food is delivered to their home.

Did you know?

Sainsbury's has run trials of vending machines which sell medicine.

Vending machines

These are often used in schools and offices for snacks and drinks. Customers put money into a machine and enter a code before receiving their goods. Costa Coffee has recently developed a range of vending machines selling their branded coffee.

Shopping channels

Channels such as QVC operate on satellite and Freeview TV channels. Potential customers can watch demonstrations of products which include everything from homeware to jewellery. Customers place orders online or over the telephone before they are delivered.

Location

The location of retail business varies according to the sub-sector and retail outlet chosen.

- **City/town** – traditional shopping areas in the centre of a town or city. This is where you will find the 'high street'. These areas have declined in recent years in many towns. Parking is often hard to find or expensive.

Activity Investigating retail locations

Print a map of your local area from a source such as Google Maps.

1. Highlight the different retail locations in your area using a different colour for each.
2. Explain why some types of retail location are more common and others are less common in your area.

- **Out of town** – areas on the outskirts of a town or city where land is cheaper. Retailers will often build superstores or hypermarkets in these locations.
- **District** – normally somewhere in the centre of a residential area. This might be a suburb of a town or city.
- **Retail parks** – large areas of land where retailers can open large outlets. They normally have a large number of free parking spaces and regular transport links provided by bus or tram.
- **Primary locations** – main shopping streets such as the high street in a town or city. Alternatively, they might be in the main concourse of large shopping centres such as the Arndale Centre in Manchester or at an airport or railway station. These locations often have higher footfall, which means that there are more potential customers, but they also have higher rents and reduced access to parking.
- **Secondary locations** – areas away from main streets. These areas normally have lower footfall, but they also have cheaper rents. This type of location is more suited to specialist retailers such as art supply stores because their customers are willing to search for these outlets.

Activity Improving retail business

In 2011, Mary Portas published a report on how to improve retail business in town and city centres. She suggested that local councils should make it easier to open market stalls, the government should make it more difficult to open betting shops and landlords should make empty shops look attractive.

1. Do you agree with Mary's recommendations? Why?
2. How would you encourage more retailers to open stores in your local town or city centre?

Take it further

1. Find out more about Mary Portas's review of the British high street. You can access this by going to www.pearsonhotlinks.co.uk and searching for this title.
2. Do you agree with her findings?

TOPIC A.7 A.8

What makes retail businesses function?

Jobs in retail business

To run effectively, a retail business needs employees to work in particular roles. Some of the common job roles in retail businesses include the following.

- **Cashiers** process transactions for customers, recording what has been purchased. They handle cash, cheques and credit cards.
- **Customer service staff** work in the front line of retail businesses, answering phone calls or working on the shop floor. Their role is to ensure that customer needs are met.
- **Retail assistants** can be divided into shop floor assistants and stockroom assistants.
- **Sales floor assistants** make sure that stock is replenished and advise customers about products. They ensure that the retail environment is safe and hygienic by cleaning as they work.
- **Sales floor supervisors** complete a rota to ensure that the sales floor is fully staffed at all times. They organise the breaks and lunchtimes of staff so that enough people are working at all times.
- **Stockroom assistants** work behind the scenes, handling stock and ensuring that it is stored correctly. They lock away valuable items, and check that items requiring special treatment such as frozen food are held in the right environment.
- **Stockroom supervisors** organise the stockroom, planning space to make sure that there is enough room for the different types of goods. They check that legal requirements such as safe handling of goods are met.
- **Receptionists** welcome customers to a shop. They might make appointments for customers to visit specialists such as opticians or sales advisers.

Why it is important that cashier's receive sufficient training before they begin to process cheques and credit cards?

Discussion point

Many retailers expect staff to do different jobs from day to day. For example, staff might be expected to move from the stockroom at busy times in order to operate tills. Do you think that it is a good idea to expect staff to know how to do different jobs? What are the advantages and disadvantages of this approach?

Did you know?

- Training is important to retailers to make sure that people do their jobs well. Asda offers over 20,000 apprenticeships to its staff every year.
- Many retailers like to promote their staff. Tesco runs a scheme called *Options* to prepare their staff for management jobs.

Just checking

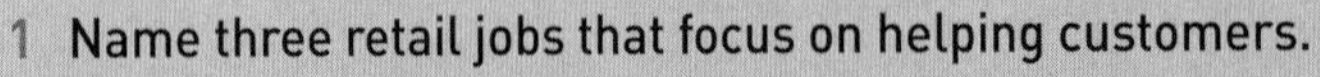

1. Name three retail jobs that focus on helping customers.
2. Describe one retail job that deals with deliveries of stock.
3. Explain two ways that supervisors help to keep retailers organised.

Supporting retail business

Retail businesses can be very large and complex. For example, Sainsbury's has many shops across the UK, each of which needs regular deliveries of stock. As the business opens new stores, it must employ companies that can fit them out. It also requires legal and financial services to support its operations.

Retailers often need to make use of people with specialist skills. Although it is important to use these people to complete specific tasks, it might not be necessary to employ them permanently. Table 6.4 lists some of the functions of supporting retail businesses.

Table 6.4 Supporting retail businesses

Transport and delivery companies	These ensure that new stock arrives on time.
Suppliers and manufacturers	It is important to have suppliers who can produce the right quantity of goods to a high standard.
Computing and financial services	Many retailers use an electronic point of sale (**EPOS**). Specialist teams design these systems, providing upgrades so they continue to work properly.
Tradespeople	Workers such as carpenters or plumbers will carry out repairs in retail outlets. Workers might be hired to support specialists such as shopfitters.
Shopfitters	Shopfitters are specialist builders and decorators who are experts in preparing the retail environment, setting up the appropriate shelving and counters.
Marketing and advertising agencies	These firms carry out research into customers' needs and plan promotional campaigns to attract more customers. They might arrange advertising or produce point-of-sale material to highlight special offers.
Legal and accountancy firms	Firms of solicitors and accountants perform essential services. Accountants carry out an **audit** of a business's accounts and prepare financial statements such as profit and loss accounts annually so that managers can monitor the financial performance of their business. **Stock takes** ensure that records are accurate. Legal firms might carry out checks on legal 'due diligence' records, e.g. temperature checks on fridges.

Activity — Thinking about stock takes

Most retailers carry out a stock take at least once a year. This is normally carried out by someone independent of the store staff and managers.

1. Suggest three reasons why it might be important to check whether or not stock records are accurate.
2. Suggest one reason why stock takes might be carried out by an independent person.

Key terms

EPOS – stands for 'electronic point of sale'. These are computer systems that record transactions and process payments.

Audit – an official check on actions taken and financial claims made by a business.

Stock take – the stock in a retail outlet is counted to ensure that records are up to date.

TOPIC A.9 A.10

Retail targets and performance

Introduction

Like any other business, retail businesses set themselves targets to achieve and monitor their performance against these targets.

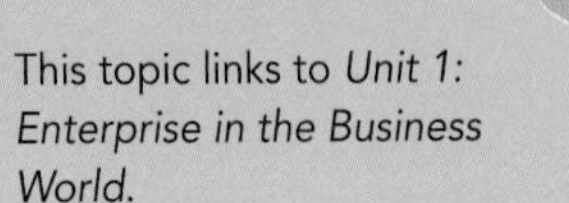

Link

This topic links to *Unit 1: Enterprise in the Business World.*

Aims and objectives

Aims are the long-terms plans that are set by a business. **Objectives** are the steps that a retailer takes to achieve their aims.

Having aims and objectives gives the retailer a clear plan to follow. Setting targets helps to monitor the performance of individual store managers.

A retailer's aims might include:

- **survival** – a smaller business might struggle against larger competitors
- **profit maximisation** – reducing business costs and increasing revenue to make as much money as possible
- **innovation** – retailers might want to find original ways to use retail outlets or unique products that are not available to their competitors
- **securing locations** – getting the best space in a retail park or high street can be a big advantage over competitors.

Retail managers set aims and objectives which they share with their staff. Department managers review their objectives with their managers weekly, monthly or quarterly. Table 6.5 shows how retailers might use SMART objectives.

Table 6.5 SMART objectives

Specific	The objective focuses on a particular **key performance indicator** (KPI).
Measurable	Focusing on a specific KPI means you can see if you have met your target, for example 5% growth.
Achievable	You cannot increase your sales KPI to 100% if you don't have room for extra stock in your store.
Realistic	The retailer must have all of the resources that it needs to meet the objective; for example, if you want 100% more sales, you must have enough stock to achieve this.
Time-related	Clear deadlines will make it easier to see if you are on target or not.

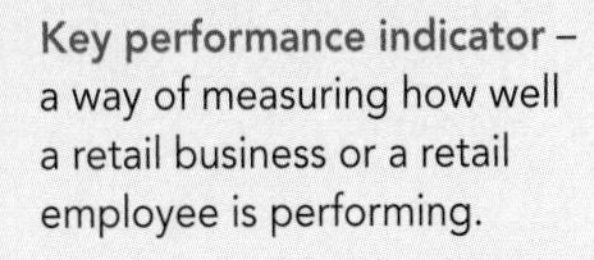

Key term

Key performance indicator – a way of measuring how well a retail business or a retail employee is performing.

Measuring performance

Key performance indicators (KPIs) provide a way of checking how well you are progressing towards your aims and objectives. They can be set for an entire business, individual stores or groups of stores, for example all of the branches in a region.

Common KPIs include the following:

- **Sales** – this is how much revenue a retailer has earned over a period of time. This might be a day, week, month or a year.
- **Profit** – this is calculated by subtracting costs from revenue. It helps retailers to understand how well they are managing their costs.
- **Sales/profit per square metre** – this is the amount of revenue that is generated for each square metre of floor space in a store. This shows how efficiently a store is managed.
- **Sales per employee** – this is how much revenue each member of staff generates. This can help to show how hard staff are working.
- **Average revenue per customer** – this is how much money the average customer spends. This is also known as 'basket size'.
- **Service level** – this can be measured in various ways, for example by counting the number of people at checkouts, or calculating the percentage of stock on sale.
- **Customer satisfaction** – this can be measured in a number of ways, for example by looking at the rate of customer complaints or the score on a customer report.
- **Stock holding** – this is how much stock is kept in stockrooms and sales floors. If this is too high, it leads to waste when goods go out of date. If it is too low, it leads to products being out of stock.
- **Returns** – this is the number of products that are brought back to the store and the reasons why.
- **Complaints** – a business might keep records of how many customers complain, the time and date of the complaint as well as what the complaint is about.
- **Environmental performance targets** – this might be how many plastic bags are given out to customers or how much packaging is recycled.

Discussion point

Is it always fair to use sales per employee or sales per customer as a KPI? Some stores are located in busy locations or in affluent areas. Do you think that achieving good figures on your KPIs is about luck, or will a good manager achieve the targets no matter where the business is located?

Did you know?

Zara and Topshop get new deliveries of stock every few days. This keeps customers interested and helps keep the level of sales in their stores high.

Assessment activity 6.1

2A.P1 | 2A.P2 | 2A.P3 | 2A.P4 | 2A.P5 | 2A.M1 | 2A.M2 | 2A.D1

The local Chamber of Commerce would like to improve the high street in your town by encouraging more retail businesses to open stores there. They would like you to produce a website that could be used to promote the opportunities for retail in your town. You should research two contrasting retailers that already operate successfully in your area. Find out about the careers opportunities in each business and investigate local businesses that provide them with support.

1. Describe the sub-sector, channels, format, size, ownership and location of two retail businesses operating in different sub-sectors.
2. Make an assessment of how appropriate the ownership of each business is.
3. Describe how each retailer uses different forms of non-outlet retailing.
4. Outline and describe two job roles in one of your selected retailers and how you can progress in those roles.
5. Explain the role of two businesses that support a local retailer. Give examples of tasks that they carry out.
6. Describe the aims and objectives of each retailer.
7. Explain how and why each retailer uses aims and objectives.
8. Prepare a conclusion evaluating how much KPIs help each business to achieve their aims and objectives.

Tips

- When you pick your retailers for this task, make sure that they use different forms of non-outlet retail.
- You must include some evidence about why each form might be appropriate or not in an assessment. You should then conclude with a clear judgement on each business.
- Make sure that you choose two different job roles, for example a supervisor and a manager.

Retail business in the UK

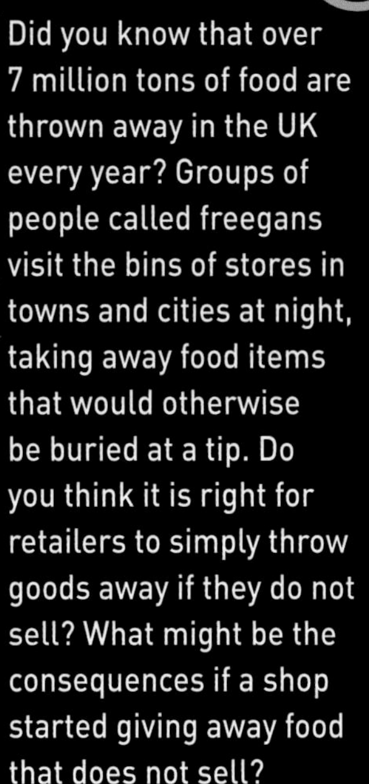

Getting started

Did you know that over 7 million tons of food are thrown away in the UK every year? Groups of people called freegans visit the bins of stores in towns and cities at night, taking away food items that would otherwise be buried at a tip. Do you think it is right for retailers to simply throw goods away if they do not sell? What might be the consequences if a shop started giving away food that does not sell?

Link

This topic links to *Unit 1: Enterprise in the Business World.*

Key terms

Carbon footprint – the amount of greenhouse gas that a business releases into the atmosphere as a result of its activities.

Greenbelt land – an area which is protected from building and development to allow people in cities access to open space and natural environments.

Brownfield land – abandoned industrial or commercial land that can be used for new developments.

Retail business and the external environment

Environmental issues

Opening a new store can lead to more people driving to visit it. This will increase traffic in local communities, causing more traffic jams and a number of road accidents.

Activity: Carrying out a traffic survey

Visit a local town centre and carry out a traffic survey at different times of the day. Compare the number of cars parked and travelling through the area every two hours. What do you notice about the number of vehicles at different times of the day? What impact will this have on other travellers such as children going to school?

The amount of heating and lighting required for a large retail development might have a substantial **carbon footprint**. There is also pollution from waste packaging.

Food miles are the distance that food travels from where it is produced to where it is sold. In order to have products such as green beans all year round, many retailers import them from warm countries such as Kenya. This increases their carbon footprint.

The amount of green space in the UK is decreasing. Building out-of-town stores on **greenbelt land** is controversial. Environmentalists feel that there are already too many supermarkets and green sites should be protected. Campaigners believe that the first choice for new retail developments should be on existing **brownfield land**.

Check the packaging on the fruit and vegetables you have at home to see where they have been produced.

Activity: Calculating food miles

Visit Pearson hotlinks to find a link about food miles. You can access this by going to www.pearsonhotlinks.co.uk and searching for this title.

Download the spreadsheet that is available. In groups, think of a meal that you might eat this week. Calculate the number of food miles required for your meal. Suggest three ways that you could reduce the food miles in your meal.

Ethical issues

Many retailers now stock fair trade products. It is quite normal for goods such as tea and coffee to meet this standard. Fair trade is when the producer (often a farmer in a poor country) is paid a fair wage for their goods. This is good for the farmer, but it costs more for the retailer, reducing their profits.

In some poorer countries, child labour is used to produce goods. If a British retailer is found to stock goods produced by children, this causes negative publicity in the press.

Corporate responsibility has become more important to retailers in the UK in recent years. Many companies set aims and objectives relating to protecting the community and the environment.

Genetically modified foods are very controversial and no British retailers admit to selling them. The public is very worried about the impact on health of eating 'Frankenstein food'.

Organic foods have become very fashionable in the last decade. It costs more to grow food without chemicals, but customers are willing to pay more for them.

Activity — Encouraging healthy lifestyles?

Are retailers causing people to put on weight or are they helping them to live healthy lifestyles? Visit Pearson hotlinks to research stories about obesity. You can access this by going to www.pearsonhotlinks.co.uk and searching for this title.

Divide the stories up according to whether they are about retailers encouraging or discouraging healthy lifestyles.

Shoppers are increasingly interested in healthy living. People who are worried about obesity don't want to buy fatty snacks such as crisps or processed food such as ready meals. This has also helped enterprising shop managers increase sales of items such as exercise bikes and step counters.

Animal research is controversial. Britain is a nation of animal lovers and few people like the idea of using cosmetics that have been tested on dogs or rabbits. Pressure groups such as PETA often protest at companies that use animal-tested products.

Activity — Investigating animal research

Visit Pearson hotlinks to read about the uses of animal research in the UK. You can access this by going to www.pearsonhotlinks.co.uk and searching for this title.

Answer the following questions:

1 What are the arguments for and against animal testing?
2 What is animal testing used for in the UK?
3 Is it right for retailers to sell products that have been tested on animals? Explain your answer.
4 In your group, hold a debate on whether it is right or wrong to test products on animals. Divide into two teams with one team arguing for animal testing and one against.

CONTINUED ▸▸

Discussion point

Is child labour a bad thing? In poor countries where there is no formal education for young people, is it better for children to earn some money in a factory or to work on family farms? Is it better to control child labour so that it is safe or to ban it completely and make children go to school? What are the benefits and drawbacks of each situation?

Did you know?

- Asda aims to reduce the amount of waste that they send to landfill by 100 per cent by 2015.
- Greenbelt land covers 13 per cent of England. The largest greenbelt is around London and it has a total area of 486,000 hectares.
- To qualify as organic, products must follow strict British and European laws. Retailers claiming to sell organic food have to be able to trace each item back to the farm where it was grown.

▸▸ CONTINUED

Community concerns

New out-of-town developments are often blamed for the decline of city centres. Major retailers usually choose to open larger stores at these sites. This leads to town centres filling up with charity shops and betting shops.

Discussion point

Are retail parks a good idea? In your group, discuss the benefits and drawbacks of allowing these developments in a community.

This type of development is often blamed for a reduction in the number of small shops and independent retailers. When large firms leave town centres, this reduces footfall which means small shops struggle to attract enough customers to survive.

New retail parks can lead to new road developments. This can often improve the transport links for communities in out-of-town locations.

New retail developments create pressure on local infrastructures as there is more demand for electricity, water and local roads.

Transport systems have to be changed to accommodate new retail developments. This often provokes criticism. Who should pay the cost of this?

Would it be good if a supermarket was to set up next to your school/college?

Activity Contributing to charity

How many retail businesses in your local area contribute to local charities? Carry out a survey of retailers in your local area and find out how many donate money or staff time to local causes. Who makes the biggest contribution, the major chains or the small independents?

Political issues

The amount of power held by large supermarkets is controversial. This is investigated by the Competition Commission, a government body which aims to protect the public. Limits are placed on how many stores some companies can open in certain areas to make sure no one company becomes too powerful.

Pressure groups often develop to argue against the opening of new out-of-town retail parks. Groups such as IRATE in Ilkley protest against these developments, writing letters to MPs and councillors.

Advertising campaigns by retailers are carefully watched. Most of the major supermarkets claim to have the lowest prices, but who actually does?

Activity Researching pressure groups

Search online for 'Tescopoly' and find out about pressure groups' arguments against supermarkets. Summarise their main points. Explain whether or not you agree with their objections.

The benefits of retail developments to communities and customers

Economic benefits

New retail developments provide employment within stores and also indirectly in local companies such as wholesalers.

Activity Supporting a new retailer

In groups, list as many businesses as you can that would support a new local retailer. For each business, describe how they will support the retailer and how often they will provide this support.

Donations and sponsorship are often provided, for example to local football clubs. Charities are often supported by retailers who encourage staff to arrange fundraising events in store.

A retail development will often attract new businesses to an area when it opens. If a large hypermarket opens, outlets such as cafes and taxi firms may open nearby to offer services to customers.

New people might come to live in an area near a new retail development, helping communities to grow and providing more customers for local businesses.

Did you know?

In America many small towns hold street festivals where local retailers and other small businesses can promote their goods and services to the community.

Social benefits

A retailer can provide meeting places for the community. People will chat while they shop. Some retailers run events such as launch nights for books where people can socialise.

Cafes and restaurants in store are often relatively cheap as a service to customers and provide a place to meet and relax.

When opening a new store, many retailers provide community facilities such as sport centres when they develop land for their store. Large superstores often have recycling facilities in their car parks.

Customer benefits

Large developments such as the Bullring in Birmingham provide facilities such as lifts and ramps for the disabled. Most large and medium-sized retailers provide wheelchairs and Shopmobility buggies for their customers.

Large out-of-town developments, such as Brent Cross in London, offer free parking to customers. This is often more convenient than paying high prices in town centre car parks.

Hypermarkets often provide cheap petrol to encourage customers to visit their stores.

Discussion point

Are retailers really a good place for social activity? Would you attend social events in a retail business or meet friends in a cafe?

Doing business with the rest of the world

The relationship between UK retailers and international markets

If a British retailer wishes to open a store abroad they must make sure that they understand their market, including the following aspects.

- **Customs:** How do people like to behave? For example, the Spanish have a siesta in the afternoon, meaning shops close for three to four hours in the day.
- **Tastes and styles:** Fashion varies greatly in different countries and it is important to sell products that meet the needs of customers.
- **Lifestyles:** People might be used to shopping in a certain way or using a particular type of goods. Tesco's Fresh and Easy stores in America struggle because American consumers are not used to the same type of ready meals as the British.
- **Location issues:** For example, will customers shop out of town or in city centres?
- **Economic and legislative environments:** For example, in India it is a legal requirement to have a local business partner.
- **Cultural considerations:** People live their lives differently in different countries. For example, the British are a nation of tea drinkers, whereas the Americans and French prefer coffee.

It is also important to choose the most appropriate method of entering the market. There are several different ways to enter foreign markets as shown in Table 6.6.

Table 6.6 Methods of entering a foreign market

Method	Description
Self-entry	All the work and investment comes from within your business, with the support of local advisers.
Acquisition	Buying a local company. This can be expensive.
Joint ventures	Working with a local partner. This means sharing your profits, but you can benefit from their knowledge and experience.
Franchising	Local firms can be offered the rights to operate stores under your brand name, allowing you access to expert local knowledge of customer needs.

Assessment activity 6.2

2B.P6 | 2B.P7 | 2B.M3 | 2B.D2

Your local Chamber of Commerce has asked you to write an article for their magazine about the issues faced by British retailers when they grow at home and abroad.

They want you to investigate two retail developments in the UK such as Bluewater in Kent and Liverpool One. You must present a balanced view of the benefits and concerns of each development. You should also investigate the issues faced by British retailers when they choose to expand abroad.

1. Explain two concerns and two benefits that have been raised about the retail developments you have investigated.
2. How have the developments benefited the community? Assess the extent to which the developments have been positive.
3. Choose one retail development and evaluate the impact that it has had on its local community.
4. Research examples of British retailers expanding abroad. Explain three different issues that British retailers should consider when they enter foreign markets.

Tip

You should include evidence that you have considered whether or not a retail development will benefit its local community. You must show that you understand potential negative impacts, such as the closure of small shops, as well as benefits, such as employment, in order to give a balanced assessment.

WorkSpace

Lowri Roberts

Owner of Siop Cwlwm

Lowri Roberts has always wanted to set up a shop dedicated to selling Welsh products. She is passionate about the Welsh language and she wants to run a business that makes a contribution to the community as well as allowing her to earn a living. She runs the shop in partnership with her mum. They each have different skills to contribute to the business. Her mum is very good at organising stock takes. Lowri makes presentations to gain funding for the business.

Lowri and her mum chose a market stall because it was a low-risk way to test their idea. The rent isn't very high and they only have to give a week's notice if they want to leave. They also sell their stock online, which means they have customers all over the country, not just in Oswestry.

Lowri runs a lot of community events to encourage people to speak Welsh. They have regular 'talking shop' days where people can come in, practise speaking the language and meet other members of the community. They enjoy making a contribution to their community. Lowri and her mum also encourage children to learn Welsh. They offer lessons in Welsh and have paid a designer to make toys such as jigsaws which sell very well.

You can find out more about Lowri's shop on her website. Access this through www.pearsonhotlinks.co.uk.

Think about it

1. Which retail channel has Lowri chosen for her business?
2. How does she benefit from operating the business as a partnership?
3. How does Siop Cwlwm make a positive contribution to its community?

Introduction

Effective business support is essential for many organisations. Whether you are visiting a hotel, a hospital, a leisure club or a school or college, you will see several people carrying out a whole range of administrative activities.

These activities are absolutely vital for the organisation to function properly. Teachers, doctors and other professionals could not do their own jobs properly without administrative assistance. Neither could senior managers in business who rely on their office staff to make travel and meeting arrangements, greet visitors, answer the telephone and carry out many other necessary tasks.

Providing business support can offer fascinating opportunities. Top Personal Assistants (PAs) and Executive Assistants have interesting and well-paid jobs in major cities throughout the world.

This unit will give you the opportunity to undertake support tasks yourself and develop your skills in a practical way, as well as learning more about the importance of this role.

Assessment: This unit will be assessed through a series of assignments set by your teacher/tutor.

Learning aims

In this unit you will:

A understand the purpose of providing business support

B use office equipment safely for different purposes

C organise and provide support for meetings.

My sister works in a support role in the HR department of a company. She helps to organise interviews and prepare information for training courses and also does confidential tasks for the HR manager. It sounds really interesting and I'd like to understand more about this type of job.

Jia-li, *15-year-old Business student*

Providing Business Support

7

This table shows you what you must do in order to achieve a **Pass**, **Merit** or **Distinction** grade, and where you can find activities in this book to help you.

Assessment criteria			
Level 1	**Level 2 Pass**	**Level 2 Merit**	**Level 2 Distinction**
Learning aim A: Understand the purpose of providing business support			
1A.1 Identify types of business support in two contrasting businesses	**2A.P1** Explain the purpose of different types of business support in two contrasting businesses **See Assessment activity 7.1, page 171**		
Learning aim B: Use office equipment safely for different purposes			
1B.2 Identify office equipment to meet different business requirements	**2B.P2** Describe the use of office equipment to meet different business requirements **See Assessment activity 7.2, page 179**	**2B.M1** Explain the appropriate uses of office equipment types, features and functions to suit different business purposes **See Assessment activity 7.2, page 179**	**2B.D1** Analyse the contribution that office equipment makes to the provision of business support **See Assessment activities 7.2, page 179**
1B.3 Demonstrate using different types of office equipment safely, with guidance and in accordance with health and safety legislation	**2B.P3** Demonstrate using office equipment safely, in accordance with health and safety legislation **See Assessment activity 7.2, page 179**	**2B.M2** Demonstrate understanding of the application of safe lifting techniques when using office equipment **See Assessment activity 7.2, page 179**	
Learning aim C: Organise and provide support for meetings			
1C.4 Draw up a checklist for organising and supporting either an internal or an external meeting	**2C.P4** Organise a meeting according to specified requirements using a checklist **See Assessment activity 7.3, page 191**	**2C.M3** Explain the organisation and support required for different types of meeting **See Assessment activity 7.3, page 191**	**2C.D2** Evaluate own contribution to providing support before, during and after the meeting and suggest improvements **See Assessment activity 7.3, page 191**
1C.5 English Produce a meeting brief and agenda for either an internal or an external meeting	**2C.P5** English Produce accurate documents required prior to a meeting and take notes during the meeting **See Assessment activity 7.3, page 191**	**2C.M4** English Produce accurate and detailed post-meeting documentation (including minutes) prepared from notes taken during meeting discussions **See Assessment activity 7.3, page 191**	
1C.6 Provide some support at either an internal or an external meeting and assist in clearing the venue after the meeting has finished	**2C.P6** Provide all required support for a meeting, including follow-up activities **See Assessment activity 7.3, page 191**		

English Opportunity to practise English skills

How you will be assessed

The unit will be assessed by a series of internally assessed tasks and practical activities. These are designed to enable you to demonstrate that you understand the types and purpose of business support, can use office equipment safely and can organise and provide support for a meeting.

You may need to carry out research tasks and must keep any notes you make carefully, as these will provide evidence to support your work. If you give a demonstration, make a presentation, support your teacher/tutor or other business people at an event or discuss what you have done to organise a meeting, then you will also obtain witness testimony and/or observation reports to confirm what you have done. It is important that you keep these safely, together with any documents you produce yourself.

Your assessment could be in the form of:

- a leaflet or display which illustrates how business support is different in two contrasting businesses
- a fact sheet or presentation which summarises the appropriate use of different types of office equipment and how this contributes to providing business support
- a demonstration of how to use office equipment safely
- a poster to illustrate safe lifting techniques
- a personal record of all the activities you have undertaken to organise and support a meeting and the documents you produced
- a reflective report in which you evaluate your contribution to the meeting, what you have learned from the experience and any improvements you would make in future.

Providing business support

Getting started

What type of support is provided by your school or college office? How does this help your tutors? What would happen if it didn't exist? Discuss this with your teacher/tutor to find out!

Types of support

Business support is vital in all organisations, both large and small, because it keeps the business running smoothly. There are various types of support and these are shown in Table 7.1.

Table 7.1 Types of business support

Support task	Assistance for the business
Dealing with visitors	Gives callers an immediate positive impression and enables visitor needs to be met promptly
Organising travel and accommodation	Enables staff to travel cost-effectively to meet customers and other external contacts
Managing diaries	Enables activities to be coordinated and staff to be found quickly when necessary
Using telephone systems to make, receive and transfer calls	Enables enquiries to be dealt with promptly and accurately, improves customer relations and responsiveness
Organising and supporting meetings	Helps meetings to run smoothly and a reliable and accurate record to be kept
Producing documents	Provides a written record of important information for those who need it
Processing and storing information, both manually and electronically	Enables rapid access to records so decisions are based on the latest available information

What administrative support is essential at a meeting?

Activity: Comparing support roles

Maria works in a large doctors' practice. Justin works in the local office of his MP. Both provide business support. In pairs, suggest two differences and two similarities between the tasks they do. Compare your ideas with other groups.

The purpose of providing business support

The aim of business support is to keep everything running smoothly. This is very important in both small and large organisations for several reasons.

- **To ensure consistency:** This means that support tasks are carried out in the same way, and to the same high standards, no matter who does them.
- **To make effective use of time:** In any thriving business, there are many tasks to do in a limited amount of time. Some will be urgent, some important, a few will be both. When tasks are prioritised and done by support staff, other staff can concentrate on meeting the priorities in their own jobs.
- **To support managers, teams, colleagues and departmental processes:** Managers must focus on their own responsibilities. They cannot achieve targets or run their own areas efficiently if they are distracted by administrative tasks. Other staff, too, will do a better job if they can rely on support staff for assistance.
- **To provide effective services to internal and external customers:** External customers may contact a business for information or advice, to complain or to buy products and/or services. Internal customers are people in the same workplace who need something, such as information or a copy of a document. Both types of customers want their request to be handled promptly and professionally. If this is done consistently the image and reputation of the business is enhanced.

Just checking

1. List four common business support activities and state how each one helps the work of the business.
2. What are the main purposes of providing business support?

Assessment activity 7.1

2A.P1

1. Research the job roles of three or four different business support staff in two contrasting businesses. Do this by talking to job holders, investigating job adverts online or in your local paper. Identify the types of support each job holder provides and the main purposes(s) of each person's job.
2. Use this information to prepare a leaflet that identifies and explains the types and purposes of business support provided in both businesses. Then present your findings to the rest of your group.

Tips

- Check with your teacher/tutor that the businesses you choose are 'contrasting', i.e. very different in some way(s).
- Make sure the jobs you investigate involve contrasting activities as this will give you more scope in your answer.

Did you know?

- You can find out more about business support activities by looking at *Executive PA* magazine online.
- In large organisations, support staff usually work within departments, such as HR, sales or finance and specialise in the type of work done there, for example organising interviews in HR, updating customer records in sales and checking expense claims in finance.

Remember

Support staff help a business to run more efficiently because they enable other staff to focus on their own job, knowing that important support tasks have been carried out properly.

TOPIC B.1

Using office equipment for different purposes

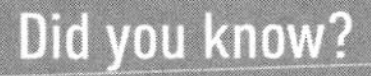

- Google Docs™ is free web-based software that allows anyone to create and share documents, spreadsheets and presentations. It is popular with many small business owners and staff, especially if they travel regularly on business.
- Many small businesses have printers that can also scan and copy documents. Some will also fax documents.
- You should always check your work carefully, so you do not make unwanted copies, and print in draft mode if possible to save ink.

Introduction

Many support tasks involve the use of office equipment. Using this correctly means that you get the best results in the shortest time. Using it safely is also important, as you will see later in this unit.

Types of office equipment

Computers

Most offices use both desktop computers and laptops. Laptops are preferred by staff who frequently travel or often work at home. Staff computers are usually connected on a network so that information can be shared by email or over an intranet. Users access communal software, such as word processing and database packages and an internet browser, such as Internet Explorer. Support staff must know how to use their computer system and the software packages needed for the tasks they undertake.

Printers

There are two main types of computer printers used in offices. The features and functions will depend upon the type and the price paid.

- **Inkjet printers** are small, cheaper and usually slower. They use ink cartridges which are expensive to replace if usage is high.
- **Laser printers** are larger and more expensive. They are quicker, quieter and the print quality is crisper. These printers use toner cartridges.

Table 7.2 Office printer features and functions

Feature	Function
Duplex printing	This means documents can be printed back to back.
Media capacity	This is the amount of paper the paper tray holds.
Media size	This is the maximum size of paper the printer will use (usually A4).
Media type	This is the type of paper you can use, e.g. plain paper, envelopes, labels, etc.
Memory	This is the number of pages that can be held in the printer memory.
Mono or colour	Most inkjets offer colour; laser printers may be mono or colour.
Networkable	This means the printer can be linked to several computers.
Print resolution	The higher the dots per inch (dpi) figure, the better the print quality.
Print speed	This is rated in pages per minute (ppm) and is slower for top-quality prints.

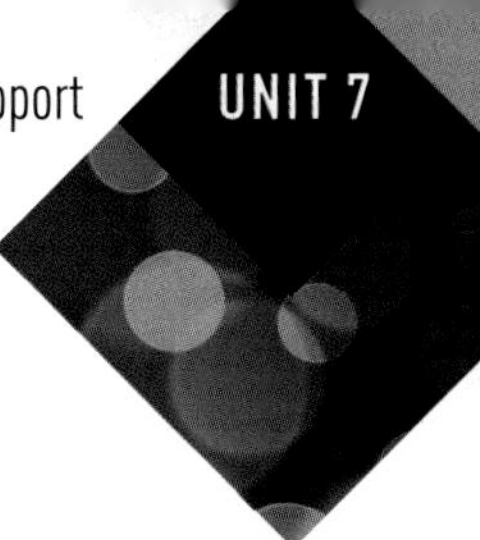

Photocopiers

Photocopiers make copies of documents, such as items received in the mail and papers in the file. They vary tremendously in terms of their size, speed and features. Some are small desktop models, others are much larger. Some are digital, use touch screen technology, provide internet access and can be linked to the computer network. Computer users can give instructions from their desk to print a document and specify how it should be produced, for example, whether it should be printed back to back.

Table 7.3 Features and functions of office photocopiers

Feature	Function
Automatic document feeder	ADFs allow multi-page documents to be stacked for copying and each page enters separately. Some also accept double-sided originals.
Copying speed	This can range from 15 pages a minute to over 100.
Duplexing	This enables two-sided copying which saves paper.
Finishing unit	This may collate multi-page documents, hole punch or staple them.
Image density adjustments	This adjusts exposure for poor text or dirty backgrounds to improve clarity.
Interrupt facility	This allows a long job to be paused while an urgent job is done.
Memory (digital copiers only)	Pages are scanned into memory before printing; routine jobs can be programmed into the machine and recalled as required.
Mono, colour or hybrid	Copies may be only black and white or colour. A hybrid saves money as the best option can be selected per task.
Paper trays and capacity	Can range from one small A4 paper tray to several different trays for different sizes of paper, e.g. a bypass tray for labels or transparencies.
Reduce/enlarge	Copies can be reduced or enlarged to fixed pre-set ratios. Some machines automatically use the best ratio.
Sample copy	This enables a test copy to be made.
User ID/counter	This calculates usage per user. Users enter a PIN to use the machine.
Zoom	This allows more precise reduction/enlargement.

Activity Investigating photocopiers

Find out about the features available on the main photocopier you use in your centre. Then watch a demonstration that ideally includes printing on different paper sizes, collating and stapling a multi-page document, and making basic adjustments to improve print quality.

▸▸ CONTINUED

Discussion point

Are automated systems and music on hold a good thing or bad? Do they lose customers or gain them? Discuss your views as a class.

Telephone systems

There are different types of business telephone systems. In a large organisation, a designated person may operate a screen-based console that receives incoming calls. In a small business, calls are usually routed direct to extensions and answered from any phone. Many firms now have VoIP (Voice over Internet Protocol). Calls are routed over a computer network instead of traditional phone lines because this is cheaper and the quality is better.

Table 7.4 Features and functions of business telephone systems

Feature	Function
Automated attendant/ interactive voice response (IVR)	Callers are greeted with a pre-recorded message and given options to select the department they want. With an IVR system, callers can obtain information and carry out some transactions. They may be asked for ID (such as an account number) before being connected.
Automatic call distribution	This distributes incoming calls evenly among a group of operators. Used by many call centres to reduce waiting times for callers.
Caller display/ identification	This shows the caller's number plus the name and company if linked to an address book feature.
Conference calls	This allows you to speak to several people at once, either extension holders and/or outside callers.
Divert or call forwarding	This allows calls to be rerouted from one extension to another or to another phone or mobile if a person is out of the office, travelling on business.
Do not disturb	This blocks calls to an extension while it is set.
Hands free/listen on hold	This enables you to replace the handset and listen and/or talk through a speaker.
Interrupt	This indicates a waiting call, usually by a bleep on the line.
Last number redial	This automatically redials the last number you called.
Message waiting	A light or bleep shows that a voicemail message is waiting. On a computerised system, the message appears on screen.
Music on hold	This plays music and/or provides information to callers waiting to be connected.
On hold/reminder call holding	This allows incoming calls to be held while the correct person is found to deal with the call/gives a prompt that the caller is still waiting to be connected.

Table 7.4 Features and functions of business telephone systems

Feature	Function
Redirect	This enables a transferred call to be rerouted if the call has to be redirected again.
Secrecy button	Depressing this button means the caller cannot hear anything you say to a colleague (and is far better than covering the mouthpiece with your hand!).
Speed dialling	This allows abbreviated dialling for long numbers and for numbers called frequently.
Voicemail/ advanced messaging services	Callers leave voice messages in individual mailboxes when people are away or engaged on another call. Messages can be retrieved from an extension or external phone. On some systems, voicemail can be sent as text messages or as emails.

Activity: Investigating telephone systems

1. Find out the standard greeting given to telephone callers by staff at your centre. How do you think this might differ in a bank or a small retail shop?
2. Investigate the telephone system in your centre. Find out which features it has and which are most commonly used.
3. In small groups, decide on three telephone system features that would benefit **a)** a health centre, **b)** a cinema, **c)** a large retail store, **d)** a small estate agency, **e)** an international business. Compare your ideas as a class.

Office chairs

Office chairs allow staff to carry out a range of tasks comfortably and safely. They are designed to support the user's back and neck, encourage good posture and prevent discomfort. The best chairs are often described as being **ergonomic**.

You can alter the height of an office chair so that your feet are flat on the floor. You should also be able to adjust the back of the chair so that your spine is supported. The best ones also have adjustable seat depth, chair arms and tension so that the chair will tilt easily according to your weight.

You will learn more about sitting properly and safely on later in this unit.

What features can you identify that will help with good posture?

Did you know?

Most businesses instruct their staff to answer external calls with a specific greeting. This may be formal or informal, depending on the type of firm and the business it carries out. On a central switchboard, the greeting will include the name of the organisation. Individual extension users should also identify themselves by name.

Key terms

Ergonomic – designed to enable people to work safely and productively.

CONTINUED ▸▸

▸▸ CONTINUED

Instruction manuals

All office equipment is sold with an instruction booklet or manual. This explains all the features and functions and includes any other information the manufacturer thinks you should know. One important section is troubleshooting, which is normally near the end. This tells you what to do if there is a problem with the equipment. The manual also includes safety advice, which is important if you are using electrical equipment.

While you may be tempted to ignore the manual and just press a few buttons to see what happens, there are dangers with this approach. As well as making a mess of a job, you could also do something that is hazardous or break the equipment.

Remember

It is normally quicker and safer to check what you should do before you start, not when you get stuck later on!

Training in usage

The best way to learn how to use equipment is to watch an expert who also explains what they are doing. They may make it look very easy, and you might forget what you are told, so it is sensible to take notes that you can refer to when you are doing the job yourself.

Did you know?

- Most manuals are also available on the manufacturer's website, together with help and guidance for users.
- Photocopier suppliers often provide training and show nominated members of staff how to solve problems such as paper jams and replenishing toner. Other users will not be allowed to do these tasks.

Activity Watching a demonstration

Watch someone experienced demonstrating a range of photocopying operations and using the telephone system at your centre. Make notes so that you remember what they did.

Problem solving

All users should know the correct procedure to follow if they have a problem with a piece of equipment. If a computer printer fails to work in your centre, then you may be expected to report it to a named tutor or contact a helpline. Before you do this, however, it is sensible to make a few basic checks, such as ensuring it is plugged in and switched on.

Why do staff need special training before they can solve photocopier problems?

Activity Solving problems

In groups, look at the manuals for the printer and photocopier you use regularly. Find out what to do if the paper jams, printing stops unexpectedly, the equipment stops working or the copies are unreadable. Produce a help sheet for users.

Did you know?

It is usually more economical for a small business to have a basic copier or multifunction device (that will also print, fax and scan documents) and to pay a copy shop or local printer to prepare coloured leaflets or posters.

Meeting different business requirements

All office equipment is chosen to meet specific business requirements. The needs of a health centre are different from a bank or a cinema, and a hairdresser will have different requirements from an estate agent, a solicitor or a retail store. Factors to consider include:

- whether the business needs to produce professional documents or leaflets for clients as this will affect the type of printer or photocopier they buy
- whether there will be a large volume of telephone calls to deal with, and whether many calls will be received 'out of hours'
- whether staff are regularly travelling on business and need to keep in touch with the office.

Activity Research office equipment

Research the type of office equipment which is routinely used in business organisations to meet different requirements, such as preparing, printing or reproducing documents, communicating with other people and providing meeting support.

You can do this by talking to the job holders you spoke to for Assessment activity 7.1 and finding out the type of office equipment that each job holder needs to use to do their work. You should also research online and you can visit large office suppliers, such as Staples, to see some items yourself.

Identify and note the main features and functions and why they are important to different users. Keep your notes safely as you will need them when you do the next Assessment activity.

TOPIC B.2

Working safely

Getting started

A government study found that in 2010/11 1.2 million working people were suffering from a work-related illness. Can you think of the main reasons why?

Remember

Make sure you are a safe worker, not a walking hazard! Don't leave your bag on the floor where someone can fall over it, or wear a rucksack without considering people behind you.

Using office equipment safely

Most people use computers every day without realising that they can cause painful ailments if they are not used correctly. This is because a computer user may be in a fixed position for hours, with their face looking at the screen, hands on the keyboard and the rest of the body immobile, resulting in musculoskeletal disorders such as repetitive strain injury (RSI) and upper-limb disorders (ULDs) to hands, wrists, arms, neck, shoulders or back. These are caused by repetitive movements, such as keying in text or using a mouse, and continual poor posture.

Laptop computers can cause more serious injuries as users sometimes rest them on their knees. The keyboard is not ergonomically designed and the screen may be small or difficult to see in bright light. This is why many businesses provide docking units for safe laptop use within the office.

The Health and Safety at Work (Display Screen Equipment) Regulations introduced minimum standards for the use of visual display screens (VDUs) and workstation design. Users are also expected to make simple changes for their own wellbeing. These include adjusting their office chairs so that their backs are well supported and their feet are flat on the floor or on a footstool, and positioning the monitor, keyboard and mouse correctly.

Figure 7.1 How will sitting correctly help to avoid workplace injury?

Activity — Thinking about posture

1. Check your own posture against the illustration shown. Score yourself against each item to see if you get 10 out of 10 or rather less!

   Visit Pearson hotlinks to download the booklet *Working with VDUs* from the HSE. You can access this by going to www.pearsonhotlinks.co.uk and searching for this title.
2. Use this to design a poster which shows good positioning of a keyboard, monitor and mouse.
3. In groups, research ergonomic office chairs online, and produce a leaflet which shows how to make the necessary adjustments so the user is sitting in the correct position. Remember to test your ideas to make sure they work!

Health and safety legislation for working safely

The Health and Safety at Work Act 1974 (HASAWA) is the main legislation relating to health and safety. This states that employers have a responsibility to provide a safe working environment, and employees must take reasonable care of their own health and safety. They must also act responsibly because other people may be affected by their actions.

Other legislation regulates the space, temperature and facilities in the workplace and how equipment is maintained and used.

Safe lifting techniques

The Manual Handling Operations Regulations state that staff must never try to lift a load which is too heavy. All organisations must provide trolleys or wheeled 'sack' trucks to move heavy items. If the load is within your capabilities, then you must lift it properly by bending your knees first, so that your legs take the strain. Your legs can cope with this, whereas your back cannot.

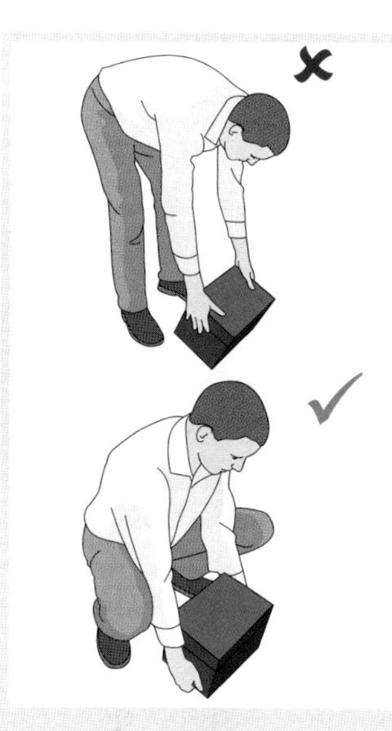

Figure 7.2 An injury to your back could mean recurrent pain for the rest of your life.

Following instructions

Under HASAWA all employees must cooperate with their employer and follow all instructions relating to health and safety. Businesses try to prevent accidents by providing equipment manuals and training staff in how to use equipment and certain substances safely. These precautions are useless if employees ignore them.

Remember

Working safely means following workplace policies and manufacturers' instructions. It also means using your common sense and concentrating when you are doing something.

Assessment activity 7.2

2B.P2 | 2B.P3 | 2B.M1 | 2B.M2 | 2B.D1

Your centre is hosting an event for young entrepreneurs. You have been asked to provide information about office equipment and demonstrate this to attendees.

1. Prepare facts sheets for three items of equipment, using your research findings. Each sheet should give information on how that item of office equipment is used to meet different business requirements and the type of features and functions that are valued by support staff. You should also summarise how that particular item of equipment contributes to effective business support.
2. During the event you must demonstrate that you can use a computer, printer, office chair, telephone and, ideally, a photocopier properly and safely. You must also carry out other support tasks, including greeting visitors and asking them to sign a visitor book, issuing and collecting visitor badges, finding and storing your facts sheets in a filing cabinet and producing documents.

   You must also demonstrate how to lift safely, how to sit properly at a computer and how to adjust your chair appropriately. Your teacher/tutor will observe you and will complete an observation report on your performance.
3. After the event, use your research and experience to prepare a summary in which you analyse how different items of office equipment contribute towards providing effective business support.

Tip

You should analyse your information. This means identifying the relevant features and functions that apply and explaining why each one is important.

Did you know?

- Your eyes regularly need a break from a computer screen. Look into the middle distance at intervals and blink more rapidly for a few seconds. Stretch your arms and wrists and straighten your fingers at the same time.
- RSI Action, the UK charity, warns that children as young as seven may now suffer from RSI. Read the guidelines on its website by visiting Pearson hotlinks to ensure you don't join them. You can access this by going to www.pearsonhotlinks.co.uk and searching for this title.
- If you use a telephone while you are on a computer, you should have a hands-free headset. This prevents you cradling the phone between your ear and neck while you type, which can cause serious injuries.

TOPIC C.1 C.2

Organising and providing support for meetings

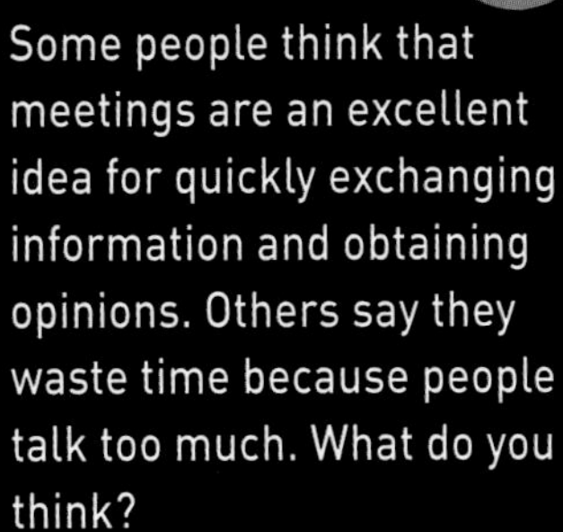

Getting started

Some people think that meetings are an excellent idea for quickly exchanging information and obtaining opinions. Others say they waste time because people talk too much. What do you think?

Types of meeting

There are different types of meeting and they vary in several ways.

- **Size** – some meetings involve only two or three people, whereas others involve a large number of people.
- **Internal/external** – some meetings only have internal staff present; others involve external contacts such as customers, suppliers or shareholders.
- **Formal/informal** – formal meetings have specific rules and procedures; others are informal and may just involve a small group of people chatting together.
- **Confidentiality** – meetings are confidential when sensitive information is being discussed, such as strategy meetings when directors are discussing future plans and meetings about HR issues such as a staff disciplinary interview.
- **Team meetings** – these are internal meetings held by the team leader to keep a team up to date with developments. Team members may be asked for ideas and contributions to solve a problem.

The type of meeting affects the organisational arrangements, including where and when it is held, the number of people present, how they are invited, the budget and the written record that is made.

Discussion point

As a group, suggest what problems could arise if word leaked out that the directors in a company had held a meeting to discuss possible redundancies because of a lack of orders.

Activity — Investigating meetings

Find out all the different types of meetings held at your centre, both formal and informal. Discuss with your tutor the steps that are taken at confidential meetings to ensure that sensitive information is kept private.

Why is it important to check equipment is working in advance of a meeting?

Organising meetings

All meetings have several aspects in common. People are invited to attend, often by the **chairperson.** They are informed about the items to be discussed and these are often listed in an **agenda.** A record is kept to summarise the decisions taken and sent to people afterwards. These are called **minutes** and are a legal requirement for some formal meetings.

Meeting brief and agenda

The purpose of the meeting affects who is invited, what is discussed, how long the meeting lasts and where it is held. It also partly determines the budget as you will see later.

A **meeting brief** may be prepared which summarises all the key facts. This is done by the chairperson and the organiser, often by using a checklist like the one below.

Checklist for a meeting brief	
Why is the meeting being held?	
What is the agenda?	
What is the budget?	
How long will the meeting last?	
When should it be held and what time will it start/end?	
Who are the key people who must attend?	
Where will the meeting be held?	
Are refreshments required?	
Are any special equipment, resources or facilities required?	
How will people be invited?	
What information/documents will they need?	
Will anyone require accommodation?	
Will someone be required to take minutes?	
What follow-up activities are required?	

Figure 7.3 A checklist will help to ensure nothing is forgotten.

The chairperson also decides the agenda. Certain standard items are usually included and, for regular meetings, some topics may have been suggested at the last meeting. Anyone who is invited to attend may also be asked for contributions.

The agenda lists the topics in the order they will be discussed. This is helpful because if someone can only attend for a short time, they know when an item will be raised or where they will be expected to contribute.

The agenda is often linked to the notice asking people to attend as this saves sending out two sets of paperwork.

Key terms

Chairperson – the leader of a meeting.

Agenda – a list of items to be discussed at a meeting.

Minutes – the official record of the discussions and decisions taken at the meeting.

Meeting brief – a summary of the main requirements for a meeting.

Did you know?

- An Annual General Meeting (AGM) is a legal requirement for all public limited companies. This is a formal meeting to which all the shareholders are invited (see Unit 1).
- Sometimes a task group is set up to organise a specific event such as an Open Day, and will hold meetings to discuss their plans. Once the event has been held, the task group is disbanded.
- Checklists are useful because you can tick off each item as you complete it, to make sure you don't forget anything.

CONTINUED ▸▸

▸▸ CONTINUED

Did you know?

- When people cannot attend a meeting themselves, they may be able to send a colleague in their place. Whether this is allowed or not should be made clear when they are invited to attend.
- Large organisations usually have a list of approved venues staff must use for meetings. This list is regularly reviewed and the prices and facilities compared as a result of feedback after the event has been held.

Checking dates

Participants in regular meetings usually know when they are expected to attend each time. Sometimes, however, the date of the next meeting is agreed at a meeting, or it may be arranged from scratch. This is more difficult because the meeting should ideally be held when everyone can attend. If this is not possible, you need to identify the key people who must be there for the meeting to achieve its purpose.

For major events where an external venue is to be used, some alternative dates should be suggested at the start because it will not be known whether a suitable venue is available on one particular date.

Confirming the budget

The budget sets the amount of money that can be spent on holding the meeting. Most organisations set a limit, which will vary according to the type of meeting and its size. For a small internal meeting the limit may be coffee/tea and biscuits. A breakfast meeting or working lunch would cost more, although this can be kept down if the catering is done internally or sandwiches are bought locally.

Meetings at an external venue, with several meals and even travel or accommodation reservations are entirely different. The budget must be agreed before any arrangements are made and quotations obtained to ensure the budget is not exceeded.

Activity Controlling meeting costs

Most organisations have procedures staff must follow to control the costs of a meeting. Find out what happens in your centre when someone wants to hold a meeting and wants to include refreshments.

Choosing and booking venues

A meeting can be a disaster if the room is unsuitable or the facilities are poor, so space, heating, lighting, ventilation and sound-proofing are very important. The room must also be clean and tidy and not cluttered with dirty cups and papers from the previous meeting.

Internal meetings are often held in special rooms set aside for that purpose. Large organisations have a board room or committee room. Customised meeting rooms usually contain a large table and several chairs. There may be side tables for refreshments and special facilities for presentations, including blackout blinds if audio/visual equipment is regularly used.

External venues include hotels and conference centres with specialist facilities, such as seminar rooms for group discussions. Some also provide accommodation for overnight guests.

Sending meeting invitations

For a formal meeting a notice may be posted or emailed to everyone who has the right to attend giving details of the date, time and venue. This usually also includes the agenda. Other documents that may be sent include:

- **a copy of the minutes** taken at the last meeting
- **papers or reports** to be discussed at the meeting, so that attendees can read them in advance.

People are often invited to informal meetings by email. In many organisations, administrators use an electronic diary package to book the meeting in people's diaries.

Did you know?

The method(s) used to invite people must be appropriate for the formality of the meeting and the timescale. People may be informed of an urgent informal meeting by text message or phone call, as well as by email.

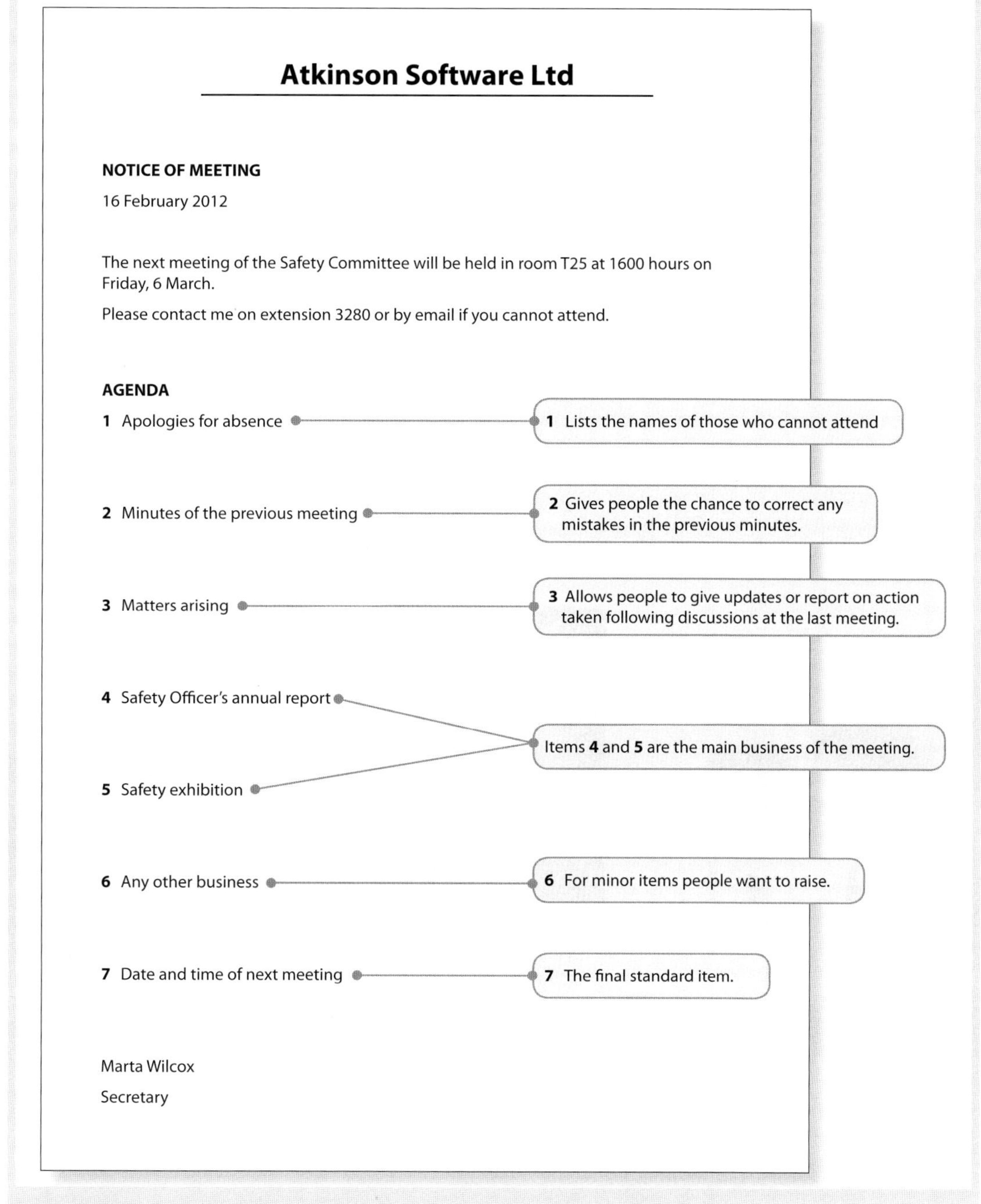

Atkinson Software Ltd

NOTICE OF MEETING

16 February 2012

The next meeting of the Safety Committee will be held in room T25 at 1600 hours on Friday, 6 March.

Please contact me on extension 3280 or by email if you cannot attend.

AGENDA

1 Apologies for absence

2 Minutes of the previous meeting

3 Matters arising

4 Safety Officer's annual report

5 Safety exhibition

6 Any other business

7 Date and time of next meeting

Marta Wilcox

Secretary

Figure 7.4 The notice and agenda is often combined into one document

CONTINUED ▸▸

Arranging catering, equipment and resources

- **Catering requirements** depend on the length and type of meeting, the time of day and the budget. Usually, a hot drink is offered at the start and jugs of water are available on the table. A working lunch may include sandwiches.
- **Basic equipment** includes a whiteboard or flipchart on which to record ideas or decisions. There may be an overhead projector or a laptop/PC and projector so that a PowerPoint presentation can be given. A radio microphone and remote mouse allow the speaker to move around freely. There may be an interactive whiteboard, and/or a video link to an external location.

Activity Researching equipment

Find out the functions and features of the equipment used during meetings at your centre and why each item is used.

Discussion point

Some people think that providing paper, pens, soft drinks, mints and biscuits is a good idea. Others believe it costs too much and people just take advantage of the 'freebies'. What do you think?

- **Resources** include the notice and agenda, notes or minutes from the last meeting and supplementary documents. Discussion groups need notepads, pens and pencils. For external meetings, information packs and name badges are often given to delegates on arrival.

Information packs for delegates

If the meeting is at an external venue, an information pack is usually sent out. This will include a map, showing people how to reach the venue, details of any transport links (such as London Underground lines) and car parking plus information on local accommodation. The pack should state if people attending the meeting are expected to pay for their own accommodation.

What equipment can you identify in this photo?

Confirming attendance and keeping a record

An accurate record must be kept of the people who will be attending a meeting for several reasons.

- Anyone who cannot attend a formal meeting should send apologies in advance. A list is kept of these people and their reason for not attending. This enables the chairperson to check that everyone expected to arrive has done so, and the meeting can start.
- Attendees at a large meeting are normally issued with name badges on arrival. These are prepared after their responses have been received.
- The number of attendees will affect the requirements for refreshments and other resources, from pens to car parking spaces.

Identifying any special requirements

Some attendees may have physical disabilities or an impairment which means they have special requirements, for example:

- wheelchair access to the meeting room and within the room itself
- a signer on the platform for anyone who is deaf
- a hearing loop system for hearing aid users
- paperwork in large print for anyone with limited vision.

You must also ask attendees if they have any special dietary requirements. This is often included on the booking form. You will need to tell the caterer if anyone is vegetarian/vegan or restricted by dietary requirements or cultural/religious beliefs. If you cannot check requirements beforehand, the safest option is a buffet with a good range of salads.

Activity Researching meeting venues

You have been asked to investigate meeting venues in your area for a one-day seminar for 50 staff. The event will start at 9 a.m. and finish at 10 p.m. Three people require accommodation overnight.

In groups, research online to find venues in your area. Check the rooms, equipment and resources plus other facilities including those for disabled attendees. Find out about catering options and calculate the likely cost.

Present your findings to the rest of the class. Then decide which venue provides the best value for money.

Just checking

1 What is a meeting brief and why is it used?
2 Identify four essential items you would need in a meeting room.
3 Explain why a formal meeting should start with apologies for absence.
4 What is meant by the term 'any other business'?

Did you know?

- Some people attending a meeting may need car parking. Often visitor spaces can be pre-booked for attendees.
- At most formal meetings, a minimum number of people must attend for the meeting to go ahead. This number is called the **quorum**.

Key terms

Quorum – the minimum number of people who must be present at a formal meeting to allow official decisions to be made.

Remember

Water and soft drinks are usually served at meetings, not alcoholic drinks.

Supporting meetings and following up meetings

Getting started

The tasks that need to be done during a meeting vary according to the size of the event and where it is being held. What differences do you think there would be between supporting an informal team meeting in the workplace and supporting a formal meeting in a conference centre?

Supporting tasks

Documentation for attendees

It is sensible to have extra copies of everything that was sent to attendees in advance of the meeting, in case people forget to bring them. This includes spare copies of the agenda and also the minutes of the last meeting held by the same group. There will also be sets of documents to be given out at the meeting.

Attendance list

This is a list of everyone expected to attend and is prepared in advance. You also need to keep a list of anyone who contacts you to say that they will not be attending, and the reason.

Checking the room

The room must be set out correctly when people arrive. It is sensible to arrive early to check that the furniture is arranged properly and there are no dirty cups or papers lying around. You need to check that the resources and drinks you ordered have arrived, and that there is somewhere for people to leave coats and umbrellas.

If you have booked an external venue then you should be able to take issues such as cleanliness and equipment for granted, but it is still worth arriving early to check.

What type of problems can occur if you don't check a room in advance?

Checking the equipment

This is essential. You do not want your boss to start an important meeting and find the flipchart has only two pages left, or the radio microphone for the guest speaker is not working and no one can find a replacement. Check every item methodically by switching it on and making sure that it works properly. If someone is giving a PowerPoint® presentation, check the projector is focused and the screen is clearly visible from all parts of the room, even when the sun is shining.

Serving refreshments

Ideally, serve a hot drink before the meeting starts and have jugs of water available so people can help themselves during the meeting. Arrange for the chairperson to pause the meeting if you need to break off when the sandwiches or more hot drinks arrive. Alternatively, ask someone else to help you.

Recording who is present and who is absent

You need to know who is present and who is not. At a large meeting, pass round a piece of paper and ask people to record their names. At a small meeting, the chairperson will check who is present and you must record this. You should already have a list of people who have sent apologies in advance. Add the name of anyone else who is missing and the reason, if known.

Did you know?

- Documents at a meeting are those that are sent out in advance, such as the agenda, and those that are given out (or tabled) at the meeting itself. The term 'tabled' simply means 'put on the table'.
- The reason why minutes of the last meeting are sent with the agenda is so that attendees can check them in advance. Therefore, they don't need to read through them at the meeting, which saves time.

Why is it important that the chairperson and meetings organiser work together?

Agreeing minutes of last meeting

If a meeting is held regularly, everyone must confirm at the start of the meeting that the minutes that were taken at the previous meeting are a correct record. If they contain a minor error, they are changed and approved 'as amended'. They are then signed by the chairperson. If they contain major errors, they must be rewritten and approved on another occasion.

Activity — Role of a chairperson

Research the role of a chairperson at a meeting. Then decide the main attributes of an effective chairperson and share your ideas with the rest of your class.

CONTINUED ▸▸

Taking accurate minutes of the meeting, if appropriate

A record of what is decided is often taken at meetings for the following reasons:

- to ensure that the important points are recorded and circulated promptly
- to remind people what they have agreed to do.

Tips on taking accurate meeting notes

- You must note all essential information, that is:
  - date of the meeting
  - names of those present/those who sent apologies
  - what has been discussed/decided
  - action points (tasks people have agreed to do)
  - date and time of next meeting.
- Rule left- and right-hand margins on an A4 lined pad and write the above information at the top.
- Write the agenda heading, the initials of the speaker in the left margin and a summary of what they say next to it.
- In the right-hand column, put the initials of people who agree to do something.
- Listen carefully to what people are saying.
- Summarise – just write down the main points of what was agreed.
- Don't panic if you miss something. Put an asterisk where the gap is and ask the chairperson for help later.
- Use 'text speak', if it helps.
- Write up your notes promptly, while the discussions are fresh in your memory.
- Use complete sentences and the past tense, i.e. 'Luke said that . . . ', not 'Luke says that'.
- Check you have spelled everyone's name correctly.
- Be prepared to redraft your notes several times.

Follow-up activities

You may think that your job is done once the meeting is finished, but there are several other tasks still to do.

Writing up minutes after the meeting

Write up your minutes promptly, especially if you have any queries, or the chairperson may forget what happened. An example of the minutes of a meeting is given opposite. You should note that:

- the chairperson is listed first and other members are then listed in alphabetical order
- the headings match those in the agenda
- the minutes are written in the past tense and specific dates are given (not 'tomorrow' or 'next year' as this could be confusing)
- the minutes are a summary (details of discussions are not included)
- the action column shows the initials of everyone who agreed to do a task.

Atkinson Software Ltd

MINUTES OF MEETING

A meeting of the Safety Committee was held in room T25 at 1600 hours on Tuesday 6th March 2012.

PRESENT
Annika Hall (Chair)
Uzma Ahmed
David Blunt
Neelam Rani
Marc Salazar (Safety Officer)
Marta Wilcox

		Action
1	**Apologies for absence** Sean Fox sent his apologies.	
2	**Minutes of previous meeting** These were agreed as a true and correct record and signed by the Chairperson.	
3	**Matters arising** David Blunt said he had received a quotation from Brands Electrical for new emergency lighting at a cost of £12,500. He would chase up the two quotes still outstanding.	DB
4	**Safety Officer's annual report** Marc Salazar circulated copies and outlined key items – in particular accident figures which were down 8 per cent from the previous year.	
5	**Safety exhibition** Annika Hall said this would be held at the NEC on 12 and 13 November and suggested two members should attend. Uzma Ahmed and Neelam Rani agreed to do so and to report back at the next meeting.	UA/NR
6	**Any other business** David Blunt said several safety signs had been vandalised at the Northfield Road depot. Marc Salazar agreed to investigate.	MS
7	**Date and time of next meeting** The next meeting will be held at 1600 hours on Friday 6th April 2012.	

Signed .... (Chairperson) Date ....

Figure 7.5 An example of minutes.

CONTINUED ▸▸

▸▸ CONTINUED

Other tasks

Clearing the venue

Always leave the room as you would wish to find it. Check all waste paper is in the bin, the table is clear, equipment is unplugged and tidied away, all spare papers and resources have been collected and the furniture is where it should be. Check, too, that no one has left anything behind.

Why is it particularly important to make sure equipment is put away safely when using an external venue for meetings?

Remember

All documents should be circulated in time for people to carry out the actions they agreed to take before the next meeting.

Circulating documents to attendees

Once the chairperson agrees that your minutes are accurate, you must send them out together with any other documents that were agreed. These are sent to everyone, whether they attended the meeting or not, so that they know what happened and have the information they need for the next meeting.

Did you know?

People who receive the minutes of a meeting usually look first to see where their name appears – and then check what they promised to do.

Monitoring completion of agreed actions

People agree to do things at a meeting for many reasons. They may want to impress their boss or feel they cannot refuse. They may genuinely want to be involved, but then find themselves very busy immediately afterwards. The danger is that action tasks may get forgotten.

For this reason, many administrators keep a separate list of the actions people promised to take. They can then check that progress has been made, and give a gentle reminder if necessary.

Activity — Investigating meeting documents

Look at two or three past agendas, related minutes and meeting papers issued at meetings at your centre (preferably in sequence). In groups, discuss the contents and check how those who attended responded to the different agenda items and action points listed.

Just checking

1. Suggest three reasons why meetings are held.
2. Why is it important to know who cannot attend a meeting?
3. Why is an action column useful in the notes of a meeting?
4. Suggest three tasks you may have to carry out if external visitors were invited to a meeting venue some distance away.

Assessment activity 7.3 *English*

2C.P4 | 2C.P5 | 2C.P6 | 2C.M3 | 2C.M4 | 2C.D2

For this assessment activity, you will form your own meetings group (or groups) and hold a series of meetings. Your first task is to make sure that you do not forget anything when you are organising and supporting these.

1 a) Prepare to organise the first meeting by drawing up a checklist with suitable headings. This should include all the aspects involved in organising and supporting a meeting that you have read about in this unit.

b) Attach to your checklist an explanation of the organisation and support that is required for different types of meetings.

2 When you are personally responsible for organising a group meeting, you will undertake the following tasks:

a) Update your checklist to ensure it includes all specified requirements. You will organise the meeting according to these requirements.

b) Produce accurate documents needed for a meeting, for example the meeting brief and agenda.

c) Take notes during the meeting.

d) Produce accurate and detailed post-meeting documentation, including minutes, for at least one meeting.

e) Provide the support required including follow-up activities when the meeting has ended.

f) Afterwards, reflect on your own contribution. Identify what went well and what did not, and think about what you could have done better at all stages, that is before, during and after the meeting. Prepare a short report, suggesting changes that would enable you to improve your contribution in the future.

Tips

- Prepare your checklist using similar headings to the ones in this book, for example: meeting brief/agenda, dates, budget, venue, equipment and resources, refreshments, documents. You might also find it easier to write about organisation and support under the headings of before, during and after the meeting.
- Identify the difference between formal and informal meetings and those held internally and in an external venue.
- A good way to start thinking about your contribution is to look back at your checklist. Compare what actually happened with what you planned to happen. What differences were there, and why? Then think about everything you have learned since you started. What advice would you give someone who was organising next week's meeting, and why?

In this unit is an activity to help you to prepare for the meetings you will hold. You will find it helpful to read this, and the Workspace case study that follows, before you undertake Assessment Activity 7.3.

▸▸ CONTINUED

Activity — Preparing for meetings

You now need to make some preparations before you hold the first meeting. As a group, decide the focus for your meetings. This could be to hold an event (see suggestions below), to raise money for charity, to form a student council, or your group or teacher/tutor may have some better ideas.

You should now plan the first meeting. Decide when and where it will be held and make any required bookings. Decide what equipment you might need (e.g. a flipchart, projector and computer) and book this. Ask for a volunteer to be meetings organiser the first time. This duty must then be done by everyone in turn.

The meetings organiser should prepare a meeting brief, notice and agenda. The notice will be straightforward. The agenda should be as follows:

1. Apologies
2. Election of chairperson
3. Rota for meetings organiser
4. Main business of meeting (e.g. selection of event, charity to support, role of student council)
5. Any other business
6. Time and date of next meeting

The first item must be done properly. Anyone unable to attend must send apologies to the meetings organiser beforehand, together with a reason.

Your group must decide a fair way to elect a chairperson. You might want to start by thinking of the qualities a good chairperson would need. Note the chairperson has the casting vote if there are any later disagreements.

The main item of business should be the key focus. Don't be too ambitious or plan to spend any money unless you know how to raise some. The meetings should be held over the next two to three months, which should give you some idea of the time you have available.

If you can't reach a decision at the first meeting, everyone should be asked to go away to think about other options, check ideas with family members and report back at the next meeting. This is what happens at many business meetings!

Finally, ask if anyone has anything to raise under AOB. The meetings organiser must then prepare the notes and circulate them, and all participants must carry out any agreed action before the next meeting.

Event suggestions include:

- A one- or two-hour workshop with visiting speakers
- An away day for the group as a whole
- A quiz event with prizes
- A visit to an interesting local business
- A mini conference lasting half a day with various activities.

It is even better if you can choose an event that will help you with other aspects of your course.

WorkSpace

Caroline Gooder

Engineering Administrator, Cummins Turbo Technologies

Cummins is a large, global organisation which employs over 1000 people in Huddersfield, West Yorkshire. It produces Holset turbochargers which improve the efficiency of an engine, and sells these mainly to large truck makers. More than 350 engineers are employed in the Engineering Department where Caroline works.

Caroline's boss is Joanne Worthington, the Engineering Global Capacity Project Leader, but she also provides administrative support to the seven engineering directors and other departmental staff.

Caroline's role includes dealing with visitors, organising travel and accommodation, organising and supporting meetings and producing documents. She organises two different types of meetings: the monthly staff meeting of the directors, and the site facilities meeting with the engineering staff. She books the meeting rooms, prepares and issues the agenda and takes the minutes. Refreshments are only arranged if external clients are present. Caroline types the minutes on a laptop in the meeting room. The image is projected on screen so that the directors can comment on items as she types them. At the end of each section Caroline notes any action required in bold type.

The meeting rooms also have conference call phones with a speaker, so that other Cummins staff can be involved in any discussions. In addition to the projector, there is also an electronic whiteboard.

Caroline's most essential item of equipment is her computer. She uses this to communicate by email, rather than telephone. Cummins has its own instant messaging (IM) service which enables her to talk to Cummins staff all over the world when they are travelling on business. The company has a policy of being paper-free so all information is held on the computer system and only printed out when absolutely necessary.

Think about it

1. What equipment does Caroline find the most useful, and why?
2. Cummins' engineers travel to many places, including China. What will Caroline have to consider before she tries to talk to someone visiting Shanghai?
3. Suggest two reasons why an interactive whiteboard is useful in a meeting room.
4. Why do you think Cummins only provides refreshments at meetings when there are external visitors?
5. Suggest three benefits for Cummins of having a paper-free policy.

Introduction

In this unit, you will learn how businesses are structured, or organised, so that people can do their jobs effectively. All businesses need to carry out certain functions and these are usually represented by specific departments, such as sales, finance and production. You will find out about different job roles and how the structure of the organisation can affect these.

All functions within an organisation are important but one key area is human resources (HR) which is responsible for ensuring the best person is recruited for each job vacancy. You will learn about the documents that inform candidates about a specific vacancy and the correct way to apply for a job. You will prepare for, and attend, a job interview and carry out a personal audit to produce your own career development plan.

Assessment: This unit will be assessed through a series of assignments set by your teacher/tutor.

Learning aims

In this unit you will:

A know about job roles and functional areas in business

B produce documentation for specific job roles

C demonstrate interview skills and plan career development.

I am really interested in this unit because one day I will be applying for jobs. I want to find out about different job roles and how businesses decide what sort of candidate they want when they have a vacancy. Knowing what they look for when people apply for a job will help me to make a good impression and do well in an interview.

Harry, *16-year-old Business student*

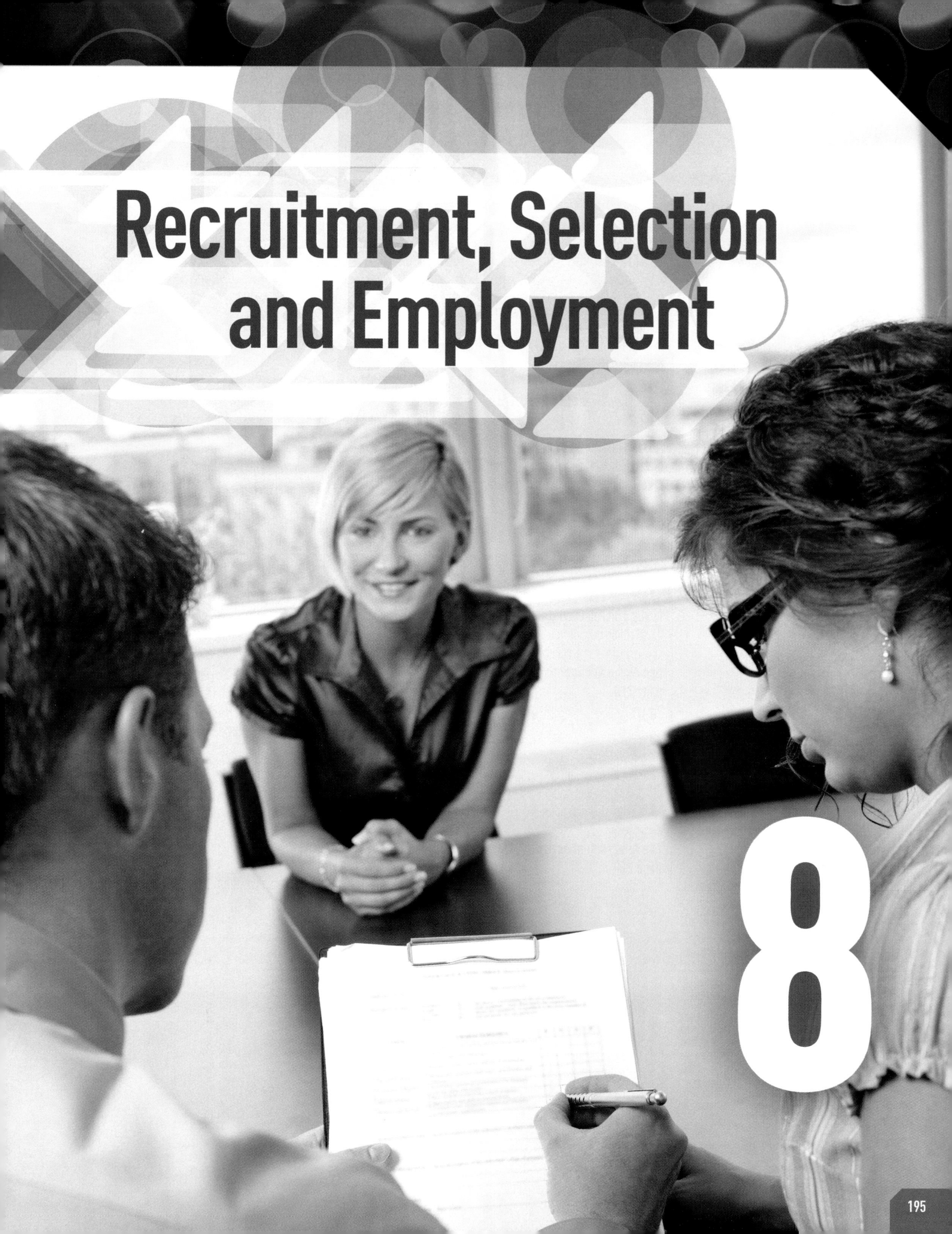

Recruitment, Selection and Employment

8

This table shows you what you must do in order to achieve a **Pass**, **Merit** or **Distinction** grade, and where you can find activities in this book to help you.

Assessment criteria			
Level 1	Level 2 **Pass**	Level 2 **Merit**	Level 2 **Distinction**
Learning aim A: Know about job roles and functional areas in business			
1A.1 Describe the purpose of two functional areas in two contrasting businesses	**2A.P1** Explain the purpose of different functional areas in two contrasting businesses **See Assessment activity 8.1, page 207**	**2A.M1** Compare two job roles and responsibilities from different functional areas in two contrasting businesses **See Assessment activity 8.1, page 207**	**2A.D1** Analyse the impact of organisational structure on job roles and functional areas in a selected business, using appropriate examples **See Assessment activity 8.1, page 207**
1A.2 Identify the responsibilities of two different job roles in a selected business	**2A.P2** Describe the responsibilities of two different job roles in two contrasting businesses **See Assessment activity 8.1, page 207**		
Learning aim B: Produce documentation for specific job roles			
1B.3 English Produce a job description for a specific job	**2B.P3** English Produce an appropriate and detailed job description and person specification for a specific job **See Assessment activity 8.2, page 218**	**2B.M2** English Produce an appropriate and detailed job description and person specification for a specific job, justifying why the documents will encourage effective recruitment **See Assessment activity 8.2, page 218**	**2B.D2** Analyse gaps in knowledge and skills that might require further training or development to match the requirements of a given person specification and job description **See Assessment activity 8.2, page 218**
1B.4 English Produce, with guidance, a curriculum vitae and letter of application to apply for a suitable job role	**2B.P4** English Produce a curriculum vitae, letter of application and completed application form to apply for a suitable job role **See Assessment activity 8.2, page 218**	**2B.M3** Justify how current knowledge and skills meet those required in a given person specification and job description **See Assessment activity 8.2, page 218**	

Assessment criteria			
Level 1	Level 2 **Pass**	Level 2 **Merit**	Level 2 **Distinction**
Learning aim C: Demonstrate interview skills and plan career development			
1C.5 English Provide some appropriate responses to interview questions for a specific job role	**2C.P5** English Provide appropriate responses to interview questions for a specific job role. **See Assessment activity 8.3, page 223**	**2C.M4** English Demonstrate prior research and preparation when providing appropriate responses to interview questions for a specific job role **See Assessment activity 8.3, page 223**	**2C.D3** Evaluate the suitability of a realistic career development plan using interview performance feedback and own reflection **See Assessment activity 8.3, page 223**
1C.6 English Produce, with guidance, a personal career development plan	**2C.P6** English Produce a realistic personal career development plan **See Assessment activity 8.3, page 223**	**2C.M5** English Produce a realistic personal career development plan showing independent research and planning **See Assessment activity 8.3, page 223**	

English Opportunity to practise English skills

How you will be assessed

This unit will be assessed by a series of internally assessed tasks. These will enable you to demonstrate that you understand how functional areas and job roles can differ between organisations. You will prepare a job description and job specification and apply for a suitable job role. You will attend an interview and produce your own career development plan.

Your assessment could be in the form of:

- a leaflet or presentation in which you explain the differences between two contrasting organisations
- a recruitment pack that you prepare for candidates
- your own application for a suitable job role and attendance at an interview
- your career development plan with reasons for the items you have included.

TOPIC A.1

Organisational structures and functional areas

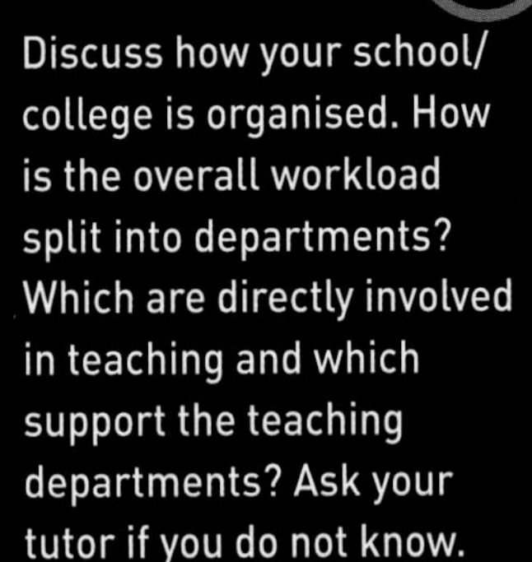

Getting started

Discuss how your school/college is organised. How is the overall workload split into departments? Which are directly involved in teaching and which support the teaching departments? Ask your tutor if you do not know.

Introduction

In all businesses, whether large or small, it is important to **coordinate** staff job roles so that everyone contributes to the overall purpose of the business and work is not duplicated unnecessarily.

Key term

Coordinate – work together in an organised and complementary way so that everyone can do their job more easily and efficiently.

Understanding organisational structures

All organisations need some form of structure. Having specific job roles means each person knows what they are responsible for doing. At a medical practice, for example, there may be doctors, nurses, a practice manager, office staff, receptionists and cleaners. Their responsibilities are different, but together they ensure the practice is run efficiently.

In most businesses, staff are divided into different groups. At your school or college, there are teaching and support staff. The way an organisation is structured depends on its size and type.

Hierarchical structures

Large organisations may have several levels of managers and supervisors. Staff have specific job roles and only carry out tasks related to their own role. There may be fixed rules and procedures and little scope for staff to use creativity and imagination. Examples include the army, local government and large supermarket chains such as Sainsbury's.

Flat structures

Flat structures have only two or three levels, for example a recruitment agency with one manager, several interviewers and a few support staff. Flat structures are used when staff need little supervision. Many creative businesses prefer this structure as staff can exchange ideas more easily.

Figure 8.1 Hierarchical organisation structure

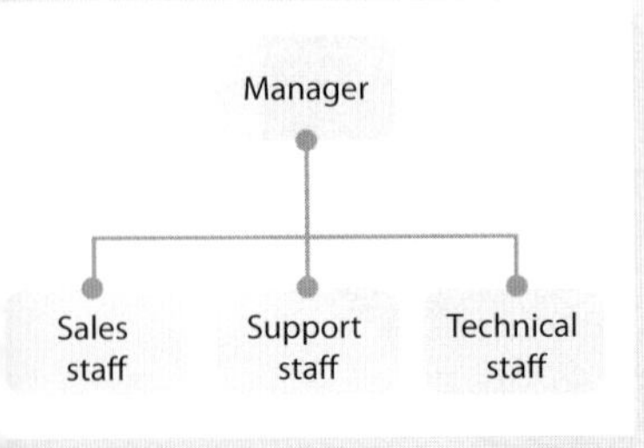

Figure 8.2 Flat organisation structure

Matrix structures

This structure is used when a business is involved with major projects such as building hospitals or installing large IT systems. Each project is undertaken by a team controlled by a project leader. All teams are supported by the departments who provide specialised services such as finance and human resources (HR). When a project is completed, the team is disbanded and assigned to a new one.

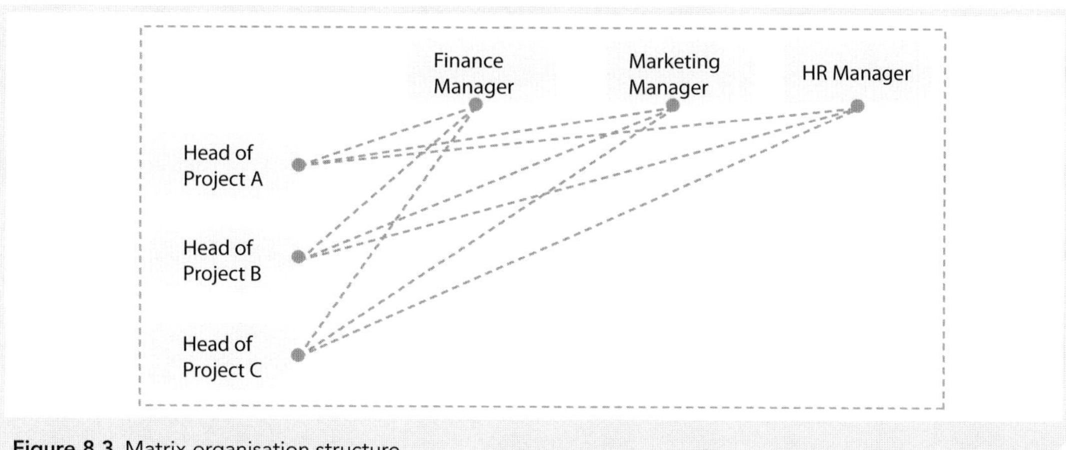

Figure 8.3 Matrix organisation structure

Did you know?

- The plane manufacturer Airbus employs 10,000 people at its factories in Filton near Bristol and Broughton in North Wales. Each person plays a part in the overall purpose of the business.
- A hierarchical structure is shaped like a pyramid because there are fewer staff at the top than at the bottom.

Functional structures

Many organisations are divided into functional areas, each based on one aspect of the organisation's overall purpose, such as finance, marketing or HR, as you will see later in this unit.

In other organisations, some of the main functions may be different and this affects what the areas are called. For example, airport functions include air traffic control, security, retail, catering and baggage handling.

Activity — Identifying different functions

Divide into groups and research the type of functions carried out by hospitals, hotels and newspapers (or magazines). Then compare your results.

Divisional structures

Some businesses structure their operations into different divisions, based on location, type of customers, what they do, or a combination of these.

Many international organisations, for example Kraft Foods, are structured by geographical area, such as the Americas, the Middle East, Asia/the Pacific and Europe. Other businesses focus on their products, for example, Alliance Boots has two divisions: Health and Beauty and Pharmaceutical Wholesale operations.

Just checking

1. What does the term 'organisation structure' mean?
2. Identify four types of organisation structure you may find in business.
3. Describe the main differences between a hierarchical organisation and a flat structure.

TOPIC A.1

Functional areas

Introduction

Many business organisations are divided into functional areas, each specialising in a group of related tasks. Some of these activities are undertaken by all businesses, such as finance, sales and HR, whereas others vary. Only a manufacturer has a production department.

Sales

Businesses earn money by selling goods and services and this is the function of the sales staff. Their responsibilities include:

- meeting or telephoning customers to promote goods and services
- responding to customer enquiries and providing technical information and advice
- preparing quotations or estimates; negotiating discounts or financial terms
- organising sales promotions and other events and keeping customer records up to date.

Discussion point

Hairdressing suppliers such as GHD, Matrix and Paul Mitchell call on salons regularly to promote and sell their products. Discuss the benefits and drawbacks of this method of selling, both for the supplier and the customer.

In what situations is it possible to negotiate a discount?

Did you know?

Quality assurance involves keeping a tight control on incoming materials and production processes to avoid producing reject products.

Production

Production is the key activity of all manufacturing businesses. Some focus on manufacturing the components that are used in the finished product, others assemble the components. Their responsibilities include:

- planning production schedules to maximise the use of available equipment
- producing or assembling the product and checking quality throughout the process to avoid producing any rejects
- resolving any delays or problems
- routinely inspecting and maintaining production machinery.

Activity Investigating production processes

In groups, research the difference between **job, batch and flow** production processes. Then find an example of each on YouTube. Products could include. crisps, bread, cars, fizzy drinks, submarines, cosmetics, paper, chocolate, glass and cruise liners. You decide which is which!

Purchasing

The purchasing department is responsible for buying materials and components for production, consumables such as stationery and small capital items such as office furniture and computers. Their responsibilities include:

- obtaining raw materials, stock and consumable items from approved suppliers
- evaluating suppliers and negotiating to obtain the best value for the business
- resolving any supply or quality problems and chasing late deliveries
- taking account of customer needs and current fashions and trends in the case of retail buyers (see Zara case study).

Did you know?

- A quotation is a price which the supplier is bound to keep to, but an estimate is an indication of cost which could change.
- The term 'supply chain' is sometimes used to describe each stage of the process from goods leaving a factory to arriving in a store.

Administration

Administrators carry out a variety of support activities in order to help business operations run smoothly. Senior administrators may also monitor budgets and interview new staff for their departments. Their responsibilities include:

- dealing with incoming and outgoing mail and telephone messages; receiving visitors
- organising, storing and retrieving paper and electronic records
- making travel arrangements and organising events such as conferences and interviews
- organising meetings and preparing meetings documents
- preparing and distributing documents by post and electronically.

Customer service

Customer service staff assist customers who have an enquiry, concern or complaint. Customer service staff must be helpful, personable and aware of customers' legal rights. Their responsibilities include:

- providing specialist information and advice about products and services
- responding to complaints and solving customers' problems
- supplying spare parts, arranging for repairs and replacing damaged goods
- giving feedback to departments to improve service and satisfaction
- ensuring the business complies with consumer laws.

Discussion point

Many customer service staff help customers who use the company's website to buy goods. Discuss the additional skills that these staff will need to help customers who are having problems ordering goods online.

▸▸ CONTINUED

Distribution

Distribution ensures that finished goods are delivered to the right place, on time and in the right condition. Their responsibilities include:

- storing and labelling goods correctly before despatch
- completing delivery documents, loading vehicles safely and despatching on an agreed date
- scheduling vehicle routes to minimise overall journey time
- dealing with problems, such as delays due to vehicle breakdown
- completing any required paperwork for shipping goods abroad.

Activity Delivering just in time

Some manufacturers such as car makers ask for deliveries to be made in a narrow time slot called 'just in time'. This system is designed to keep the stock of components to a minimum. Suggest two benefits of doing this.

Finance

There are two main tasks undertaken by finance: providing information to help managers run the business (management accounting), and keeping accurate records of financial transactions undertaken by the business (financial accounting). Their responsibilities include:

- preparing and sending invoices and checking that correct payments are received
- checking and paying invoices received
- preparing the payroll and ensuring staff are paid correctly and on time
- producing departmental budgets and budget reports
- producing cash flow forecasts and other financial reports
- producing the annual statutory accounts (including the profit and loss account and balance sheet).

Human resources (HR)

Discussion point

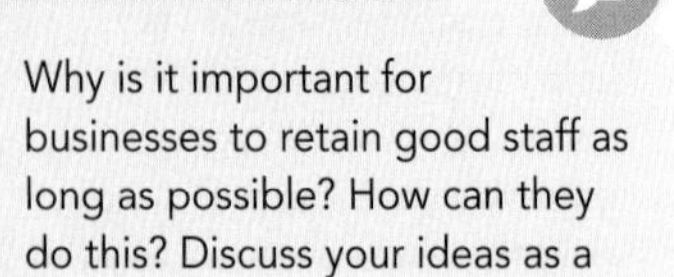

Why is it important for businesses to retain good staff as long as possible? How can they do this? Discuss your ideas as a group.

The human resources (HR) of a business are its employees. HR staff are responsible for all aspects of recruitment and training. Their responsibilities include:

- advertising job vacancies and promotion opportunities, dealing with job applications and arranging interviews
- issuing a contract of employment to new staff and arranging induction
- maintaining staff records including leave entitlement and absenteeism due to sickness
- arranging staff training and development activities
- checking health and safety and keeping accident records
- liaising with staff associations or trade unions
- ensuring compliance with current employment legislation.

ICT (Information and Communications Technology)

Even small businesses today have a computer system or network and most also have a website. The ICT department's responsibilities include:

- maintaining current computer systems and software
- advising on and installing updates, upgrades and new equipment and software (including maintaining security against viruses and hackers)
- training and assisting users
- maintaining the company website in conjunction with the marketing department
- operating a backup system so that critical data can be restored quickly.

What other ways can you think of to advertise a product?

Marketing

Marketing is all about identifying and meeting customer needs and promoting products to potential customers. The responsibilities of the marketing department include:

- conducting market research to obtain customer views on products and services
- summarising market research findings to managers and designers
- promoting products and services by advertising and promotional methods (press, TV, online, direct mail, sponsorship and trade shows), and coordinating publicity campaigns
- producing and distributing leaflets and catalogues
- designing, updating and promoting the company website.

Research and development (R & D)

Research, development and design are three stages in bringing a new or adapted product to the market. The responsibilities of people working in this area include:

- identifying future customer needs, and keeping up to date with technological and scientific developments through research
- developing outline drawings together with a model and/or a prototype for any new products
- designing detailed drawings and specifications so that the item can be produced.

Did you know?

- Induction programmes aim to familiarise new employees quickly with the company, what it does and its rules and procedures.
- Beyoncé and Jay-Z applied to patent their baby's name, Blue Ivy, to stop anyone else from using it. Normally patents are used to prevent people copying new product ideas.
- The pharmaceutical (drugs) industry spends billions of pounds on R & D, yet only 1 in 10,000 potential drugs actually reach the market.

Activity — Researching functions

With the agreement of your teacher/tutor, arrange to research functional areas in a local business. Divide into groups and prepare to interview someone who is involved with marketing, HR, finance, ICT and administration. Prepare questions in advance and then present your findings to the rest of the class.

Just checking

1. Why would you find a production department only in some businesses?
2. What is the difference between the sales department and the marketing department?
3. Why is the finance department so important?
4. What is the main function of the HR department?

TOPIC A.1

Purposes of functional areas and links between them

Getting started

Most businesses aim to make a profit, but not all of them. Your school or college is one example. Can you suggest three other types of organisation with aims other than making a profit?

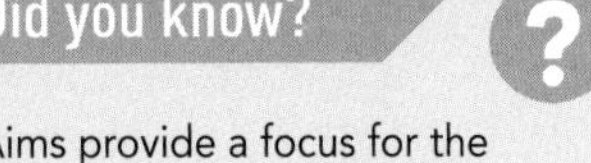

Did you know?

Aims provide a focus for the business. They may include providing excellent service, growing in size or simply surviving if times are hard. Objectives are targets that help the business to achieve its aims.

Supporting business aims and objectives

The purpose of functional areas is to ensure that vital business activities are carried out promptly and efficiently so that the business achieves its aims and objectives. Specific areas support certain types of aims and objectives.

- Sales and marketing are involved achieving targets linked to developing new markets or increasing sales.
- R & D and production are involved developing new products and may use feedback from sales, marketing or customer service.
- ICT maintains communication links between different functional areas.
- Finance supports financial targets such as keeping costs low and monitoring budgets.

Links between functional areas

No functional area in a business organisation can work in isolation. In a small firm, people responsible for different functions usually interact informally and on a continuous basis. Sales staff know which customers pay their bills promptly and which ones still owe money. Managers know, without being told, which members of staff are hard-working. A customer query can be answered quickly by asking others in the office for advice. In a larger organisation, people may work in separate areas and rarely meet each other, but they still need information and support to work effectively. The main departmental links in an organisation are shown in Table 8.1.

Table 8.1 Information flows between functional areas

Functional areas	Examples of links with...
Sales	production about delivery dates for customers finance about customer credit ratings, discounts or late payments marketing about sales promotions
Production	purchasing about raw materials required sales if there are delays or production problems
Purchasing	finance to confirm that deliveries are received
Distribution	sales/customer service if there are delivery problems finance to confirm deliveries are despatched so invoices can be sent
HR	all departments about staff vacancies and training finance about salary increases and bonuses
R & D	production, marketing and customer service about new or adapted products
Finance	all departments about budgets and financial targets
ICT	all departments about maintenance or security
Administration	all departments whenever information is required or to organise meetings between departments.

Case study

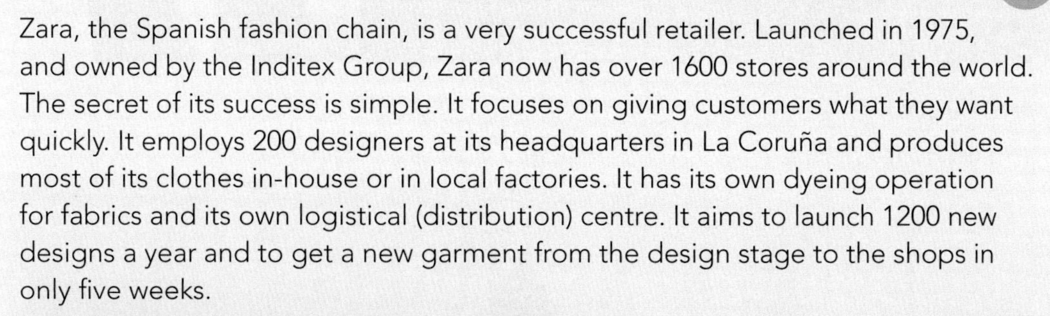

Zara, the Spanish fashion chain, is a very successful retailer. Launched in 1975, and owned by the Inditex Group, Zara now has over 1600 stores around the world. The secret of its success is simple. It focuses on giving customers what they want quickly. It employs 200 designers at its headquarters in La Coruña and produces most of its clothes in-house or in local factories. It has its own dyeing operation for fabrics and its own logistical (distribution) centre. It aims to launch 1200 new designs a year and to get a new garment from the design stage to the shops in only five weeks.

Zara does not have a hierarchical structure because it wants decisions to be made quickly. This is not possible if there are many levels of managers. Store managers and staff compile new orders quickly, based on demand in their own store. Twice a week, customers can expect new deliveries in the stores, all located in prime locations.

Find out more about the company and see what it would be like to work in one of its stores by visiting Pearson hotlinks. You can access this by going to www.pearsonhotlinks.co.uk and searching for this title.

1 Identify two main aims Zara has.

2 Identify how design, production, distribution and the retail stores all contribute towards achieving Zara's aims and objectives.

3 Unlike many fashion retailers, Zara has not **outsourced** its production to Asia to save money. Instead, it keeps control over its supply chain from design to distribution. What does it gain by doing this?

4 How does Zara's organisation structure benefit **a)** its operations, **b)** its customers?

5 Zara stores are in expensive prime locations, yet it spends less on advertising than most of its competitors. Suggest two reasons for this strategy.

Key term

Outsource – hire an outside firm to do a task, such as distributing goods or installing an ICT system.

TOPIC A.2

Job roles and responsibilities

Introduction

In most large organisations, staff are employed at several different levels.

Figure 8.4 Job roles at different organisational levels

Key terms

Policy – the general direction which the business wants to move in.

Strategy – how the business intends to achieve its objectives.

Supervisor – the person who works above you and who gives you instructions. You are his or her 'subordinate'.

What do people at these levels do?

Table 8.2 Job roles and responsibilities you may find at each level

Job role	Responsibilities	This involves...
Director	Looking after shareholders' interests Deciding **policy** or **strategy**	Deciding where the business is going Agreeing how it should get there Being successful so shareholders get a good return on their investment
Manager	Motivating staff, setting targets Recruiting and dismissing staff Allocating work, communicating Planning and decision making Problem solving	Focusing on the objectives their department must achieve Organising the work to produce the required results Quickly solving any problems that may prevent this
Supervisor and team leader	Managing operatives Motivating staff Allocating tasks	Allocating work and checking it is being done Solving day-to-day problems
Operational and support staff/assistant	Day-to-day general work or clerical duties	Completing tasks on time and to the right quality standards

Impact on roles of different organisational structures

Zara does not want a hierarchical structure because it wants staff to be able to make rapid decisions about stock (see case study). Many retail chains make these types of decision at head office, and this is an example of how organisational structures can impact on different job roles. Other examples are given in Table 8.3.

Table 8.3 The impact of organisational structure on job roles

Structure	Impact
Small firm/ flat structure	Usually informal, all staff may undertake different tasks, be expected to work flexibly and make suggestions. No specific functional areas – staff roles cover main functions required. Owner/ manager undertakes a wide range of tasks and is known to all staff.
Matrix structure	Team members report to team leader who is responsible for the success of a project. Some members may belong to more than one team.
Hierarchical structure	More formal, specific job roles, salary grades and rules. Training programmes provided for staff. Instructions from above are passed on by managers and supervisors. There is less flexibility and permission is required to make major changes.

Did you know?

- The number of staff a manager is responsible for is called their '**span of control**'. Normally this is between eight and twelve. It is easier to supervise staff doing routine operations, such as packing, than complex or varied jobs.
- You can find out about the organisational structure and the responsibilities of different job holders in many large businesses by looking at the careers section of their website.

Assessment activity 8.1

2A.P1 | 2A.P2 | 2A.M1 | 2A.D1

You have been asked to contribute to a local careers exhibition by preparing an information leaflet on functional areas and job roles in business.Your leaflet will also show how the organisational structure can affect job roles and functional areas. You may work in small groups to research specific businesses, but the information leaflet you produce must be all your own work.

Prepare for this task by choosing two contrasting businesses. Find out the titles of their functional areas, the work they do and how they link with each other. Then investigate the organisational structure of each business. You might find it helpful to draw charts to illustrate these.Then investigate two different job roles in each organisation. Make sure they are from different functional areas so they are easier to compare. Find out the responsibilities of each job holder.

- Start your leaflet by explaining the purpose of the different functional areas in each business. If one of your businesses is too small to have functional areas, explain the main functions carried out by different employees.
- Identify and describe the responsibilities of two different job roles in each business.
- In a separate section, compare two job roles and responsibilities. They should be in different functional areas and different businesses.
- For one of the businesses you have investigated, analyse the impact of the organisational structure on both the job roles and functional areas. Use appropriate examples from your research to provide evidence for your conclusions.

Tip

You will find this activity easier if your two businesses are totally different, for example a small charity and a large retailer, or a large manufacturing organisation and a small service provider such as a solicitor or estate agent.

Recruitment

Getting started

Discuss why obtaining the best person for a job is so important, and what can go wrong if a bad decision is made.

Why vacancies arise in a business

There are several reasons why vacancies arise:

- **An employee leaves:** People may retire, move away from the area or find a job which suits them better, pays more or involves less travel.
- **High staff turnover:** This can happen if working conditions are poor, the hours are long or the wages are lower than at similar companies.
- **Extra work:** As businesses expand, they often need extra staff. This can include managers and supervisors as well as support staff.
- **Sickness:** If staff members are ill and need to stay off work for some time, temporary cover may be needed to ensure their work is done.
- **Different job roles required:** If a business starts to carry out new types of work, then job roles will change.
- **Maternity and paternity cover:** Maternity leave enables expectant mothers to take up to 12 months' leave; new fathers can have up to two weeks' leave. Parents of young children can apply for parental leave. Employers can fill these vacancies on a temporary basis.

Ways of recruiting staff

Businesses can fill a vacancy in several ways:

Jobcentre Plus: This is a government-funded service that accepts job advertisements by phone or email. They focus on helping people who are unemployed to find work.

Consultants: They specialise in filling senior positions that need someone with specialist skills and experience. Some are called 'headhunters' because they try to poach top executives from one company to work for another.

Why is it important to ask all candidates the same questions?

Recruitment agencies: They advertise permanent and temporary vacancies on behalf of their business clients, who only pay a fee if a permanent vacancy is filled. Temporary staff ('temps') are usually paid by the agency which charges the client a higher rate.

From within the business itself: This happens if there are suitable internal applicants who can apply for promotion. The business must still follow a proper recruitment procedure to ensure equal opportunities for all applicants.

Advertising: Many businesses advertise vacancies, which may involve posting them online at sites such as Fish4jobs, or advertising them in a local or national newspaper or relevant trade journal.

Activity — Investigating Jobcentre Plus and recruitment agencies

Find out more about Jobcentre Plus by visiting Pearson hotlinks. You can access this by going to www.pearsonhotlinks.co.uk and searching for this title.

Research some recruitment agencies (either locally or online) to find out what kind of vacancies they advertise.

Types of recruitment

The first decision the business must make is whether to recruit from within the organisation (internal), or to look outside (external) for applicants. There are advantages and disadvantages to both methods, as shown in Table 8.4.

Table 8.4 Advantages and disadvantages of internal and external recruitment

Recruitment option	Advantages	Disadvantages
Internal	• Candidates' strengths and weaknesses are known. • Cheaper to advertise. • Vacancy can be filled more quickly. • Staff see that there are opportunities for advancement.	• Only suitable when there is a potential promotion involved. • The person appointed is unlikely to bring fresh ideas to the job. • It still leaves a job to fill within the company as the internal candidate must be replaced.
External	• External person has outside experience and new ideas. • Suitable for basic level jobs where there is no promotion opportunity.	• Not easy to judge applicants – some people are good at selling themselves at interview. • May not fit into the existing team. • May take time to fill vacancy. • New employees may need training.

Cost and legal considerations

- **Cost:** The costs involved depend on the method of recruitment. An agency advertises and carries out preliminary interviews, but charges a fee if they provide a candidate who is appointed. If the business itself carries out the recruitment tasks, costs involve staff time preparing the documentation and interviewing, and paying for press advertising. For some vacancies, travelling expenses may be paid to candidates.
- **Legal considerations:** By law, all applicants must be treated fairly and equally at all stages of recruitment. A business can ensure this happens, by only allowing candidates who meet an essential list of requirements to be interviewed. All applicants must be asked the same questions at the interview.

Activity — Researching equal opportunities policies

Find out about the equal opportunities policies at your centre to ensure all staff and learners are treated fairly.

Just checking

1 Identify four reasons why a vacancy may occur in a business.
2 Why must all candidates be treated in the same way?
3 Identify two advantages and two disadvantage of filling a job vacancy with an internal candidate.

Did you know?

- Some businesses are busier at certain times of the year. For example, many retail stores recruit extra staff on temporary contracts over Christmas, and some holiday companies recruit temporary staff over the summer months.
- Online recruitment saves money. Advertisements in the press are expensive, but promoting vacancies on the company website is free.
- In the UK it is unlawful to treat someone differently or unfairly because of gender, race, disability, age, religion and beliefs, sexual orientation or transsexuality.

TOPIC B.2 B.3 B.4

Job descriptions and person specifications

Introduction

Job descriptions and person specifications help applicants to understand more about a potential job, and therefore help to prevent unsuitable applications that would waste people's time.

Key terms

Job description – a statement that lists the main elements of a job and the tasks done by the job holder.

Person specification – linked to the job description, it states the skills and abilities needed to do the job effectively.

Did you know?

When someone is leaving, businesses often review the job role and update the duties to include any new requirements.

Job descriptions and person specifications can be developed in several ways.

- **By department:** Staff in the department where the vacancy arises may prepare a description of what the job entails. This allows departmental staff to contribute ideas and suggestions.
- **By job holder:** The current job holder may list the tasks and duties that are involved. The benefit is that this person will know the job better than anyone, but may exaggerate some of the tasks or duties!
- **By interview:** The job holder may be interviewed to find out what is involved. This enables their views to be considered, but also allows for extra input by a specialist. This is useful if the business wants to change or update the job role.

Contents of a job description

A **job description** summarises the main facts about a job. It helps an applicant to understand exactly what type of work they will be asked to do. An example is shown in Figure 8.5.

SAFETY FIRST LTD – JOB DESCRIPTION	
Job title	Customer Services Team Member
Contract type	Permanent
Location	Main Street, Danesbury DN3 9JL
Description of business	Safety First provides safety equipment and protective clothing.
Purpose of job	To ensure all customers are satisfied with the products and service they receive.
Main tasks	Answering customer queries by phone and email; processing customer orders; informing customers about any issues with their orders; resolving customer problems; processing refunds; updating customer records; liaising with other team members.
Hours of work	37.5 hours per week
Pay and benefits	£12,000 – £13,500 per annum
Promotion prospects	After appropriate training and experience, the successful candidate may be eligible for promotion to Team Leader.
Lines of reporting Responsible to: Responsible for:	 Customer Services Team Leader N/A

Figure 8.5 A job description for a customer service team member

Contents of a person specification

A **person specification** lists the essential and desirable qualifications, skills and attributes of the person required. Applicants chosen for interview are normally those who have all the essential requirements and several of the desirable ones, too.

Depending upon the vacancy, the person specification may include information on:

- attainments, e.g. qualifications, membership of professional bodies
- competency profiles, e.g. what the candidate should be able to do
- special aptitudes or skills, e.g. numeracy, problem solving
- essential and desirable attributes, e.g. previous relevant experience and product knowledge, relevant interests
- disposition, e.g. leadership qualities
- circumstances, e.g. whether mobile or not.

SAFETY FIRST LTD – PERSON SPECIFICATION		
Department	Customer Service	
Job title	Customer Services Team Member	
Vacancy no.	474	
	Essential	**Desirable**
Attainments	Educated to GCSE level	Level 2 Business or
	IT literate	Customer Service qualification
Competency profile	Can deal effectively with customers	Able to use database software
	Can contribute to the work of the team	
Special aptitudes	Good communication skills	Good numeracy skills
Disposition	Good organisational skills	Calm and patient
	Friendly personality	

Figure 8.6 A person specification for a Customer Services Team Member

Activity — Identifying attributes

1 In groups, identify two jobs where each of the following attributes would be important: **a)** high level of qualifications; **b)** good at maths; **c)** interest in animals; **d)** ability to travel; **e)** patience; **f)** good IT skills. Compare your ideas.

2 Research job descriptions and person specifications online for vacancies in large companies such as Boots and Marks & Spencer. Expect them to vary in layout and content.

Assessment activity 8.2 — Preparation

Research job vacancies that would appeal to, and be relevant to you. You can use printed and online sources, or your own experience if you have a part-time job. Find out as much information as possible about the organisations and how the jobs contribute to the overall purpose of the businesses.

You are working in a business and need to draft an appropriate and detailed job description and person specification for your chosen job. To encourage effective recruitment, check that the essential and desirable requirements are appropriate for the candidates you want to attract.

Keep your documents safely. You will use them again when you complete Assessment activity 8.2.

Applying for jobs

Introduction

Businesses vary in the way they advertise jobs and in their application process. You may have to request a job description and person specification, or they may be available online. You may be required to complete an application form, or send your CV and a covering letter of application.

Application forms

Although these are important documents, many applicants make careless mistakes, from incorrect spellings to missing out important information. This may mean they are immediately eliminated from the application process.

Table 8.5 Dos and don'ts when completing an application form

Do...	Don't...
... print out (or photocopy) the form to practise on	... complete the original until your practice form is perfect
... read the form through first	... try to do it in a rush
... collect all important information, e.g. examination results, before you start	... guess anything important, such as grades or dates
... check whether you must use a black pen, or can submit the form online	... use an old pen that might put blobs of ink on the form
... check where you should use block capitals	... write your town or postcode in the wrong place
... write neatly and think about what you are doing	... put the current year for your date of birth
... check whether you need to include names of referees	... include someone's name without permission
... use the space for answers wisely	... make any spelling errors
... check where you need to sign and date the form	... complete any section marked 'for official use'
... ask someone to help you check the form	... sulk if they criticise anything
... proofread the form carefully	... cross out errors – use a tiny amount of correction fluid
... make a copy before you post it.	... attend an interview without rereading the form.

Activity Completing an application form

Many sample application forms are available online. Print one out, complete it and ask your tutor to check you have done it correctly.

Curriculum vitae

A curriculum vitae (CV) is a summary about you and your achievements. It must look professional and be printed on good-quality white A4 paper. It should be quite short – one or two pages at the most – and divided into sections under clear headings to include the following information.

- **Your personal details:** Your name, address, phone number and email address are vital. Your date of birth is optional.
- **Your education:** Put this in date order with your most recent qualification or course first. Include your school or college, dates attended, qualifications obtained, or examinations where you are still awaiting the result.

Activity Preparing a profile

Some people start their CV with their name and then write a brief personal profile. This short, opening statement summarises their strengths to attract the reader's attention. Read some examples online and try doing it yourself. Then compare statements to see whose are best.

- **Your work history:** This should be in date order, with the most recent job first. Include part-time or temporary jobs you have undertaken, giving examples of your responsibilities.
- **Other useful information:** This makes your CV stand out from the rest. Include any positions of responsibility you have held, hobbies, sports, voluntary work or organisations you belong to, and any other relevant information (such as fluency in a language).
- **Referees:** Many CVs say 'references available on request'. This means if you are offered an interview you will have to provide names. One should be a current teacher/tutor and the other someone who knows how you work, such as a work experience supervisor. Always obtain permission before you give someone's name.

Why is it important to include your hobbies on your CV?

Activity Creating your own CV

Find out more about CVs on the National Careers Service website by visiting Pearson hotlinks. You can access this by going to www.pearsonhotlinks.co.uk and searching for this title.

Use the CV builder to prepare your own and obtain expert advice if you need it.

Letters of application

Most employers expect you to write a letter of application, to which you will attach your CV. This letter must tempt the reader to read your CV. Your letter should 'sell yourself' to the prospective employer so there must be no spelling, punctuation or grammatical errors.

CONTINUED ▸▸

▸▸ CONTINUED

Activity Checking Jack's letter

Jack writes a covering letter of application to send to Safety First Ltd. Read the letter on the next page, and then identify where he relates his application to the essential and desirable requirements in the person specification. Could he have done any better? Discuss your ideas as a group.

Other requirements

Most job applicants are expected to produce documents to support their application, for example copies of qualification certificates. They may also need to provide evidence of a CRB (Criminal Records Bureau) check. This lists all convictions held on a person's police record and is essential for anyone working with young people or vulnerable adults.

Pre-application tests

Did you know?

You can find many examples of psychometric tests online if you want to practice.

Prospective employers use application forms, CVs and letters of application to assess candidates applying for a job. They may also use other forms of assessment, such as:

- **Online psychometric tests:** These use questionnaires to assess a person's knowledge, abilities, attitude and personality traits.
- **Physical fitness test:** This applies to jobs where fitness, strength and stamina are needed, such as the police, fire service and armed forces.
- **Sight test:** Some jobs require first-class vision such as air traffic controllers and driving instructors. Sight tests also check for colour blindness, which is necessary for jobs where colour awareness is important, such as interior designers and personal shoppers.
- **Health checks:** These are often essential for candidates for senior positions where long absences could cause serious problems.

Next steps after applying for a job

When applications are received, they are logged, and once the closing date has passed, they are assessed by HR or a senior manager.

- **Shortlisting** means identifying which candidates meet all the essential requirements and should be interviewed.
- **Invitation to interview or assessment centre:** Shortlisted candidates are invited to attend an interview or an assessment centre where they are tested against criteria for the job.
- **Feedback:** After the interview or assessment, the best candidate(s) for the job(s) are identified and offered the position. Unsuccessful applicants should be given the opportunity to receive constructive feedback on their performance.

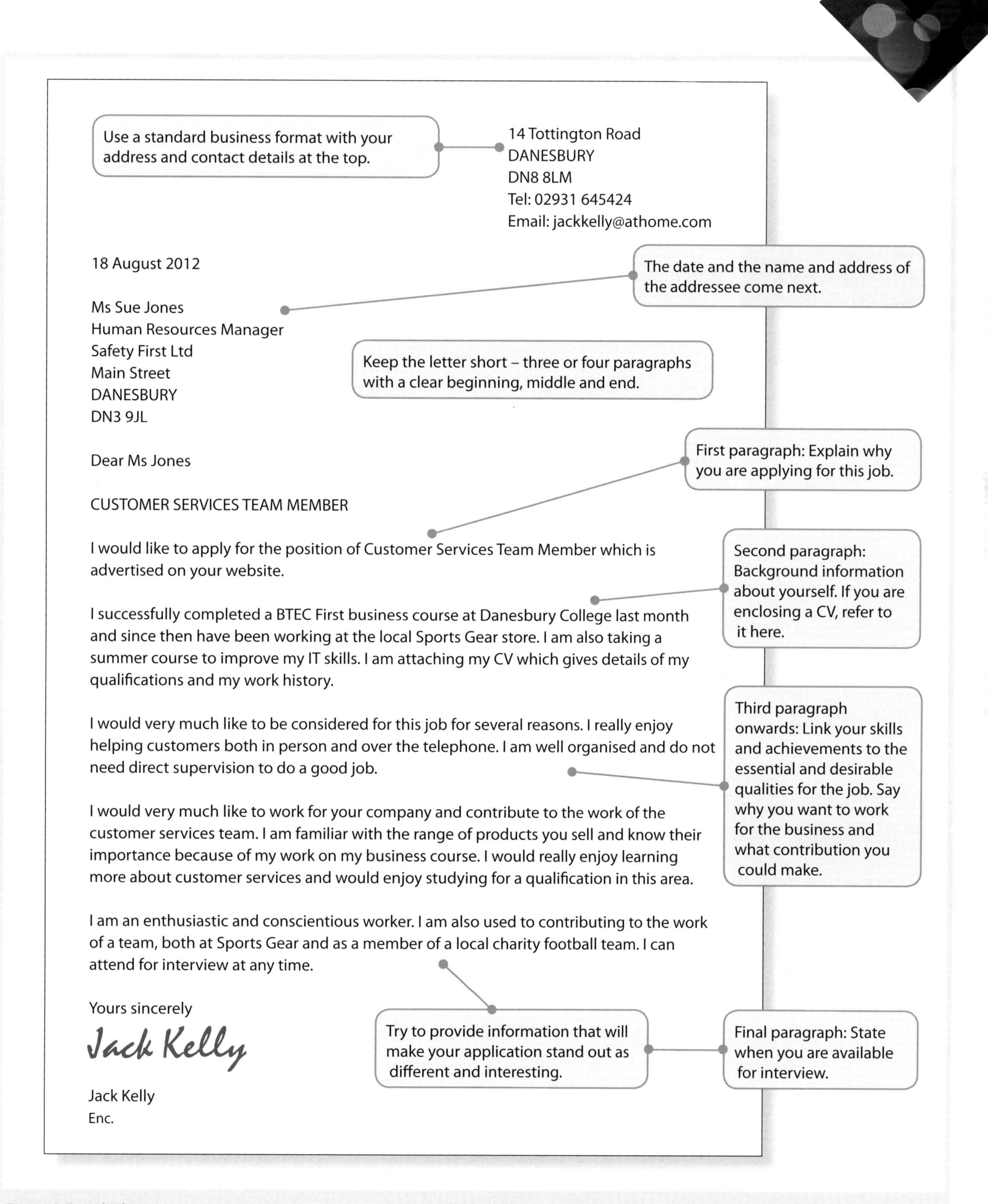

14 Tottington Road
DANESBURY
DN8 8LM
Tel: 02931 645424
Email: jackkelly@athome.com

18 August 2012

Ms Sue Jones
Human Resources Manager
Safety First Ltd
Main Street
DANESBURY
DN3 9JL

Dear Ms Jones

CUSTOMER SERVICES TEAM MEMBER

I would like to apply for the position of Customer Services Team Member which is advertised on your website.

I successfully completed a BTEC First business course at Danesbury College last month and since then have been working at the local Sports Gear store. I am also taking a summer course to improve my IT skills. I am attaching my CV which gives details of my qualifications and my work history.

I would very much like to be considered for this job for several reasons. I really enjoy helping customers both in person and over the telephone. I am well organised and do not need direct supervision to do a good job.

I would very much like to work for your company and contribute to the work of the customer services team. I am familiar with the range of products you sell and know their importance because of my work on my business course. I would really enjoy learning more about customer services and would enjoy studying for a qualification in this area.

I am an enthusiastic and conscientious worker. I am also used to contributing to the work of a team, both at Sports Gear and as a member of a local charity football team. I can attend for interview at any time.

Yours sincerely

Jack Kelly

Jack Kelly
Enc.

Figure 8.7 Jack's letter

TOPIC C.1

Job interviews

Getting started

Some people dread interviews because they are scared of failing. Yet learning to cope with failure and move on is an essential life skill. How good are you?

Before the interview

If you are asked to attend an interview, you may be thrilled but nervous too. You want to do well, but may worry because you do not know what to expect or how to impress your interviewer(s). The answer is good preparation so that you can do your best.

Research into the business and the job role

What do you know about the organisation? Have you checked the website and looked at online press reports to find out as much as possible? Find out as much as you can about the business and the job role. If you have received a job description and person specification, these will help. If you know someone who works there, talk to them, but be aware they could be biased one way or another!

Activity Preparing for interview

Read the WorkSpace case study to see how one HR manager recommends that you prepare.

Remember

The interviewers will refer to the job description and person specification to identify appropriate questions to ask.

Did you know?

If you cannot answer a question, be honest. This is far better than bluffing!

Questions, questions

- **Questions to ask** should *not* focus on holidays or pay rises. Instead try to fill in any gaps in your knowledge and show that you have done your research and are committed to working hard. Good examples include:
  - I saw on your website that you support the local community by doing various projects. Can all staff get involved with these?
  - Would your organisation support me if I wanted to carry on studying on a part-time basis?
- **Anticipating questions that you might be asked** helps you to have some good answers ready. Usually the first questions are the easiest as these are meant to relax you. Later they will get slightly harder. Typical questions include:
  - What did you enjoy most at school/college?
  - Why did you decide to apply for this job?
  - How could you contribute to the success of this business?
  - How would you describe yourself?

Prepare an answer for each question you think you may be asked and ask someone to give you a practice interview beforehand.

Activity Deciding on questions for Jack

In groups, decide what questions you would ask Jack if you were interviewing him for the job of Customer Services Team Member at Safety First Ltd. Look back at the job description and person specification for clues. Then compare your ideas with other groups.

Preparing for an interview

Think about your appearance. Remember that the interviewer is probably of your parents' generation, so dress with this in mind. Choose an outfit you like which is comfortable, ideally one that boosts your confidence.

Making sure your clothes are freshly washed and pressed, and check your hair and nails are clean too. Good personal hygiene is essential, and this means having fresh breath too.

Check the day, date and time of the interview, and allow plenty of time to get there. Check where the business is located and the bus or train times. If it is somewhere unfamiliar, do a practice run to find the premises a day or so before.

Behaviour during the interview

Displaying confidence

Experts say that confidence is a state of mind, but this is not much use if you are feeling just the opposite. Instead, focus on the practical.

- Wear clothes that boost your confidence.
- Rehearse so that you are well prepared.
- Remind yourself that an interview is a two-way process. Perhaps you will find out you do not want to work for the company.
- Remember you can only do your best. You cannot control who else has applied.
- Tell yourself an interview is an opportunity to sell yourself to an employer. If they decide not to buy, it is their loss.

Remember that you will feel more confident if you are well prepared.

Body language

Confident people stand tall and look people in the eye. They have a firm (but not terrifying!) handshake. They sit upright, do not fidget and smile at appropriate times. They send positive signals to people watching them. For an example of confidence in action watch Barack Obama on YouTube.

Tone and clarity of voice

There is no point rehearsing appropriate answers if the interviewer cannot tell what you are saying because you are not speaking clearly. Avoid slang, but speak naturally and don't mutter or shout. Your tone must be respectful, but this does not mean you have to grovel. Just be polite!

CONTINUED ▸▸

▸▸ CONTINUED

Active listening

You should pay attention to the questions to make sure that you understand what you are being asked. If you are not sure what the question means, it is better to say, 'I'm sorry, but could you repeat that, please?' than to answer the wrong question.

Showing interest

At the interview, you should use appropriate body language, tone of voice and questions to show that you are very interested in working for the business. The questions you ask can show an in-depth interest in the work involved.

Activity — Using body language

In groups, suggest four ways in which you can show boredom or interest through your body language. Then compare your ideas as a class.

Assessment activity 8.2 — *English*

2B.P3 | 2B.P4 | 2B.M2 | 2B.M3 | 2B.D2

On your own, finalise the draft job description and person specification for the specific job role that you researched earlier. Present these to your class and your tutor, explaining why your documents will encourage effective recruitment. Divide into small groups, decide which of the jobs appeals most to your group, and prepare an attractive job advertisement. Advise applicants to apply by completing an application form and submitting their CV and a letter of application. Then prepare an application form that candidates can complete, and circulate the advertisement to the rest of your class.

1. On your own, apply for one of the advertisements circulated by producing your CV, application letter and completed application form. Prepare a personal statement that justifies how your current knowledge and skills meet those required in the job description and person specification.
2. Prepare a checklist or personal statement that justifies your choice of job by showing how your current knowledge and skills meet those required in the job description and person specification.
3. Research the job role and prepare your responses to possible interview questions. Prepare interview notes in which you analyse any gaps in your knowledge and skills that might require further training or development. Keep these safely.

WorkSpace

Sonya Clarkson

Head of Employment Services, East Lancashire Hospitals NHS Trust

When Sonya Clarkson's personal circumstances prevented her from going to university, she promptly focused on finding a career she would enjoy. She knew she liked dealing with people, so HR was a natural choice. She obtained a job as an HR Assistant and worked hard, studying part-time for three years to obtain the Chartered Institute of Personnel and Development (CIPD) Diploma and then an MA degree. She steadily climbed the ranks and is now Head of Employment Services for a large NHS Trust. Her experience means she can quickly spot when young candidates have the potential and commitment to build a successful career.

To impress Sonya, you must think carefully about your future career path. Assess your strengths and weaknesses so that you know which skills to develop. Sonya recommends getting feedback so that you do this honestly. Setting career goals for the short, medium and long term means you can seize the right opportunities to help you progress.

Read the job description and person specification for a job carefully and be realistic about whether you have the skills or not. If you apply, then you must be able to justify your claims.

Sonya is always impressed by applicants who ask to speak to her informally to find out more about the job, organisation and team they will be working with.

Finally, Sonya expects interviewees to make an effort to stand out – by preparing well, dressing smartly, being friendly and open, and interested in the job and the organisation.

1 How has Sonya demonstrated that she sees setbacks as potential learning experiences and can set realistic goals?
2 Identify two skills that you possess. Then prepare a statement for each that demonstrates that you have applied that skill.
3 Research an organisation that interests you, and prepare two questions you can ask an interviewer to demonstrate your knowledge and to find out more.

Personal audit

Getting started

A survey of 1000 UK students carried out by accounting firm Ernst and Young found they were good at problem solving, making friends and having a sense of humour. They were less keen on taking risks, showing determination and making themselves stand out from the crowd. However, 87 per cent were positive about achieving their career aspirations. Are you the same?

Key term

Personal audit – a summary of your knowledge, skills, attributes and interests.

Remember

Sonya Clarkson recommends getting feedback from someone after you have prepared a personal audit to check you have done it honestly.

Personal audit

A **personal audit** is a useful first stage in preparing for employment. It involves assessing your current knowledge and skills, then identifying areas where you are strong and those you need to develop.

Knowledge and skills

You can gain knowledge in many ways. Studying for qualifications is just one. Going to work (either part-time or work experience), or helping out in a family business will increase your knowledge. Similarly, you may travel or learn a language.

Skills may be technical or practical, such as being able to swim, ride a bike, drive a car, draw or use a computer. In business, your communication and numeracy skills are vital. Potential employers will expect you to have proof of knowledge or skills you claim to possess, such as exam certificates and school or college reports.

Interests

Sometimes your interests and leisure activities can be relevant to a job application. Demonstrating team-working skills through sport may be useful for a job, but playing computer games would not normally be relevant, unless you are applying to work in a games shop.

Activity — Carrying out a personal audit

Carry out a personal audit, using the format shown opposite, or using a pre-prepared form provided by your centre. Then discuss your conclusions with your teacher/tutor.

Matching knowledge and skills

Many people apply for jobs with no hope of an interview because they do not have the necessary experience and/or qualifications. All good job advertisements clearly state the essential knowledge and experience required. As an applicant, you need to check you possess these. You may be successful without all the desirable attributes, providing you can persuade the interviewer that you are keen to develop these areas.

You need to match your knowledge and skills to jobs you would like to do in the future. Look at the requirements in advertisements, and then identify the knowledge and skills you need to develop so that you can apply with confidence for the position.

Just checking

1. Identify two benefits of carrying out a personal audit.
2. Why is it useful to identify and list your personal interests?

PERSONAL AUDIT

Name .... Date ....

KNOWLEDGE

Knowledge gained	**Evidence**
....	....
....	....
....	....
....	....

SKILLS

Communication skills

Speaking to people face to face
Listening carefully
Joining in a group discussion
Using correct punctuation and spelling
Speaking clearly on the telephone
Expressing my ideas and opinions
Persuading other people
Writing clearly and concisely

Technical skills

Using ICT equipment
Using a range of software
Keyboarding
Using office equipment
Using the internet
Producing professional documents

Practical and work skills

Working with details
Finding and correcting own mistakes
Organisational ability
Planning how to do a job
Making decisions
Punctuality
Tidiness
Meeting deadlines
Using initiative to solve problems
Accepting responsibility

Numeracy

Simple calculations
Accuracy
Percentages

INTERESTS

Identify knowledge you have gained from other sources, such as work experience, e.g. first aid or how to do stock-taking for a retail firm.

For each skill listed, score yourself from 1–5 where 1 = I am very good at this skill; 2 = I am good, but it could be improved; 3 = I definitely need to improve this skill; 4 = I would have to work hard to develop this skill; 5 = I have not had the chance yet to develop this skill.

List your interests and identify how each of these has contributed to your personal development.

Figure 8.8 Example of a personal audit form

Career development

Getting started

Sonya Clarkson in the WorkSpace case study decided she wanted a career not a job. What is the difference? And does it matter? What is your view?

Information and advice

Many learners have only a vague idea about possible careers. It is all too easy to drift into a job if one comes your way, or to be influenced by family or friends. While their input can be invaluable, there are many other useful sources that can reveal types of work and jobs that you might not have thought about. Your main options are listed in Table 8.6.

Table 8.6 Sources of careers information and advice

Source of advice	Type of advice available
Careers advice services	Most schools and colleges have careers advisers who provide information about career paths. You can also contact a specialist adviser online at the National Careers Service.
Advertisements	You can find job advertisements in newspapers and online. Those in your local paper will identify opportunities in your own area.
Word of mouth	Ask people you know about the work they do, particularly family and friends.
Careers fairs	Here you can visit stands set up by employers and educational establishments to talk about types of jobs and courses.
Teachers/tutors	Your teachers/tutors know about the careers previous learners have followed. They can advise you, knowing your strengths and weaknesses, which is an advantage.
Previous and current employers	You will have your own views about the type of work you are doing. What do you like and dislike about it?
Network connections	Networks are people you know and (sometimes) people they know. They can be useful if there is someone you know who is doing the type of work you are interested in.

Employment and government agencies

Employment agencies such as Adecco, Reed and Kelly Services specialise in finding employees for clients and provide useful advice online. Visit Pearson hotlinks to find a link to the National Careers service website.

You can access this by going to www.pearsonhotlinks.co.uk and searching for this title.

Activity Researching careers

Check out the Career Tools and the Careers Advice provided by the National Careers Service and find out more about those that interest you.

Developing a career plan

Your career plan is your rough map to the place where you one day want to be. It is 'rough' because you may change your mind several times as you progress. It identifies your aims and ambitions, and helps you to decide which courses to take and to identify opportunities which would give you useful experience. Your options include:

- **Choosing between an academic or vocational pathway:** Academic courses focus on specific subjects such as maths or physics; vocational courses are aimed at particular careers, such as business or engineering. Some are full-time courses; others are designed so that people can learn as they are working, such as apprenticeships which include taking NVQ qualifications.
- **Full- or part-time employment:** Full-time employment means working around 40 hours per week. A part-time job means you could study for additional qualifications in your spare time. Many students in higher education have part-time jobs so that they can earn money.
- **Training needs, development plans, personal targets:**
  - Your training needs relate to the skills you need to develop to work in a certain job or for a particular employer.
  - Development plans identify the activities that would help you to improve your abilities, such as learning a language.

  Personal targets are the aims you set yourself to achieve your needs and plan.
- **Professional and career-specific qualifications:** Most major careers have professional qualifications linked to them (see WorkSpace case study). There are specific qualifications in many professions including accountancy, law, teaching and food hygiene.

Did you know?

- LinkedIn is a social media site where professionals can find and contact each other online.
- If you leave school at 18 and study for a degree, you will be in higher education. If you study after leaving school, but not at degree level, this is called further education.

Discussion point

Some young people offer to work for nothing to get experience in an industry. Is this a good idea or not?

Activity — Designing a career development form

In small groups, design a form for a career development plan. Allow space for your name, date of plan, career aims (short, medium and long term), current strengths, skills and weaknesses, and training/qualification needs (short, medium and long term). Include an action plan (with dates for review). Compare the forms as a class and choose the best one.

Assessment activity 8.3 — *English*

2C.P5 | 2C.P6 | 2C.M4 | 2C.M5 | 2C.D3

- Produce a realistic personal career development plan for yourself. This should show evidence of independent research and planning and identify how you would realistically achieve the skills you are currently lacking.
- You have been asked to attend an interview for the job role for which you applied. Attend as requested by your teacher/tutor, and provide appropriate responses to the questions you are asked. These should show that you have researched the role and have prepared well.
- After the interview, write a report in which you evaluate the suitability of your career plan. Do this by referring back to your interview performance feedback, your own reflection on this, and the gaps in your knowledge and skills that you identified in Assessment activity 8.2. Identify any changes you would make.

Tip

Your career development plan must show evidence that you have researched career paths you are interested in, and identified the qualifications and skills you will need to attain.

Glossary

A

Advertising budget – the amount of money that you make available to spend on adverts.

Agenda – a list of items to be discussed at a meeting.

Assets – items the business owns or money it is owed.

Audit – records of stock or transactions are checked to make sure that they are accurate.

B

B2B market – a business to business market in which one company sells products to another.

B2C market – a business to consumer market in which companies sell products directly to the public.

Body language – the messages communicated through facial expressions, gestures and posture.

Brownfield land – abandoned industrial or commercial land that can be used for new developments.

Budgetary control – checking performance against the plan and taking action if there are problems.

Budgeting – planning future expenditure and revenue targets with the aim of ensuring a profit is made.

Business format – the way a business is legally owned and operated.

C

Capital – the amount of money invested in the business by the owner.

Carbon footprint – the amount of greenhouse gas that a business releases into the atmosphere as a result of its activities.

Cash balance – the amount of money forecast to be in the bank account after the net cash flow figure has been added or subtracted from the existing bank balance.

Cash inflows – the amounts of money entering a business's bank account.

Cash outflows – the amounts of money leaving a business's bank account.

Chain of production – the steps taken to turn raw materials into a finished product.

Chairperson – the leader of a meeting.

Code of practice – a set of guidelines that set standards of service customers can expect.

Consistent (customer service) – providing the same service over and over again to a high standard every time.

Coordinate – work together in an organised and complementary way so that everyone can do their job more easily and efficiently.

Cost of sales – the cost of producing a product.

Cross-selling – suggesting a related product to a customer to increase the overall sale, for example a hairspray to go with a haircut.

Customer profile – the main features of a particular group of customers.

D

Debtors (or trade receivables) – people who owe money to the business for goods or services they have received. Trade payables are traders to whom the business owes money because they have supplied goods or services.

Differentiate – make your business noticeably different from your competitors.

Direct distribution – selling your product direct to the market yourself.

Distribution channels – the route that a product or service takes to get to the market, e.g. manufacturer to wholesaler to retailer.

E

Economy – the national system of producing and consuming goods.

Economy – the system by which a country's money and goods are produced and used.

Entrepreneur – someone who starts up a new business in order to make a profit, often in a way that involves financial risks (our word 'enterprise' comes from this French word).

EPOS – stands for 'electronic point of sale'. These are computer systems that record transactions and process payments.

Ergonomic – designed to enable people to work safely and productively.

Exchange rates – the value of an individual currency against other currencies.

Expenditure – money that a business spends.

External customers – outside businesses and individuals who want to make a purchase.

Face-to-face customer service – when the customer receives service in front of a member of staff.

F

Fairtrade – products which pay a fair wage to the producer.

Financial year – the trading period over which a business collects information for their annual income statement (for example, a business might have a financial year that starts on 1 May and ends on 30 April).

Fixed costs (or indirect costs) – expenditure on items which does not change with the number of items sold or produced.

Floating – launching a public limited company on the Stock Exchange.

Front-line customer service staff – those people who are a customer's first point of contact with the business.

G

Greenbelt land – an area which is protected from building and development to allow people in cities access to open space and natural environments.

Gross profit – the money made from selling a product (the sales revenue) after the cost of producing that product (cost of sales) has been deducted.

I

Income – money which is paid into a business.

Interest rates – the cost of borrowing money.

Internal customers – colleagues who work in the same organisation and need you to do something.

Interpersonal skills – being able to speak to customers and read their body language.

J

Job description – a statement that lists the main elements of a job and the tasks done by the job holder.

K

Key performance indicator – a way of measuring how well a retail business or a retail employee is performing.

L

Legislation – relates to the laws of the land which everyone must obey.

Liabilities – amounts of money which a business owes.

Limited liability – the owners are only responsible for debts up to the amount they have invested in the business.

Loss – occurs when expenditure is more than revenue.

M

Manufacturer – a business which transforms raw materials into finished goods, ready to be sold.

Market – the customers for a particular product or service.

Market research – finding out customer views and opinions.

Marketing mix – the combination of product, price, place and promotion. This is often referred to as the 4 Ps.

Mass market – all the consumers in one market

Medium – how you choose to advertise to your target market.

Meeting brief – a summary of the main requirements for a meeting.

Message – what you want to tell your customers.

Microbusiness – a business which has fewer than ten staff.

Minutes – the official record of the discussions and decisions taken at the meeting.

N

Net cash flow – the difference between the cash inflow and outflow figures over a particular time period.

Net profit – the money made from selling a product after all costs (expenditure) have been deducted from the gross profit.

Niche market – a small group of customers for a specialised item

Non-verbal communication – the process of communication through body language, facial expressions, gestures, eye contact and tone of voice.

Non-verbal communication – the other ways that you communicate, including your facial expression and body language.

O

Operating costs (or running costs) – money spent on a regular basis to keep a business running.

Organisational procedures – step-by-step instructions issued to staff to ensure consistent standards.

Outsource – hire an outside firm to do a task, such as distributing goods or installing an ICT system.

Overdraft – this occurs if a business pays more out of its bank account than it has in credit. The bank may allow this but will make an extra charge.

Overheads – the everyday running costs of the business.

P

Perception – what a customer or consumer thinks about something.

Person specification – linked to the job description, it states the skills and abilities needed to do the job effectively.

Personal audit – a summary of your knowledge, skills, attributes and interests.

Pitch – the proposal made by a salesperson to sell their products to a potential customer.

Policy – the general direction which the business wants to move in.

Profit – occurs when revenue is more than expenditure.

Q

Quorum – the minimum number of people who must be present at a formal meeting to allow official decisions to be made.

R

Regulations – these interpret the law and state simply what people have to do to abide by the law.

Remote customer service – when a business offers customer service by telephone or online.

Reserves – money that has been saved from previous profitable years.

Retail sector – the section of the national economy made up of retail businesses.

Retailer – a business which sells goods directly to the public.

S

Sales environment – the place where sales are made.

Segment – to identify and divide customers into groups sharing certain characteristics.

Service deliverer – a member of staff who delivers customer service.

Service specification statement – issued by an organisation giving details of the level of service to be expected.

Share capital – the amount of money invested in the business by the shareholders.

SMEs – stands for 'small and medium enterprises'.

Social enterprise – a business which uses its profits or surplus to fulfil social objectives, such as helping others.

Start-up costs – the amount of money spent setting up a business before it starts trading.

Stock take – the stock in a retail outlet is counted to ensure that records are up to date.

Strategy – how the business intends to achieve its objectives.

Sub-sector – a specific category of products or services offered by a retailer.

Supervisor – the person who works above you and who gives you instructions. You are his or her 'subordinate'.

Supply chain – the stages that goods pass through between the producer that makes them and the retailer that sells them.

Target customer – the customer that a business aims to supply.

Total costs – the total amount of money spent running a business over a certain period of time (e.g. a month).

U

Unlimited liability – the owners are personally responsible for all debts, even if this means selling personal possessions.

Up-selling – promoting a more profitable alternative to increase the value of the sale.

V

Value for money – belief that the price paid is fair.

Variable costs (or direct costs) – costs which vary according to the number of items sold or produced.

Verbal communication – what you say and how you say it.

W

Wholesaler – a business which sells large quantities of goods to other businesses.

Wholesaler – a company which sells goods in bulk to retail businesses.

Word of mouth reputation – customers tell their friends, family and colleagues about their experiences with an organisation.

Working capital (or net current assets) – money the business can raise quickly which is calculated by deducting current liabilities (all current debts owed by the business) from current assets (all money owed to the business at the current time).

Index

S

T

U

V

W